GLENN GOULD
VARIATIONS

GLENN GOULD

By Himself and His Friends

Edited with an Introduction by John McGreevy

QUILL

NEW YORK

*Checking out pianos at Columbia's 30th Street studio,
New York City, 1957. (CBS Don Hunstein)*

Library of Congress Catalog Card Number: 84-60614

ISBN 0-688-03905-7

Printed in the United States of America

First Quill Edition

1 2 3 4 5 6 7 8 9 10

To the memory of Glenn Gould:

In the deserts of the heart
Let the healing fountain start,
In the prison of his days
Teach the free man how to praise.

W.H. AUDEN

CONTENTS

FOREWORD

Glenn Gould is certainly one of the greatest losses we have suffered in recent years. It must be over 25 years since we made music together and became close friends. When I heard him play, I had a feeling that I was myself playing because his music-making appealed so exactly to my own musical sense.

I regret that since he no longer wished to travel, we were unable to make music and records again.

For the next generation he will be regarded as an outstanding example of a musician who combined the musical impact of his playing technique with impeccable taste. He created a style which led the way to the future.

I shall never forget our collaboration.

HERBERT VON KARAJAN

Salzburg, February 1983

Portrait of the artist as a young pianist. (© Karsh, Ottawa)

LIST OF
ILLUSTRATIONS

ACKNOWLEDGMENTS

My first thanks are to the contributors. In particular I am grateful to Geoffrey Payzant, Glenn Gould's biographer, who has given unqualified advice. His knowledge of Gould's life and work have been invaluable. I am also grateful to Costa Pilavachi, music director of the National Arts Centre, Ottawa, for suggesting I undertake the task in the first place, and to my guardian angel at Doubleday, Janet Turnbull, who has helped in every possible way, but has made no attempt to restrict complete editorial freedom. A special debt is owed to Ray Roberts and Ruth Pinko for going through Glenn Gould's papers and delivering such gems as are now a part of this book. My thanks to Susan Koscis at CBS Records in New York, an enthusiastic supporter from the beginning, and Josephine Mangiaracina for sorting through thirty years of photographs at CBS. I am deeply grateful to photographers Arnold Newman, Yousuf Karsh and Don Hunstein for allowing us to include examples of their consumate art. My thanks to the following for permission to use previously published articles. "Apollonian," *The New Yorker*; "Growing up Gould," *Saturday Night* magazine; "Glenn Gould's Toronto," Lester and Orpen Dennys; "Bach's The Art of the Fugue," Amsco Music Publishing Company; "The Music Itself: Glenn Gould's Contrapuntal Vision," *Vanity Fair*; "Glenn Gould: Bach in the Electronic Age," The Macmillan Company; "Glenn Gould Interviews Glenn Gould About Glenn Gould," *Piano Quarterly*; "Stokowski in Six Scenes," *Piano Quarterly*. Finally I wish to thank Greg Kozdrowski for his many hours of hard labour typing the manuscript and ensuring that I met an impossible deadline.

INTRODUCTION

This book is a labour of love, a tribute to a great artist and rare human being: Glenn Gould. A luminous presence has graced our lives and moved on. For a brief moment we were dazzled by his virtuosity. All of those who caught a glimpse of this extraordinary phenomenon witnessed one of the most remarkable human performances of our time. Profound as the sense of loss is over the death of Glenn Gould, there is solace in knowing that the world continues to be illuminated by his incomparable art.

Fabulously gifted, Glenn invariably found the appropriate medium which allowed him to give fullest expression to his unique array of talents—he was a pianist, a composer, an essayist, a radio documentarian, and a film scorer. And, moralist that he was, he worked with the fervour of a mediaeval monk in the refinement of his vision. Forsaking the trappings of a "normal life," he devoted himself exclusively to the exploration of an inner universe.

Glenn was by nature an ecstatic. His search for ecstasy took on the dimensions of a moral cause, revealing something of the infinite. The creations which emerged from his quest leave the spectator corroborated in the hope that, despite the world and its terrors, here is a paradigm of perfection.

Shocked as we were by his untimely death (he was just 50), we discovered that he had recently re-recorded J. S. Bach's *Goldberg Variations*, that masterwork which had brought Glenn his initial renown.

That he had revisited this work and then died so soon after, makes his life take on a poetic, almost symbolic quality.

It seemed to me appropriate to include a few of Glenn Gould's own pieces in this book, if only to rekindle the memory of a remarkable mind in action. When Glenn tackled a subject, be it a great composer, a city, or, indeed, himself (like many great artists, he was his own favourite subject), he brought the same fascination with the imaginative process as engaged him in the recording studio. Nor could I resist including a selection from the wealth of photographic material that captures his lifetime. Enormously photogenic, Glenn was entirely relaxed in front of the camera and he enjoyed an intimacy with the medium such as he rarely experienced in front of a concert audience.

Any future biographer of a man as complex as Glenn Gould will be faced with a formidable task. Perhaps only Glenn himself could have undertaken such a work of synthesis. He sometimes made references to the book he would one day write. One can only speculate about its contribution to an already vast outpouring of creative achievement.

For now, let the reader be content with this "appreciation" from his friends as they reflect on Glenn Gould's pursuit of the ineffable.

JOHN MCGREEVY

Toronto, August 1983

GLENN GOULD
VARIATIONS

THE TRUTH ABOUT A LEGEND
Leonard Bernstein

One day in 1962, I received a call from Glenn in Toronto. He was to play Brahms' D Minor Concerto with me and the New York Philharmonic the following week in Carnegie Hall. He said, "Oh boy, have I got some surprises for you; I have made such discoveries about this piece." I thought, "Well, wonderful." Any discovery of Glenn's was welcomed by me because I worshipped the way he played: I admired his intellectual approach, his "guts" approach, his complete dedication to whatever he was doing, his constant inquiry into a new angle or a new possibility of the truth of a score. That's why he made so many experimental changes of tempi. He would play the same Mozart sonata-movement *adagio* one time and *presto* the next, when actually it's supposed to be neither. He was not trying to attract attention, but looking for the truth. I loved that in him.

A week before he was to come to New York, he made that call to announce that he had some *really* new ideas about the Brahms, and to prepare me for them. I said, "Along what order? You're not making a big cut? You're not taking a huge repeat that Brahms didn't write?" Because he had made it sound so extraordinary I didn't know what to expect. He said, "No, it's just a matter of tempo here and there, but I just want to warn you because you might be a little shocked." I told him nothing he could do would shock me because I knew him too well by now, and I was almost unshockable.

He arrived and set forth three unbelievable tempi for the three

Preparing for a recording session with conductor Leonard Bernstein, New York City, 1957. (CBS) 17

movements. In the first place, they were so slow that the first movement alone took about as much time as it should take to play the whole concerto. It was all in six—the whole first movement had to be beaten in six. There was no sense of *alla breve*, which, of course, is the point of the movement—or, rather, there was no sense of that fine line between 6/4 in *two* and 6/4 in *six*. It's a kind of tightrope which you walk so that at any moment you can veer toward one side or the other —be more flowing, or be more *sostenuto*, whatever —according to the needs of the music. This, however, was no tightrope. This was having fallen off the tightrope into the safety net called *adagissimo*—and this for an *allegro*, mind you. I said I was perfectly willing to go along with it, *pour le sport*, so to speak, as maybe he had something there.

I also said that I thought we'd have an empty house before we got to the slow movement. Glenn laughed. "Wait till you hear how the slow movement goes, which is also in 6/4. It's exactly the same as the first movement's 6/4. It's just like *repeating*!" That was his major discovery: the two movements were really both aspects of the same movement, and therefore both 6/4's had to be the same. After an hour of this, we finally got to the finale, which is a 2/4 Hungarian thing, and no matter how much you hold back in the Hungarian manner, you can't possibly do it in four. It's a 2/4 thing, and you can subdivide or hold back all you want, but you can go only so far.

I did forewarn the orchestra a little about this. I said, "Now, don't give up, because this is a great man, whom we have to take very seriously." There were some very odd looks when we began the rehearsal, but they were wonderfully cooperative and went right along with it. Of course, they did get tired: it *was* very tiring. After the rehearsal I asked him, "Are you sure you're still convinced about the 'slowth' of this piece?" And he said, "Oh, more than ever; did you hear how wonderfully the tension built?"

In those days, we had our first concert of each weekly series on Thursday night, which was a kind of dress rehearsal in which I talked to the audience. It was a chic night, *the* night to be there. You could never get a ticket for Thursday night. I sometimes had a piano, and illustrated points about the music being played as I do on a television show, all in order to bring the audience closer to the music. That night

I thought, "What am I going to talk to them about?"—when obviously the main subject of the evening was going to be our performance of a Brahms concerto and Glenn's interpretation of it. So I said to Glenn backstage, "You know, I have to talk to the people. How would it be if I warned them that it was going to be very slow, and prepare them for it? Because if they don't know, they really might leave. I'll just tell them that there is a disagreement about the tempi between us, but that because of the sportsmanship element in music I would like to go along with your tempo and try it." It wasn't to be a disclaimer; I was very much interested in the results—particularly the audience reaction to it. I wrote down a couple of notes on the back of an envelope and showed them to Glenn: "Is this okay?" And he said, "Oh, it's wonderful, what a great idea."

So I went out, read these few notes, and said, "This is gonna be different, folks. And it's going to be very special. This is the Glenn Gould Brahms concerto." Out he came, and indeed he played it exactly the way he had rehearsed it, and wonderfully too. The great miracle was that nobody left, because of course it had become such a *thing* to listen to. The house came down, although, if I remember correctly, it took well over an hour to play. It was very exciting. I never loved him more.

The result in the papers, especially the *New York Times*, was that I had betrayed my colleague. Little did they know—though I believe I did say so to the audience—that I had done this with Glenn's encouragement. They just assumed that I had sold him down the river by coming out first to disclaim his interpretation. It was, on the contrary, a way of educating the audience as part of Thursday night's procedure. All this was not only misunderstood, but repeated and repeated and multiplied exponentially by every other newspaper that wrote about it.

Then Harold Schonberg, the ex-chief critic of the *Times* who wrote the infamous review, wrote a Sunday piece in the form of a letter to "Dear Ossip"— Gabrilovitch, I assume. "Dear Ossip, you vill nyever guess vat last night in Carnyegie Hall hhappent!" sort of thing. The piece was based on this notion of betrayal. He has never let that notion die, and because it's so juicy it has undergone a kind of propagation all over the world. However, the "juicy" part is what did *not* happen. (For me, the juicy part is what *did* happen.) Of course, a defense is very weak, once a legend is born. It's rather like the *Radical Chic* Black Panther legend, which I can never seem to set straight. I have the feeling, even now, that trying to make this story about Glenn clear by telling the truth can't really erase the now legendary, but false, version.

Glenn laughed about it. He has that kind—*had* that kind of...(I can't get used to this idea of putting him in the past tense)—Glenn had strong elements of sportsmanship and teasing, the kind of daring which accounts for his freshness, the great sense of inquiry which made him suddenly understand Schoenberg and Liszt in the same category, or Purcell and Brahms, or Orlando Gibbons and Petula Clark. He would suddenly bring an unlikely pair of musicians together in some kind of startling comparative essay.

At some point, early on—I think when he was doing the Beethoven C Minor Concerto with me—Glenn and I were going to do some work at my apartment, so I invited him to dinner first. This was the first time Felicia, my wife, had actually met him. As you know, Glenn had a "cold complex." He had a fur hat on all the time, several pairs of gloves and I don't know how many mufflers, and coat upon coat. He arrived and began taking off all, or at least *some* of these things, and Felicia met and loved him instantly. "Oh," she said, "aren't you going to take off your hat?" He had a fur astrakhan cap on, and he said, "Well, I don't think so." At length, he did, and there was all this rotting, matted, sweaty hair that hadn't been shampooed in God knows how long. It was *disappearing* because it was so unhealthy. Before I knew it, Felicia—before "Have a drink" or anything —had him in the bathroom, washed his hair and cut it, and he emerged from the bathroom looking like an angel. I've never seen anything so beautiful as Glenn Gould coming out of that bathroom with his wonderful blond *clean* hair.

There was a marvelous relationship that sprang up instantly between Glenn and Felicia which lasted through the years. I remember when

during the summer of 1955—several years before we met Glenn—
Felicia was waiting to give birth to our son, Alexander. The doctors
had miscalculated, so we had an extra month to wait. It was June;
there was a heat wave in New York; she was in her ninth month and
very easily tired and disgruntled. One of the great sources of comfort
to us during that month was Glenn's first recording of the *Goldberg
Variations* which had just come out. It became "our song."

Of course, the haircut Felicia gave Glenn didn't change his lifestyle
at all. I remember we had a recording session a week after the dinner,
and he had the fur cap and gloves back on along with all the rest of it.
He'd whip the gloves off, record a few bars and then whip them on
again, or he'd stop suddenly in the middle of a take and race downstairs
to the men's room to run his hands under hot water. He'd come back,
gloves on, and start again. He was very unpredictable, but always very
approachable. He had a strange combination of dogmaticism and great
humor, which don't usually go together. The humor never, to my
knowledge, went away.

The one time I saw him on his own turf, so to speak, was when I was
making a Canadian tour with the New York Philharmonic, and we
stopped in Toronto. Naturally I had to call up Glenn. I went to see him
at his apartment, which was a shambles— months of mail stacked up
along with newspapers and test pressings. You had to pick your way
between piles of things. There he was in the midst of all this, at his
special Chickering piano, which he had prepared to sound rather like a
fortepiano, or as much like a harpsichord as possible. I wanted to see
his apartment and said, "Oh, this must be the bedroom," but he
wouldn't let me go in—apparently it was an even worse mess.

In any case, he said, "Let's go and do my favorite thing." So we
went down and got into his car, he being wrapped up in all his furs and
gloves and hats, with all the windows up, the heat turned on full blast,
and the radio turned on to a good music station, also full blast. We
drove around the city of Toronto, just listening to the radio and
sweating. I couldn't stop sweating, but he loved it. I said, "Do you do
this often?" He said, "Every day."

This was a man who was fascinated by the Arctic and the North
Pole. In fact, at that very time he was making the incredible documen-

tary about the North. He'd been there twice and was just about to go again because he was so fascinated by it. For this man, who was so afraid of the cold, to be *attracted* to the cold, is a paradox that only twelve Freuds could figure out.

Here was a man you could really come to love. We became very close friends, but when he stopped playing in public, I saw less and less of him. I regret that, because it was a real relationship, based on a mutual appreciation of the sense of inquiry. He had an intellect that one could really play against and learn from. He was about fifteen years younger than I, I think, but I never felt that he was my junior, in any sense. He was a real peer, in every sense. When he died, I just couldn't bear it.

At a mixing session in a CBC studio, Toronto, 1974. (CBC Robert C. Ragsdale)

GLENN GOULD INTERVIEWS GLENN GOULD ABOUT GLENN GOULD
Glenn Gould

Being Volume One, Number One, of the complete Gould-Gould conversations.

glenn gould: Mr. Gould, I gather that you have a reputation as a—well, forgive me for being blunt, sir—but as a tough nut to crack, interview-wise?

Glenn Gould: Really. I've never heard that.

gg: Well, it's the sort of scuttlebutt that we media-types pick up from source to source, but I just want to assure you that I'm quite prepared to strike from the record any question you may feel is out of line.

GG: Oh, I can't conceive of any problems of that sort intruding upon our deliberations.

gg: Well then, just to clear the air, sir, let me ask straight-out: Are there any off-limit areas?

GG: I certainly can't think of any—apart from music of course.

gg: Well, Mr. Gould, I don't want to go back on my word. I realize that your participation in this interview was never contractually confirmed, but it was sealed with a handshake.

GG: Figuratively speaking of course.

gg: Of course, and I had rather assumed that we'd spend the bulk of this interview on musically related matters.

GG: Well, do you think it's essential? I mean, my personal philosophy of interviewing—and I've done quite a bit of it on the air as you perhaps know—is that the most illuminating disclosures derive from areas only indirectly related to the interviewee's line of work.

gg: For example?

GG: Well, for example, in the course of preparing radio documentaries, I've interviewed a theologian about technology, a surveyor about William James, an economist about pacifism, and a housewife about acquisitiveness in the art market.

gg: But surely you've also interviewed musicians about music?

GG: Well, yes, I have, on occasion, in order to help put them at ease in front of the mike. But it's been far more instructive to talk with Pablo Casals, for example, about the concept of the *Zeitgeist* which, of course, is not unrelated to music—

gg: Yes, I was just going to venture that comment.

GG:—or to Leopold Stokowski about the prospect for interplanetary travel which is, I think you'll agree and Stanley Kubrick notwithstanding, a bit of a digression.

gg: Well, this does pose a problem, Mr. Gould, but let me try to frame the question more affirmatively. Is there a subject you'd particularly like to discuss?

GG: Well, I hadn't given it much thought really, but, just off the top, what about the political situation in Labrador?

gg: Well, I'm sure that could produce a stimulating dialogue, Mr. Gould, but I do feel that we have to keep in mind that HIGH FIDELITY is edited primarily for a U.S. constituency.

GG: Oh, quite. Well, in that case perhaps aboriginal rights in western Alaska would make good copy.

gg: Yes. Well, I certainly don't want to bypass any headline-grabbing areas of that sort, Mr. Gould, but since HIGH FIDELITY is oriented toward a musically literate readership, we should, I think, at least begin our discussion in the area of the arts.

GG: Oh, certainly. Perhaps we could examine the question of aboriginal rights as reflected in ethnomusicological field studies at Point Barrow.

gg: Well, I must confess I had a rather more conventional line of attack, so to speak, in mind, Mr. Gould. As I'm sure you're aware, the virtually obligatory question in regard to your career is the concert-versus-media controversy, and I do feel we must at least touch upon it.

GG: Oh, well, I have no objections to fielding a few questions in that area. As far as I'm concerned, it primarily involves moral rather than musical considerations in any case, so be my guest.

gg: Well, that's very good of you. I'll try to make it brief and then, perhaps, we can move farther afield.

GG: Fair enough!

gg: Well now, you've been quoted as saying that your involvement with recording—with media in general, indeed—represents an involvement with the future.

GG: That's correct. I've even said so in the pages of this illustrious journal, as a matter of fact.

gg: Quite so, and you've also said that, conversely, the concert hall, the recital stage, the opera house, or whatever, represent the past—an aspect of your own past in particular perhaps as well as, in more general terms, music's past.

GG: That's true, although I must admit that my only past professional contact with opera was a touch of tracheitis I picked up while playing the old Festspielhaus in Salzburg. As you know, it was an exceedingly drafty edifice, and I—

gg: Perhaps we could discuss your state of health at a more opportune moment, Mr. Gould, but it does occur to me—and I hope you'll forgive me for saying so—that there is something inherently self-serving about pronouncements of this kind. After all, you elected to abandon all public platforms some—what was it?—ten years ago?

GG: Nine years and eleven months as of the date of this issue actually.

gg: And you will admit that most people who opt for radical career departures of any sort sustain themselves with the notion that, however reluctantly, the future is on their side?

GG: It's encouraging to think so, of course, but I must take exception to your use of the term "radical." It's certainly true that I did take the plunge out of a conviction that, given the state of the art, a total immersion in media represented a logical development—and I remain so convinced—but quite frankly, however much one likes to formulate past-future equations, the prime sponsors of such convictions, the strongest motivations behind such "departures," to borrow your term, are usually related to no more radical notion than an attempt to resolve the discomfort and inconvenience of the present.

gg: I'm not sure I've caught the drift of that, Mr. Gould.

GG: Well, for instance, let me suggest to you that the strongest motivation for the invention of a lozenge would be a sore throat. Of course, having patented the lozenge, one would then be free to speculate that the invention represented the future and the sore throat the past, but I doubt that one would be inclined to think in those terms while the irritation was present. Needless to say, in the case of my tracheitis at Salzburg, medication of that sort was—

gg: Excuse me, Mr. Gould, I'm sure we will be apprised of your Salzburg misadventures in due course, but I must pursue this point a bit further. Am I to understand that your withdrawal from the concert stage, your subsequent involvement with media, was motivated by the musical equivalent of a—of a sore throat?

GG: Do you find that objectionable?

gg: Well, to be candid, I find it utterly narcissistic. And to my mind, it's also entirely at odds with your statement that moral objections played a major role in your decision.

GG: I don't see the contradiction there unless, of course, in your view discomfort, per se, ranks as a positive virtue.

gg: My views are not the subject of this interview, Mr. Gould, but I'll answer your question, regardless. Discomfort, per se, is not the issue; I simply believe that any artist worthy of the name must be prepared to sacrifice personal comfort.

GG: To what end?

gg: In the interests of preserving the great traditions of the musical/ theatrical experience, of maintaining the noble tutorial and curatorial responsibilities of the artist in relation to his audience.

GG: You don't feel that a sense of discomfort, of unease, could be the sagest of counselors for both artist and audience?

gg: No, I simply feel that you, Mr. Gould, have either never permitted yourself to savor the—

GG:—ego-gratification?

GG: The privilege, as I was about to say, of communicating with an audience —

GG: —from a power-base?

gg: —from a proscenium setting in which the naked fact of your humanity is on display, unedited and unadorned.

GG: Couldn't I at least be allowed to display the tuxedoed fallacy, perhaps?

gg: Mr. Gould, I don't feel we should allow this dialogue to degenerate into idle banter. It's obvious that you've never savored the joys of a one-to-one relationship with a listener.

GG: I always thought that, managerially speaking, a 2800-to-1 relationship was the concert-hall ideal.

gg: I don't want to split statistics with you. I've tried to pose the question with all candor and—

GG: Well then, I'll try to answer likewise. It seems to me that, if we're going to get waylaid by the numbers game, I'll have to plump for a zero-to-one relationship as between audience and artist, and that's where the moral objection comes in.

gg: I'm afraid I don't quite grasp that point, Mr. Gould. Do you want to run it through again?

GG: I simply feel that the artist should be granted, both for his sake and for that of his public—and let me get on record right now the fact I'm not at all happy with words like "public" and "artist"; I'm not happy with the hierarchical implications of that kind of terminology—that he should be granted anonymity. He should be permitted to operate in secret, as it were, unconcerned with—or better still, unaware of—the presumed demands of the marketplace—which demands, given sufficient indifference on the part of a sufficient number of artists, will simply disappear. And given their disappearance, the artist will then abandon his false sense of "public" responsibility, and his "public" will relinquish its role of servile dependency.

gg: And never the 'twain shall meet, I dare say!

GG: No, they'll make contact, but on an altogether more meaningful level than that which relates any stage to its apron.

gg: Mr. Gould, I'm well aware that this sort of idealistic role-swapping offers a satisfying rhetorical flourish, and it may even be that the "creative audience" concept to which you've devoted a lot of interview space elsewhere offers a kind of McLuhanesque fascination. But you conveniently forget that the artist, however hermetic his life style, is still in effect an autocratic figure. He's still, however benevolently, a social dictator. And his public, however generously enfranchised by gadgetry, however richly endowed with electronic options, is still on the receiving end of the experience, as of this late date at least, and all of your neomedieval anonymity quest on behalf of the artist-as-zero and all of your vertical panculturalism on behalf of his "public," isn't going to change that, or at least it hasn't done so thus far.

GG: May I speak now?

gg: Of course. I didn't mean to get carried away, but I do feel strongly about the—

GG: —about the artist as superman?

gg: That's not quite fair, Mr. Gould.

GG: —or about the interlocutor as comptroller of conversations, perhaps?

gg: There's certainly no need to be rude. I didn't really expect a conciliatory response from you—I realize that you've staked out certain philosophical claims in regard to these issues—but I did at least hope that just once you'd confess to a personal experience of the one-to-one, artist-to-listener relationship. I had hoped that you might confess to having personally been witness to the magnetic attraction of a great artist visibly at work before his public.

GG: Oh, I have had that experience.

gg: Really?

GG: Certainly, and I don't mind confessing to it. Many years ago, I happened to be in Berlin while Herbert von Karajan led the Philharmonic in their first-ever performance of Sibelius' Fifth. As you know, Karajan tends—in late-Romantic repertoire particularly—to conduct with eyes closed and to endow his stick-wielding with enormously persuasive choreographic contours, and the effect, quite frankly, contributed to one of the truly indelible musical/dramatic experiences of my life.

gg: You're supporting my contention very effectively indeed, Mr. Gould. I know of course that that performance, or at any rate one of its subsequent recorded incarnations, played a rather important role in your life.

GG: You mean because of its utilization in the epilogue of my radio documentary *The Idea of North*?

gg: Exactly, and you've just admitted that this "indelible" experience derived from a face-to-face confrontation, shared with an audience, and not simply from the disembodied predictability purveyed by even the best of phonograph records.

GG: Well, I suppose you could say that, but I wasn't actually a member of the audience. As a matter of fact, I took refuge in a glassed-in broadcast booth over the stage and, although I was in a position to see Karajan's face and to relate every ecstatic grimace to the emerging musical experience, the audience—except for the occasional profile shot as he might cue left or right—was not.

gg: I'm afraid you're splitting subdivided beats there, Mr. Gould.

GG: I'm not so sure. You see, the broadcast booth, in effect, represented a state of isolation, not only for me vis-à-vis my fellow auditors, but vis-à-vis the Berlin Philharmonic and its conductor as well.

gg: And now you're simply clutching at symbolic straws.

GG: Maybe so, but I must point out—*entre nous*, of course—that when it came time to incorporate Karajan's Sibelius Fifth into *The Idea of North*, I revised the dynamics of the recording to suit the mood of the text it accompanied, and that liberty, surely, is the product of—what shall I call it?—the enthusiastic irreverence of a zero-to-one relationship, wouldn't you say?

gg: I should rather think it's the product of unmitigated gall. I realize, of course, that *The Idea of North* was an experimental radio venture—as I recall, you treated the human voice in that work almost as one might a musical instrument—

GG: That's right.

gg: —and permitted two, three, or four individuals to speak at once upon occasion.

GG: True.

gg: But whereas those experiments with your own raw material, so to speak, seem perfectly legitimate to me, your use—or misuse—of Herr Von Karajan's material is another matter altogether. After all, you've confessed that your original experience of that performance was "indelible." And yet you blithely confess as well to tampering with what were, presumably, carefully controlled dynamic relationships—

GG: We did some equalizing, too.

gg: —and all in the interest of—

GG: —of my needs of the moment.

gg: —which, however, were at least unique to the project at hand.

GG: All right, I'll give you that, but every listener has a "project at hand," simply in terms of making his experience of music relate to his life style.

gg: And you're prepared to have similar unauthorized permutations practiced on your own recorded output by listener or listeners unknown?

GG: I should have failed in my purpose otherwise.

gg: Then you're obviously reconciled to the fact that no real aesthetic yardstick relates your performances as originally conceived to the manner in which they will be subsequently audited?

GG: Come to that, I have absolutely no idea as to the "aesthetic" merits of Karajan's Sibelius Fifth when I encountered it on that memorable occasion. In fact the beauty of the occasion was that, although I was aware of being witness to an intensely moving experience, I had no idea as to whether it was or was not a "good" performance. My aesthetic judgments were simply placed in cold storage—which is where I should like them to remain, at least when assessing the works of others. Perhaps, necessarily, and for entirely practical reasons, I apply a different set of criteria on my own behalf, but—

gg: Mr. Gould, are you saying that you do not make aesthetic judgments?

GG: No, I'm not saying that—though I wish I were able to make that statement—because it would attest to a degree of spiritual perfection that I have not attained. However, to rephrase the fashionable cliché, I do try as best I can to make only moral judgments and not aesthetic ones—except, as I said, in the case of my own work.

gg: I suppose, Mr. Gould, I'm compelled to give you the benefit of the doubt.

GG: That's very good of you.

gg: —and to assume that you are assessing your own motivations responsibly and accurately—

GG: One can only try.

gg: —and given that, what you have just confessed adds so many forks to the route of this interview, I simply don't know which trail to pursue.

GG: Why not pick the most likely signpost, and I'll just tag along.

gg: Well, I suppose the obvious question is: If you don't make aesthetic judgments on behalf of others, what about those who make aesthetic judgments in regard to your own work?

GG: Oh, some of my best friends are critics, although I'm not sure I'd want my piano to be played by one.

gg: But some minutes ago, you related the term "spiritual perfection" to a state in which aesthetic judgment is suspended.

GG: I didn't mean to give the impression that such a suspension would constitute the only criterion for such a state.

gg: I understand that. But would it be fair to say that in your view the critical mentality would necessarily lead to an imperiled state of grace?

GG: Well now, I think that would call for a very presumptuous judgment on my part. As I said, some of my best friends are—

gg: —are critics, I know, but you're evading the question.

GG: Not intentionally. I just don't feel that one should generalize in matters where such distinguished reputations are at stake and—

gg: Mr. Gould, I think you owe us both, as well as our readers, an answer to that question.

GG: I do?

gg: That's my conviction; perhaps I should repeat the question?

GG: No, it's not necessary.

gg: So you do feel, in effect, that the critic represents a morally endangered species?

GG: Well now, the word "endangered" implies that—

gg: —please, Mr. Gould, answer the question; you do feel that, don't you?

GG: Well, as I've said, I—

gg: You do, don't you?

GG: (pause) Yes.

gg: Of course you do, and now I'm sure you also feel the better for confession.

GG: Hmm, not at the moment.

gg: But you will in due course.

GG: You really think so?

gg: No question of it. But now that you've stated your position so frankly, I do have to make mention of the fact that you yourself have by-lined critical dispatches from time to time. I even recall a piece on Petula Clark which you contributed some years back to these columns and which—

GG: —and which contained more aesthetic judgment per square page than I would presume to render nowadays. But it was essentially a moral critique, you know. It was a piece in which I used Miss Clark, so to speak, in order to comment on a social milieu.

gg: So you feel that you can successfully distinguish between an aesthetic critique of the individual—which you reject out of hand—and a setting down of moral imperatives for society as a whole.

GG: I think I can. Mind you, there are obviously areas in which overlaps are inevitable. Let's say, for example, that I had been privileged to reside in a town in which all the houses were painted battleship gray.

gg: Why battleship gray?

GG: It's my favorite color.

gg: That's a rather negative color, isn't it?

GG: That's why it's my favorite. Now then, let's suppose for the sake of argument that without warning one individual elected to paint his house fire-engine red—

gg: —thereby challenging the symmetry of the town-planning.

GG: Yes, it would probably do that too, but you're approaching the question from an aesthetic point of view. The real consequence of his action would be to foreshadow an outbreak of manic activity in the town and almost inevitably—since other houses would be painted in similarly garish hues—to encourage a climate of competition and, as a corollary, of violence.

gg: I gather, then, that red in your color lexicon represents aggressive behavior.

GG: I should have thought there'd be general agreement on that. But as I said, there would be an aesthetic/moral overlap at this point. The man who painted the first house may have done so purely from an aesthetic preference and it would, to use an old-fashioned word, be "sinful" if I were to take him to account in respect of his taste. Such an accounting would conceivably inhibit all subsequent judgments on his part. But if I were able to persuade him that his particular aesthetic indulgence represented a moral danger to the community as a whole, and providing I could muster a vocabulary appropriate to the task— which would not be, obviously, a vocabulary of aesthetic standards— then that would, I think, be my responsibility.

gg: You do realize, of course, that you're beginning to talk like a character out of Orwell?

GG: Oh, the Orwellian world holds no particular terrors for me.

gg: And you also realize that you're defining and defending a type of censorship that contradicts the whole post-Renaissance tradition of Western thought?

GG: Certainly. It's the post-Renaissance tradition that has brought the Western world to the brink of destruction. You know, this odd attachment to freedom of movement, freedom of speech, and so on is a peculiarly occidental phenomenon. It's all part of the occidental notion that one can successfully separate word and deed.

gg: The stick-and-stones syndrome, you mean?

GG: Precisely. There's some evidence for the fact that—well, as a

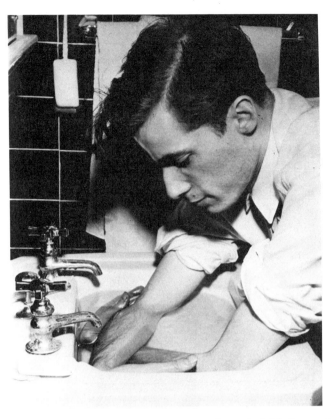

Warming up before a concert, Toronto, 1955. (Canada Wide Features)

Relaxed pedal work sans shoes. (CWF)

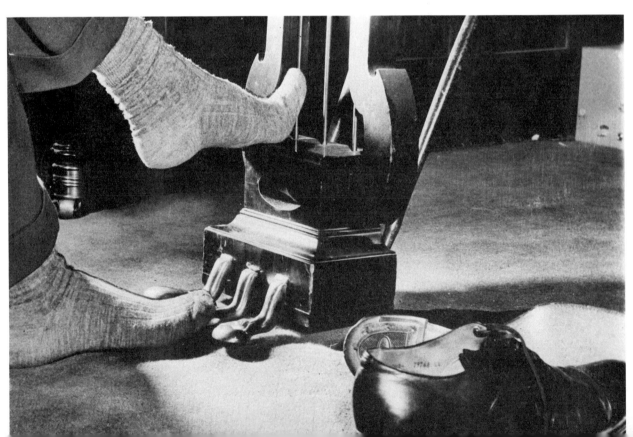

Intense finger work with mittens. (CWF)

The famous chair receives a last-minute adjustment.

matter of fact, McLuhan talks about just that in the *Gutenberg Galaxy*—that preliterate peoples or minimally literate peoples are much less willing to permit that distinction.

gg: I suppose there's also the biblical injunction that to will evil is to accomplish evil.

GG: Exactly. It's only cultures that, by accident or good management, bypassed the Renaissance which see art for the menace it really is.

gg: May I assume the U.S.S.R. would qualify?

GG: Absolutely. The Soviets are a bit roughhewn as to method, I'll admit, but their concerns are absolutely justified.

gg: What about your own concerns? Have any of your activities violated these personal strictures and, in your terms, "menaced" society?

GG: Yes.

gg: Want to talk about it?

GG: Not particularly.

gg: Not even a quick for-instance? What about the fact that you supplied music for *Slaughterhouse-Five*?

GG: What about it?

gg: Well, at least by Soviet standards, the film of Mr. Vonnegut's opus would probably qualify as a socially destructive piece of work, wouldn't you say?

GG: I'm afraid you're right. I even remember a young lady in Leningrad telling me once that Dostoyevsky, "though a very great writer, was unfortunately pessimistic."

gg: And pessimism, combined with a hedonistic cop-out, was the hallmark of *Slaughterhouse*, was it not?

GG: Yes, but it was the hedonistic properties rather than the pessimistic ones that gave me a lot of sleepless nights.

gg: So you don't approve of the film?

GG: I admired its craftsmanship extravagantly.

gg: That's not the same thing as liking it.

GG: No, it isn't.

gg: Can we assume then that even an idealist has his price?

GG: I'd much prefer it said that even an idealist can misread the intention of a shooting script.

gg: You would have preferred an uncompromised Billy Pilgrim, I assume?

GG: I would have preferred some redemptive element added to his persona, yes.

gg: So you wouldn't vouch for the art-as-technique-pure-and-simple theories of Stravinsky, for instance?

GG: Certainly not. That's quite literally the last thing art is.

gg: Then what about the art-as-violence-surrogate theory?

GG: I don't believe in surrogates; they're simply the playthings of minds resistant to the perfectability of man; besides, if you're looking for violence surrogates, genetic engineering is a better bet.

gg: How about the art-as-transcendental-experience theory?

GG: Of the three you've cited, that's the only one that attracts.

gg: Do you have a theory of your own then?

GG: Yes, but you're not going to like it.

gg: I'm braced.

GG: Well, I feel that art should be given the chance to phase itself out. I think that we must accept the fact that art is not inevitably benign, that it is potentially destructive. We should analyze the areas where it tends to do least harm, use them as a guideline, and build into art a component that will enable it to preside over its own obsolescence.

gg: Hm.

GG: —because, you know, the present position, or positions, of art—some of which you've enumerated—are not without analogy to the ban-the-bomb movement of hallowed memory.

gg: You surely don't reject protest of that kind?

GG: No, but since I haven't noticed a single ban-the-child-who-pulls-wings-from-dragonflies movement, I can't join it either. You see, the Western world is consumed with notions of qualification; the threat of nuclear extinction fulfills those notions and the loss of a dragonfly's wing does not. And until the two phenomena are recognized as one, indivisible, until physical and verbal aggression are seen as simply a flip of the competitive coin, until every aesthetic decision can be equated with a moral correlative, I'll continue to listen to the Berlin Philharmonic from behind a glass partition.

gg: So you don't expect to see your death wish for art fulfilled in your lifetime.

GG: No, I couldn't live without the Sibelius Fifth.

gg: But you are nevertheless talking like a sixteenth-century reformer.

GG: Actually, I feel very close to that tradition. In fact, in one of my better lines I remarked that—

gg: —that's an aesthetic judgment if ever I heard one!

GG: A thousand pardons—let me try a second take on that. On a previous occasion, I remarked that I, rather than Mr. Santayana's hero, am "the last puritan."

gg: And you don't find any problem in reconciling the individual-conscience aspect of the Reformation and the collective censorship of the puritan tradition? Both motifs, it would seem to me, are curiously intermingled in your thesis and, from what I know of it, in your documentary work as well.

GG: Well, no, I don't think there's an inevitable inconsistency there because, at its best—which is to say at its purest—that tradition involved perpetual schismatic division. The best and purest—or at any rate the most ostracized—of individuals ended up in Alpine valleys as symbols of their rejection of the world of the plains. As a matter of fact, there is to this day a Mennonite sect in Switzerland that equates separation from the world with altitude.

gg: Would it be fair to suggest that you, on the other hand, equate it with latitude? After all, you did create *The Idea of North* as a metaphoric comment and not as a factual documentary.

GG: That's quite true. Of course, most of the documentaries have dealt with isolated situations—Arctic outposts, Newfoundland outposts, Mennonite enclaves, and so on.

gg: Yes, but they've dealt with a community in isolation.

GG: That's because my magnum opus is still several drawing boards away.

gg: So they are autobiographical drafts?

GG: That, sir, is not for me to say.

gg: Mr. Gould, there's a sort of grim, I might even say gray, consistency to what you've said, but it does seem to me that we have come a rather long way from the concert-versus-record theme with which we began.

GG: On the contrary, I think we've performed a set of variations on that theme and that, indeed, we've virtually come full circle.

gg: In any event, I have only a few more questions to put to you of which, I guess, the most pertinent would now be: Apart from being a frustrated member of the board of censors, is any other career of interest to you?

GG: I've often thought that I'd like to try my hand at being a prisoner.

gg: You regard *that* as a career?

GG: Oh certainly, on the understanding, of course, that I would be entirely innocent of all charges brought against me.

gg: Mr. Gould, has anyone suggested that you could be suffering from a Myshkin complex?

GG: No, and I can't accept the compliment. It's simply that, as I indicated, I've never understood the preoccupation with freedom as it's reckoned in the Western world. So far as I can see, freedom of movement usually has to do only with mobility, and freedom of speech most frequently with socially sanctioned verbal aggression, and to be incarcerated would be the perfect test of one's inner mobility and of the strength which would enable one to opt creatively out of the human situation.

gg: Mr. Gould, weary as I am, that feels like a contradiction in terms.

GG: I don't really think it is. I also think that there's a younger generation than ours—you are about my age, are you not?

gg: I should assume so.

GG: —a younger generation that doesn't have to struggle with that concept, to whom the competitive fact is not an inevitable component of life, and who do program their lives without making allowances for it.

gg: Are you trying to sell me on the neotribalism kick?

GG: Not really, no. I suspect that competitive tribes got us into this mess in the first place, but, as I said, I don't deserve the Myshkin-complex title.

gg: Well, your modesty is legendary of course, Mr. Gould, but what brings you to that conclusion?

GG: The fact that I would inevitably impose demands upon my keepers—demands that a genuinely free spirit could afford to overlook.

gg: Such as?

GG: The cell would have to be prepared in a battleship gray decor—

gg: I shouldn't think that would pose a problem.

GG: Well, I've heard that the new look in penal reform involves primary colors.

gg: Oh, I see.

GG: —and of course there would have to be some sort of understanding about the air-conditioning control. Overhead vents would be out—as I may have mentioned, I'm subject to tracheitis—and, assuming that a forced-air system was employed, the humidity regulator would have to be—

gg: Mr. Gould, excuse the interruption but it just occurs to me that, since you have attempted to point out on several occasions that you did suffer a traumatic experience in the Salzburg Festspielhaus—

GG: Oh, I didn't mean to leave the impression of a traumatic experience. On the contrary, my tracheitis was of such severity that I was able to cancel a month of concerts, withdraw into the Alps, and lead the most idyllic and isolated existence.

gg: I see. Well now, may I make a suggestion?

GG: Of course.

gg: As you know, the old Festspielhaus was originally a riding academy.

GG: Oh quite; I'd forgotten.

gg: And of course, the rear of the building is set against a mountainside.

GG: Yes, that's quite true.

gg: And since you're obviously a man addicted to symbols—I'm sure this prisoner fantasy of yours is precisely that—it would seem to me that the Festspielhaus—the Felsenreitschule—with its Kafka-like setting at the base of a cliff, with the memory of equestrian mobility haunting its past, and located moreover in the birthplace of a composer whose works you have frequently criticized, thereby compromising your own judgmental criteria—

GG: Ah, but I've criticized them primarily as evidence of a hedonistic life.

gg: Be that as it may. The Festspielhaus, Mr. Gould, is a place to which a man like yourself, a man in search of martyrdom, should return.

GG: Martyrdom? What ever gave you that impression? I couldn't possibly go back!

gg: Please, Mr. Gould, try to understand. There could be no more meaningful manner in which to scourge the flesh, in which to proclaim the ascendence of the spirit, and certainly no more meaningful meta-phoric *mise en scène* against which to offset your own hermetic life style, through which to autobiographically define your quest for martyrdom, as I'm sure you will try to do, eventually.

GG: But you must believe me; I have no such quest in mind!

gg: Yes, I think you must go back, Mr. Gould. You must once again tread the boards of the Festspielhaus; you must willingly, even gleefully, subject yourself to the gales which rage upon that stage. For then and only then will you achieve the martyr's end you so obviously desire.

GG: Please don't misunderstand; I'm touched by your concern. It's just that, in the immortal words of Mr. Vonnegut's Billy Pilgrim, "I'm not ready yet."

gg: In that case, Mr. Gould, in the immortal words of Mr. Vonnegut himself, "so it goes."

THE MUSIC ITSELF: GLENN GOULD'S CONTRAPUNTAL VISION
Edward W. Said

G lenn Gould is an exception to almost all the other musical performers in this century. He was a brilliantly proficient pianist (in a world of brilliantly proficient pianists) whose unique sound, brash style, rhythmic inventiveness, and, above all, quality of attention seemed to reach out well beyond the act of performing itself. In the eighty records he made, Gould's piano tone is immediately recognizable. At any point in his career you could say, this is Gould playing, and not Alexis Weissenberg, Vladimir Horowitz, or Alicia de Larrocha. His Bach stands in a class by itself. Like Gieseking's Debussy and Ravel, Rubinstein's Chopin, Schnabel's Beethoven, Katchen's Brahms, Michelangeli's Schumann, it defines the music, makes that artist's interpretation the one you have to have if you are to get at the composer definitively. But unlike all those pianists and their individual specialties, Gould playing Bach—no less sensuous, immediate, pleasurable, and impressive as music making than any of the others I've mentioned—seems like a species of formal knowledge of an enigmatic subject matter: it allows one to think that by playing the piano Gould is proposing some complex, deeply interesting ideas. That he did all this as the central focus of his career made that career more of an aesthetic and cultural project than the short-lived act of playing Bach or Schoenberg.

Most people have treated Gould's various eccentricities as something to be put up with, given that his performances were often so extraordinarily worthwhile. Exceptional critics, Samuel Lipman and

Edward Rothstein principally, have gone further than that, saying that while Gould's uniqueness manifested itself in different, but usually erratic ways—humming, strange habits of dress, playing that is unprecedented in its intelligence and grace—it was all part of the same phenomenon: a pianist whose work was an effort to produce not only performances but also statements and criticisms of the pieces he played. And indeed Gould's numerous writings, his departure from concert life in 1964, his single-minded attention to the details of record production, his garrulous, rococo way of being a hermit and ascetic, reinforce the notion that his performances could be connected to ideas, experiences, and situations not normally associated with the career of a virtuoso pianist.

That Gould's career truly began in 1955 with this recording of Bach's Goldberg Variations is, I think, apparent, and the move, in some sense, foreshadowed nearly everything he did thereafter, including his rerecording of the piece not long before his death. Until he put out the record, few major pianists except Rosalyn Tureck had played the Goldberg in public. Thus Gould's opening (and lasting) achievement was, in alliance with a major record company (a liaison Tureck never seemed to have), to place this highly patterned music before a very large public for the first time, and in doing so to create a terrain entirely his own—anomalous, eccentric, unmistakable.

You have the impression first that here is a pianist possessed of a demonic technique in which speed, accuracy, and power are subordinated to a discipline and calculation that derive not from a clever performer but from the music itself. Moreover, as you listen to the music you feel as if you are watching a tightly packed, dense work being unfolded, resolved almost, into a set of intertwined lines held together not by two hands but by ten fingers, each responsive to all the others, as well as to the two hands and the one mind really back of everything.

At one end of the work a simple theme is announced, a theme permitting itself to be metamorphosed thirty times, redistributed in modes whose theoretical complexity is enhanced by the pleasure taken in their practical execution. At the other end of the Goldberg, the theme is replayed after the variations have ceased, only this time the literal repetition is (as Borges says about Pierre Menard's version of the *Quixote*) "verbally identical, but infinitely richer." This process of proceeding brilliantly from microcosm to macrocosm and then back again is Gould's special accomplishment in his first Goldberg: by doing it pianistically he also lets you experience the sort of understanding normally the result of reading and thinking, not simply of playing a musical instrument.

I don't at all mean to denigrate the latter. It is simply that from the beginning Gould tried to articulate music in a different mode than was the case when, say, Van Cliburn—his near contemporary, a fine pianist—played Tchaikovsky or Rachmaninoff concertos. Gould's choice of Bach at the outset, and his subsequent recording of most of Bach's keyboard works, is central to what he was trying to do. Since Bach's music is pre-eminently contrapuntal or polyphonic, this fact imparts a really astonishingly powerful identity to Gould's career.

For the essence of counterpoint is simultaneity of voices, preternatural control of resources, apparently endless inventiveness. In counterpoint a melody is always in the process of being repeated by one or another voice: the result is horizontal, rather than vertical, music. Any series of notes is thus capable of an infinite set of transformations, as the series (or melody or subject) is taken up first by one voice then by another, the voices always continuing to sound against, as well as with, all the others. Instead of the melody at the top being supported by a thicker harmonic mass beneath (as in largely vertical nineteenth-century music), Bach's contrapuntal music is regularly composed of several equal lines, sinuously interwoven, working themselves out according to stringent rules.

Quite apart from its considerable beauty, a fully developed contrapuntal style like Bach's has a particular prestige within the musical universe. For one, its sheer complexity and frequent gravity suggest a formidable refinement and finality of statement; when Beethoven, or Bach, or Mozart writes fugally the listener is compelled to assume that an unusual importance is given the music, for at such moments everything—every voice, every instant, every interval—is, so to speak, written out, worked through, fully measured. One cannot say more in music (the tremendous fugue at the end of Verdi's *Falstaff* comes to mind) than in a strict fugue. And consequently the contra-puntal mode in music is, it seems, connected to eschatology, not only because Bach's music is essentially religious or because Beethoven's *Missa Solemnis* is highly fugal. For the rules of counterpoint are so demanding, so exacting in their detail as to seem divinely ordained; transgressions of the rule—forbidden progressions, proscribed har-monies—are specified in such terms as *diabolus in musica.*

To master counterpoint is therefore in a way almost to play God, as Adrian Leverkühn, the hero of Thomas Mann's *Doctor Faustus,* under-stands. Counterpoint is the total ordering of sound, the complete management of time, the minute subdivision of musical space, and absolute absorption for the intellect. Running through the history of Western music, from Palestrina and Bach to the dodecaphonic rigors of Schoenberg, Berg, and Webern, is a contrapuntal mania for inclu-siveness, and it is a powerful allusion to this that informs Mann's Hitlerian version of a pact with the devil in *Faustus,* a novel about a polyphonic German artist whose aesthetic fate encapsulates his nation's overreaching folly. Gould's contrapuntal performances come as close as I can imagine to delivering an inkling of what *might* be at stake in the composition and performance of counterpoint, minus perhaps any grossly political import. Not the least of this achievement, however, is that he never recoils from the comic possibility that high counterpoint may only be a parody, pure form aspiring to the role of world-historical wisdom.

In fine, Gould's playing enables the listener to experience Bach's contrapuntal excesses—for they are that, beautifully and exorbi-tantly—as no other pianist has. We are convinced that no one could *do* counterpoint, reproduce and understand Bach's fiendish skill, more than Gould. Hence he seems to perform at the limit where music, rationality, and the physical incarnation of both in the performer's fingers come together. Yet even though Gould's playing of Bach is so concentrated on its task, he manages also to suggest different kinds of power and intelligence that would appear in later recordings. In the course of recording Bach's keyboard works integrally, Gould produced a disc of Liszt's transcription of Beethoven's Fifth Symphony and, still later, his own versions of orchestral and vocal music by Wagner, late romantic music that was contrapuntal in its own overripe way, made even more artificial by being set in a chromatic polyphony that Gould forced out of the orchestral score and onto the piano keyboard.

These records, like all of Gould's playing, accentuate the overwhelming unnaturalness of his performances, from his very low chair to his slump, to his semi-staccato, aggressively clear sound. But they also illustrate the way in which Gould's predilection for contrapuntal music gave him an unexpectedly novel dimension. Sitting at his keyboard, doing impossible things all alone, no longer the concert performer but the disembodied recording artist, didn't Gould seem to become his own self-confirming, self-delighting hearer, a man who replaced the God that Albert Schweitzer suggested that Bach was writing for?

Certainly Gould's choice of music to play bears this out. He has written of his preference not only for polyphony in general, but also for the composer, like Richard Strauss, "who makes richer his own time by not being of it; who speaks for all generations by being of none." Gould's dislike of middle-period Beethoven, Mozart, and most of the nineteenth-century romantics whose music was intensely subjective or fashionable and too instrument-specific, is balanced by his admiration for pre- and post-romantics like Orlando Gibbons and Anton Webern, as well as for polyphonists (Bach and Strauss) whose all-or-nothing attitude to the instruments they wrote for made for a total discipline lacking in other composers. Strauss, for example, is Gould's choice as the major twentieth-century musical figure. Not only was Strauss eccentric, he was also concerned "with utilizing the fullest riches of late-romantic tonality *within* the firmest possible formal disciplines"; thus, Gould continues, Strauss's "interest was primarily the preservation of the *total* function of tonality—not simply in a work's fundamental outline, but even in its most specific minutiae of design." Like Bach then, Strauss was "painstakingly explicit at every level of... architectural concept." You write music in which every note counts, and if like Strauss you have an orchestra in mind, all the instruments are treated with an explicit function in mind for each: whereas if like Bach you write simply for a keyboard instrument, or in the *Art of the Fugue* for four unspecified voices, each voice is carefully disciplined. There are no strummed *oompahs* (although, alas, they do exist in Strauss), no mindlessly regular chordal accompaniments. The formal concept is articulated assertively and consciously, from the large structure to the merest ornament.

There is a good deal of exaggeration in these descriptions, but at any rate Gould's playing aims to be as explicit and detailed as he thinks the music he plays is. In a sense his performances extend, amplify, make more explicit the scores he interprets, scores that do not as a matter of principle include program music. Music is fundamentally dumb: despite its fertile syntactic and expressive possibilities, music does not encode references, or ideas, or hypotheses discursively, the way language does. So the performer can either be (or play) dumb, or, as in Gould's case, the performer can set himself a great deal to do. If this might mean controlling the performance space to the extent of articulating, taking over his environment (by dressing and appearing to be against the grain), conducting the orchestra despite a conductor's presence, humming over and above the piano's sound, talking and writing as if to extend the piano's reach into verbal language via a whole slew of essays, interviews, record jacket notes, then Gould did so enthusiastically, like a mischievous, unstoppably talkative little prodigy.

The most impressive of the numerous Gould events I attended was his appearance in Boston in October 1961 with Paul Paray and the Detroit Symphony Orchestra. In the first half Gould did the Fifth Brandenburg with the Detroit's leading violinist and flutist. He was partially hidden from view, but his arms and head were visible, bobbing and swaying to the music, although his playing was suitably small-scaled, admirably light, and rhythmically propulsive, perfectly conscious of the other performers. Music with eyes, ears, and a nose, I remember thinking. (All of Gould's recorded concerto performances—especially the Bach concertos—are the same in one respect: so athletically tensile and rhetorically inflected is his playing that an electric tension is kept up between what seems often to be a heavy, rather plodding orchestra and a darting, skipping piano line that dives in and out of the orchestral mass with marvelous aplomb.) After the intermission Gould reemerged to play the Richard Strauss *Burleske*, a horrendously busy one-movement work that is not exactly a repertoire staple; Gould incidentally never recorded the piece. Technically his performance with the Detroit was stunning; one wouldn't have believed it possible that an essentially Bach-ensemble pianist would all of a sudden have become a whirlwind post- and hyper-Rachmaninoff-style virtuoso.

But the real wonder was more bizarre still, and as one reflects on Gould's later career, what he did in the Strauss besides playing the piano seems like a prefiguring of subsequent developments. As if to enlarge his part as a soloist, Gould conducted the orchestra extravagantly, if not intelligibly. Paray was there too, and he of course was the actual conductor. Gould, however, conducted to himself (plainly disconcerting though the sight of him was), doubtless confusing the orchestra and, unless Paray's occasionally murderous glances at Gould were part of some prerehearsed routine, annoying Paray. Conducting for Gould seemed to be an ecstatic, imperialistic widening of his reading of the *Burleske*, at first through his fingers, then by means of his arms and head, then finally by pushing out from his personal pianistic space into the orchestra's territory. Watching Gould do all this was a skewed lesson in the discipline of detail, the artist being led where the fanatically detailed, expansively inclined composer led him.

There is more to a Gould performance than that. Most critics who have written about him mention the clean dissections he seems to give the pieces he plays. In this he strips the piano literature of most of its inherited traditions, whether these have come down in the form of liberties taken with tempi or tone, or from declamatory opportunities that issue as a sort of professional deformation from the great line of piano virtuosos, or again that are ingrained in patterns of performance certified by famous teachers (Theodor Leschetizky, Rosina Lhevinne, Alfred Cortot, etc.). There is none of this in Gould. He neither sounds like other pianists, nor, so far as I can determine, has anyone succeeded in sounding like him. It is as if Gould's playing, like his career, is entirely self-made, even self-born, with neither a preexisting dynasty nor an extra-Gouldian destiny framing it.

The reason for this is partly the result of Gould's forthright egoism, partly the result of contemporary Western culture. Like many of the composers and pieces he has played, Gould wants to appear beholden to no one as he goes his own way. Not many pianists will take on and make sense of so formidable a mass as both books of Bach's *Well-Tempered Clavier*, all his partitas, the two- and three-part inventions, the toccatas, the English and French suites, the *Art of the Fugue*, all the keyboard concertos including the Italian, plus such oddities as Bizet's *Variations chromatiques*, Sibelius's sonatas, pieces by Byrd and Gibbons, Strauss's *Enoch Arden* and his *Ophelialieder*, the Schoenberg concerto, transcriptions of Wagner's "Siegfried Idyll" and Beethoven's Pastoral Symphony. What Gould sustains in all this is (to use a phrase he once applied to Sibelius) a style that is "passionate but antisensual." It allows the listener to observe Gould's "gradual, lifelong construction of a state of wonder and serenity" not only as an independent aesthetic phenomenon, but also as a theatrical experience whose source is Gould himself.

In 1964 Gould left the concert world and was reborn as a creature of the technology he exploited to permit more or less infinite reproduction, infinite repetition ("take-twoness," he called it), infinite creation and re-creation. No wonder he referred to the recording studio as "womblike," a place where "time turns in upon itself," where a new "art form with its own laws and its own liberties…and its quite extraordinary possibilities" is born with the recording artist. A highly readable book by Geoffrey Payzant, *Glenn Gould, Music and Mind*, copiously describes this rebirth, as well as Gould's skill in managing to keep the spotlight on himself. Gould's post-concertizing afterlife was passionate, antinatural antisensuality carried very far indeed, and it certainly flowed from his cheery penchant for being lonely, original, unprecedented, and somehow immensely gregarious, someone who curiously never tired of himself.

In less metaphysical terms, what occurred in his career after 1964 was a displacement in emphasis. In the concert hall the emphasis had been on the reception by an audience of a live performer, a commodity directly purchased, consumed, and exhausted during two hours of concert time. Such a transaction had its roots in eighteenth-century patronage and the class structure of the *ancien régime*, although during the nineteenth century, music performance became a more easily acquired mass commodity. In the late twentieth century, however,

Gould acknowledged that the new commodity was a limitlessly reproducible object, the plastic disc or tape; as performer, Gould had transferred himself back from the stage to the studio, to a site where creation had become production, a place where he could manage to be creator and interpreter simultaneously without also directly submitting to the whims of a ticket-purchasing public. There is no small irony in the fact that Gould's new bonds were with technicians and corporate executives, and that he spoke of his relationship with them (and they of him) in emotionally intimate terms.

In the meantime, Gould was able to push his contrapuntal view of things a bit further. His aim as an artist would be, like Bach or Mozart, to organize the field completely, to subdivide time and space with utmost control, to "speculate the elements" (Mann's phrase in *Doctor Faustus*) in such a way as to take a row of elementary notes and then force them through as many changes as possible, changes that would come from splicing bits of tape together to make new wholes, from displacing sequences (for instance, the different enunciations of the Goldberg theme in Gould's 1981 version were recorded out of order), from using different pianos for different sections of the same music, recording and living without paying attention to the time of day, making an informal studio space into the opposite of the concert hall's crippling formality. This, Gould said, was giving additional enrichment to the idea of process, to carrying on more or less forever.

It was also, perhaps poignantly, a way of trying to undermine the biological and sexual bases of the human performer's life. For the late-twentieth-century musical artist, recording would be a form of immortality suited not only to noncomposer (nineteenth-century-style composers being now both rare and rarefied), but to what the German cultural critic Walter Benjamin called the age of mechanical reproduction. Gould was the first great musical performer of the twentieth century unequivocally to choose that fate. Before Gould, performers like Stokowski and Rubinstein had self-consciously lived in the hybrid world of wealth and romantic cliché created by spectators, impresarios, and ticket sellers. Gould saw that such a choice, however admirable it was for those two, wouldn't do for him. Yet for someone so self-aware, Gould never reflected on the unflattering complicities of an enterprise such as his, which depended ultimately on giant corporations, and anonymous mass culture, and advertising hype for its success. That he just did not look at the market system, whose creature to some degree he was, may have been cynical prudence, or it may have been that he somehow couldn't fit it into his playing. It was as if the real social setting of his work was one of the things that Gould's contrapuntal skills were not meant to absorb, however much these skills assumed the system's complaisance.

Yet he was far from being a pastoral idiot-savant despite his affinity for the silence and solitude of the North. As the critic Richard Poirier has said of Frost, Lawrence, and Mailer, Gould was a performing self whose career was the cultivated result of immense talent, careful choice, urbanity, and, up to a point, self-sufficiency, all of them managed together like a polyphonic structure in relief. The last record to be released in Gould's lifetime— the rerecorded Goldberg Variations—in almost every detail is a tribute to an artist uniquely able to rethink and replan a complex piece of music in a new way, and yet keep it (as much as the earlier version) sounding recognizably like a performance by Glenn Gould.

Child and partner of the age of mechanical reproduction, Gould set himself the task of being at home with what Mann calls "the opposing hosts of counterpoint." Despite its limitations, Gould's work was more interesting than nearly all other performing artists of this era. Only Rachmaninoff, I think, had that special combination of lean intelligence, magnificent dash, and perfectly economical line that Gould produced in nearly everything he played. Technique in the service of an inquiring understanding, complexity resolved without being domesticated, wit relieved of philosophical baggage: Glenn Gould plays the piano.

GROWING UP GOULD
Robert Fulford

"Sit up, Glenn. Sit up straight, *please.*" Florence Gould had a talent for exasperation and she was a much exasperated, much put-upon woman. She was proud of her twelve-year-old son, her only child, but her pride was mixed with vexation. He wouldn't accept the rules of posture, for one thing, and he wouldn't exercise outdoors when she wanted him to. He looked sickly, and she worried constantly about his diet. He was likely to catch cold, or so she thought, if he became overheated or tired. He didn't always keep a civil tongue, and his opinions were often outrageous as well as clever. He could explain, without being asked, just why Caruso—on the evidence of a few scratchy recordings—was never much of a singer. He seemed to know, from birth, almost everything about everything, particularly music, and if he didn't know it today he would probably learn it tomorrow. And he wouldn't sit up straight, like a sensible boy. In the living room, year after year, on the plush chesterfield beside the piano, he slouched so much that his body was almost horizontal.

Florence Gould was a part-time voice teacher who claimed descent from the Norwegian composer Edvard Grieg. She and her husband, Bert, an amateur violinist and a dedicated supporter of the Kiwanis music festivals, appreciated music of the better sort. To judge by their conversation, they regarded it as morally worthy and important—on a level, perhaps, with prayers and United Church sermons and fair dealing in business and not swearing. They weren't prepared, however, for the arrival in their midst of Glenn Gould: it was rather like having a

The passionate state of mind. Glenn Gould, mid-1950s. (Glenn Gould Estate) 57

mountain range appear suddenly in the back yard. At three, sitting on his mother's lap before the piano, Glenn demonstrated that he had perfect pitch; at five he was able to play simple tunes she taught him and even make up a few of his own. Soon a proper piano teacher had to be called in, and by the age of eleven Glenn was in the hands of Alberto Guerrero, an avuncular Chilean in his fifties who had had a concert career in Latin America before the First World War and was now a teacher at the Conservatory of Music in Toronto. Guerrero remained Glenn's teacher for nine years, until the master happily acknowledged that he had no more to teach the pupil. By the time Guerrero died, in 1959, he had seen Gould become one of the greatest virtuosi in the world.

Florence and Bert Gould were determined that their son should have "a normal childhood"—as if anything in the life of a genius could ever be normal. In their household the phrase "child prodigy" was spoken as a dark curse, if at all. So long as they could, they would protect their son from premature exposure to the world of professional music. Mozart's unhappy life was cited as a cautionary tale. Concert managers would not be allowed to exploit *this* young talent; Glenn would not be dragged before audiences as a curiosity, like so many poor boys and girls. Glenn's talent, and his health too, had to be protected even from Glenn himself. His parents decided that he must not be allowed to practise too much, and in consultation with his teacher a limit was set—no more than four hours a day. This rule required strict enforcement: if left alone, presumably, the boy would have ruined his health by sitting at the piano all day and all night.

Bert Gould's prosperity as a furrier meant that money from concert appearances was never a serious temptation. Without noticeable strain the family was able to spend about $3,000 a year, in 1940s currency, on Glenn's musical education. His talent was developed in the privacy available only to the modestly well-to-do. Nevertheless, musical Toronto soon learned about him. He was never one of those artists of legend who go unappreciated in their native towns. People who mattered—right up to Sir Ernest MacMillan, conductor of the Toronto Symphony Orchestra—understood from the beginning that they had something exceptional on their hands. And slowly, carefully, Glenn was allowed to appear in public. From 1942 to 1949 he studied organ as well as piano, and it was as an organist that he made his début (school concerts and Kiwanis festivals aside) in a Casavant Society concert at Eaton Auditorium on December 12, 1945, the year he was thirteen. Everyone who heard him was enormously impressed. A child who can handle a giant pipe organ at all is a rarity; a child who can do it with "astonishing technique" and "interpretive intuition" (as the Toronto *Evening Telegram* said) is a miracle.

That day I sat beside Glenn on the organ bench, turning pages of his score. In grade three Glenn and I had been placed side by side in our class at Williamson Road Public School in the Beach district of Toronto; soon we realized, in comparing addresses, that my family was about to move into the house next to his on Southwood Drive, just behind the schoolyard. (This made it possible for me to take part, a couple of years later, in perhaps the first of Glenn Gould's many experiments in sound reproduction technology—the stretching between our houses of two tin cans on a thread and the attempt to communicate thereby.) From that point until our early twenties we were friends, and during much of childhood and adolescence we were each other's best friend. In the 1950s we drifted apart, toward different interests, different passions. But knowing him that long was a unique experience. Glenn's soaring talent, his limitless ambition, his rich humour, his marvellous quick understanding of everything and everyone—these constituted my first meeting with genius. His death in October, after a stroke, left me turning the pages of memory.

"Normal" or not, his childhood was dominated by music. By the last years of public school he was coming to class part-time so that he could spend much of the day at the Conservatory, with his teacher, or by himself at the piano. In high school he was more often absent than present, and was sometimes tutored in private by one of the teachers.

If his genius was a surprise to his parents it was even more of a surprise to his contemporaries at Malvern Collegiate, the high school we attended. Few of the students there could even have named an eminent pianist of the day, yet somehow most of us understood that Glenn was to be such a person. Of course we lacked the knowledge to

distinguish between the best young pianist in the east end of Toronto and the best young pianist in the world, but something about Glenn made us certain he would be a great man.

His fellow students certainly found him peculiar: he could sometimes be seen conducting an invisible orchestra as he walked home from school, both arms flailing in the wind as he hummed the parts—"pa-puh, pa-puh, duh-*pa.*" They seldom made fun of him, however: they tended to view him with wary respect. His mother badly wanted him to have "normal" (i.e., non-musical) friends, and in retrospect I imagine that our friendship owed something to her encouragement. Whatever her desires, he took part in none of the usual pastimes of boys; I cannot remember a moment when he was not an outsider. He never to my knowledge told dirty jokes or speculated about the sexuality of girls. He played no sports, and if anyone threw a baseball or football to him—either out of ignorance or to tease him—he pulled his hands back and turned away, letting the ball fall to the ground. His long, slender hands were for more important things, and he protected them carefully.

His musical tastes were fastidious from the beginning, and by his late teens he had staked out what was to be the ground of his taste during the first flowering of his career. He liked the eighteenth century and the twentieth but had little time for the nineteenth and no patience at all for anything that carried the name "romantic."

His fastidiousness did not extend to his schoolwork. His handwriting was atrocious, to the dismay of our public school teachers, and I can remember when he and I ruefully agreed that either one or the other of us would always place last in penmanship. In some subjects, though, he was amazingly quick. Like most good musicians, he was immediately at home in mathematics. In grade ten geometry he gobbled up the textbook, rushing nimbly through the whole year's work by October, pausing occasionally to explain something to me. He liked literature but disliked memory work, which was then a part of the teaching of English. When a poem was assigned to us to memorize he sometimes set it to music and we sat side by side on the piano bench, singing it incompetently till we had mastered the words.

Gould seemed never to doubt his value as a musician, and early in

Glenn Gould age 15 with his favourite accompanyist, Nicky. (Glenn Gould Estate)

adolescence his imagination was soaring toward that distant world he would soon occupy so triumphantly. In his mind the great musicians of Europe and North America were already his peers, even if they hadn't yet heard of him. When he was nineteen or twenty, still unknown outside Canada, he played for me a record of a Bach partita by one of the greatest Bach interpreters of the age and then played his own version. He explained to me why his was superior, and in my ignorance I felt as if I understood him. Then as later, he was a natural lecturer who knew his audience; he was rehearsing, unknowingly, for those brilliant interviews and articles in which he would prove himself one of the most articulate musical performers of the century, but he was also moving emotionally toward an acceptance of his destiny. A few years later he returned from a concert in Berlin and read to my wife and me a quotation from one of the leading German critics. The critic had said that Gould was the best pianist who had appeared in Berlin since Busoni, and of course Gould had immediately looked up the date of Busoni's death. It turned out to be 1924, and Glenn giggled in delight. Even German culture had accepted him, and on the terms on which he wanted to be accepted. Later he changed those terms—he would do no more concerts, he would make records of astounding originality—but still he was accepted.

There were always critics who found Gould's interpretations (of Beethoven, for example) eccentric, but I doubt that he took them seriously. His view of critics as a class was apparently set by the more or less amateurish scribblers who wrote for the Toronto papers in his youth. He loved to tell the story of the elderly lady who wrote reviews for a Toronto daily and, while expressing admiration of his talent, asked him not to play Mozart: she said he played it so softly that her hearing aid wouldn't pick it up. Later, in New York, he met the critic of *The New Yorker*—a man of small musical reputation—and reported with a wild gaiety that the man had actually condescended to him. At times he seemed to love the spectacle of the music world—the gossip, the backbiting, the outrageously inflated egos—almost as much as he loved the music itself. He even took a harmless pleasure from contemplating the jealousy that his talent naturally aroused in his contemporaries.

In the early 1950s, before he made his Town Hall début in New York at the age of twenty-two, Glenn and I were partners in a pocket-sized company called New Music Associates. We put on three concerts at the Royal Conservatory, at each of which Glenn was the major attraction. One was devoted to Arnold Schoenberg's work, another to the works of Schoenberg and his pupils Alban Berg and Anton von Webern, and a third to Bach, Glenn explaining that really Bach was essentially a modern musician and therefore could be sponsored by New Music Associates. I sold the tickets, arranged for the publicity and the printing, and lined up friends to act as ushers; Glenn looked after the music. The concerts were well attended, the music well received (at one of the concerts Maureen Forrester made her Toronto début), but we abandoned the company. Glenn had performed the *Goldberg Variations* for the first time in public at the Bach concert, and they soon became the beginning of his success as a recording artist. By the mid-1950s he no longer yearned for the musical life, or tried to promote it; triumphantly, he embodied it.

Late-night rehearsal session, late 1950s. (CBS)

SHATTERING A FEW MYTHS
John Beckwith

Geoffrey Payzant's book, *Glenn Gould, Music and Mind*, states that Gould participated in the annual music competition-festival in Toronto in 1944, and a newspaper account of this event is cited as the first public notice of Gould's exceptional abilities. Did Gould take part in subsequent festivals during his student years? About the 1945 festival I am not certain, but I can recall he was top-place winner in the open Bach-Prelude-and-Fugue category in 1946. He played *WTC I, 22* in B flat minor. Second place went to a pupil of Lubka Kolessa's named Tova Boroditsky, who performed *WTC I, 20* in A minor. I came in third, with *WTC I, 18* in G sharp minor. I was at the end of my teens while Gould was at the start of his. What do I recall about the occasion? First, the extraordinary clarity of the lines and the singing tone of the B flat minor Prelude as Gould played it—which is how I still hear that wonderful piece. Second, my own keyboard behavior in the final round—fluent in the Prelude but with nervous stumbles in the Fugue. My feelings? I suppose there may have been some resentment at "losing" to a thirteen-year-old, though I think I also felt exhilarated to have reached the final round for the first time in my life. Of one more thing I am sure: there were definitely more than three contestants.

The eloquence, the elevated seriousness, of his teenage piano performances in fact left indelible impressions. Aside from that Bach Prelude, I recall the first movement of the Beethoven G major Concerto from his performance of the solo part with the student orchestra in May 1946—not just its ease and technical fluency, but the real depth of expression held in those songful lines and those triple trills, even then full of the warm luminosity that was such a later trademark of his. Then there was the Beethoven D minor Sonata (Opus 31, no. 2) which he played in his Eaton Auditorium concert in October 1947 (his first, I think, under Walter Homburger's management). The central adagio movement is so full of silence in its opening theme that with most players one simply loses interest. Gould conveyed the feeling of forward-driving energy through the silences, so that their later filling-out with variational filigree came as an especially beautiful evolution. The Sunday afternoon concerts in the sculpture court of the Art Gallery of Toronto (now the Art Gallery of Ontario) were another regular part of the local performing circuit and from Gould's solo appearance there around 1949, my memory insists on preserving his encore rendition of—of all pieces—Chopin's post-humous E minor Valse. He articulated it within an inch of its life; the ending was like *Gang Busters.*

What was Gould like in student days? I lately discovered two early communications from him. A 1950 note, issued from "Marine Head-quarters, Uptergrove, Ont.," is all in rhymed couplets. In part it reads:

> I've been studying Ernst Křenek's Sonata #3,
> I'm sure that the score you'll be dying to see.
> It's done in four movements, and it sure is not meek,
> The first one embodies the 12 tone technique.

A late-1951 prose communication relates his satisfaction with his performance of Beethoven's B flat Concerto with the Toronto Symphony—or rather, with that "great and grossly underestimated work" itself. Listing this and a few other concerts and broadcasts, he comments:

> I have now got a pile of records for you to hear of broadcasts that I've done and we'll have to get together as soon as you get back.

(I was then studying in France.) The interesting aspect of this rather commonplace sentence is that it refers to "records." In fact, I under-stand an aircheck disc of that Beethoven performance has been recently located. Gould did not own a portable tape recorder until 1952 or 1953; few people then had them. I remember the Gould instrument both because it was a novelty and because on one hilarious occasion (it must have been in 1953), he, Ray Dudley and I recorded on it a three-handed *prestissimo* version of Chopin's A minor Etude (Opus 10, no. 2), with the intention of out-Horowitzing Horowitz. This card, incidentally, is signed "G. Gould, D. A.—which is infinitely superior to a S.M.R." This is evidently an indication that the CBC had then just boosted Gould from its "Sunday Morning Recital" radio series to the late-evening series called "Distinguished Artists."

Three myths persist.

Myth 1. To non-Canadians, it may appear that Glenn Gould was unknown and unappreciated prior to his 1955 successes in Washington and New York and his first *Goldberg Variations* recording of that same year. This is not so. Between 1945 and 1955 Gould was certainly recognized as an exceptional artist, played many solo recitals, made guest appearances with all the major Canadian orchestras; after 1950 he was heard with increasing regularity on national network radio. He performed as solo artist and also with a trio during the concert season in the very first year, 1953, of the Shakespeare Festival at Stratford, Ontario. I recently looked up the 1955 survey *Music in Canada* and found he was already (at age twenty-three) referred to as one of the most outstanding musicians the country had produced. The fact that Homburger managed him from the time he was fifteen is surely a sign that he was known, valued, and appreciated locally and nationally.

Myth 2. From his later reclusiveness one might assume Gould did not enjoy his success. This too is incorrect. The little joke about "D. A." illustrates the contrary attitude; in fact, he was pleased to be recognized. Further illustrations come to mind. In 1955 I held a staff job in CBC radio, and I remember Gould dated a girl in the department briefly. He used to drop in quite often, and one day he brought with him the proofs of the record-jacket for his first Columbia disc—the thirty photographic variations taken in the recording studios to go with the thirty *Goldbergs*. I remember how very delighted and excited he was with this design. There are many intriguing aspects to his international success: he achieved it with his own choice of repertoire, began it from an exceptional position of strength, and maintained it always within his own limits as occupant of the driver's scat. But that he was not human enough to enjoy and take a modicum of honest pride in all this, is simply too much of a distortion.

Over Myth 3 I will take longer. It must be, in fact, the main *raison d'être* of these recollections. From some of Gould's own comments in articles and interviews, and from an early passage of the Payzant study, it may appear that his early formation as a pianist owed almost everything to the recordings of such players as Schnabel and Tureck. This is an incomplete picture. In particular it ignores the strong influence of his teacher (who was also mine) the Chilean-Canadian pianist Alberto Guerrero (1886-1959).

Believing Myth 3 one would need the naïveté of the parents in *The Music Man* whose kids are told by the Robert Preston character to "think the Minuet in G" as a means of playing it on their band instruments.

Gould was a genius, and not only had what is called by pianists a "natural technique" but also was an extraordinarily quick learner. Many things he clearly did teach himself. However, whatever teaching means, the young Gould was also clearly taught many things by Guerrero. Guerrero's own pianism had, among other unusual features, the following: he sat lower in relation to the keyboard and played with flatter fingers than most players; his performances of light rapid passages had not only fluency and great speed but also exceptional clarity and separation of individual notes. To those who studied with Guerrero, Otto Ortmann's comparison of "flat-finger stroke" and "curved-finger stroke" in his important study *The Physiological Mechanics of Piano Technique* (1929; chapter xvii) rings familiarly, as do the arguments in favor of what Ortmann calls (in chapter xx) "pure finger-technique" as opposed to "weight technique." The 1940s were a period when Guerrero was applying many of Ortmann's ideas (as I learned later from Myrtle Rose Guerrero; Guerrero did not make us read Ortmann). One practice-technique for finger-separation consisted of playing the music for each hand separately, very slowly, but making the sound by tapping each finger with the non-playing hand. One learned from this how very precise and economical the muscle-movements needed for fast playing really could be. It was indeed a "pure finger-technique" in that virtually no hand-action was applied—the fingers did it all. One heard the result in Guerrero's memorable Bach and Mozart performances but also in works like the Chopin *Barcarolle* or Debussy's *Feux d'artifice*.

Guerrero's uniqueness as a teacher, however, was not as much technical as musicianly. As others have said of him, he was not so much a teacher of piano as a teacher of *music*. (It may be significant in this regard that a number of composers are among his former pupils—Oskar Morawetz, Bruce Mather, and R. Murray Schafer especially come to mind.) He had a view of music as a profoundly serious commitment, and he somehow got you to keep this in mind while he helped you through your sometimes-unseemly physical and mental grapplings with the notes.

In this description of some aspects of Guerrero's thinking, teaching, and playing, are there not many characteristics which later became fundamental to Gould's art? Gould's physical appearance at the keyboard was in my view more like Guerrero's than was any other pupil's—the finger-angle very similar, the low-seated position similar too, though lower still in his mature years. His "pure finger-technique" was also highly reminiscent of Guerrero's; his famous quick non-legato touch could be called an extension of it. (Another fellow pupil confirmed to me that in fact Gould did use the slow tapping technique in his practice in student days.) His basic attitude to music stemmed from Guerrero's example initially, divergent though they were in outlook and taste later on.

Gould disagreed with his teacher on Mozart, and the latter's love of traditional opera was something he did not really learn to share. But the Bach keyboard repertoire was in many ways the core of Guerrero's work and must be accorded a similar centrality in Gould's. One of my most vivid recollections of Guerrero is his performing analysis of the C major Invention. He claimed to have spent one summer practicing this two-page piece and nothing else, and I believed him. He revealed in it a microcosm of beautiful compositional logic, and I was moved to learn and perform all the Inventions and Sinfonias, as Gould later did. This may not have been orthodoxy in piano repertoire, but it was an unforgettable musical inspiration.

Was Guerrero's style of performing Bach harpsichord-like? In many ways, yes, it was. In that generation, the harpsichord meant Wanda Landowska, who was certainly an idol of Guerrero's. I guess I myself was encouraged to learn the *Goldberg Variations* partly by Guerrero and partly by listening to her 78-rpm recording. Gould came to hear my performance in 1950 in the basement theater of the Royal Ontario Museum, and was very enthusiastic backstage afterwards. I wish I could say therefore that I influenced his own decision to learn this piece. I did not; but Guerrero no doubt did. Guerrero himself knew the *Variations* intimately and had performed them in Toronto in the 1930s. At one stage of his teaching Guerrero advocated slow staccato practice to a metronome, after observing that Landowska, visiting Toronto for a series of CBC broadcast concerts, had only two items of furniture in her studio—her harpsichord and a little stand for her metronome. (The studio was in the apartment of Guerrero's daughter and son-in-law, so I guess the story was true.) Later, Gould would always say that Landowska's performances were for him "too romantic," but in student days he may have absorbed something of her approach both through recordings and through Guerrero's influence. Certainly she was a performer in the creative Stokowski-like mold Gould admired so much, and one deduces she was a performer with a highly developed sense of the possibilities of recording techniques, perhaps the one earlier keyboard artist to be compared with Gould in that respect.

Again, Gould's enthusiasm for Schoenberg derived in part from Guerrero's. Guerrero had performed the Opus 11 and Opus 19 pieces on several occasions, and was amazed at Gould's reaction when he showed them to him at a lesson in 1947 or 1948. The first response was rejection. Strongest arguments against Schoenberg and atonality were raised, Guerrero being put on the defensive. But, a few weeks later, Gould showed up with some pieces of his own in the same style, for which Guerrero was full of praise. (I remember them too; they were very good, and surely merited preservation, though Gould claimed

Glenn Gould age 13 with his teacher Alberto Guerrero. (Page Toles)

they were later destroyed.) That was the start of an unusual absorption the early culmination of which came in the two Toronto concerts which Robert Fulford has referred to—one of Schoenberg's music in October 1952 and one of music by Webern and Berg in January 1954. Organized by Gould, with a few of the works conducted by Victor Feldbrill, these were singular events, in a period before Toronto had any modern-music performance outlets to speak of. With his love for explication already evident, Gould prepared introductory essays for the various works; but rather than printing these or reading them himself (believe it or not, then he was too shy), he engaged a well-known mellow-voiced CBC announcer, Frank Herbert, to read them to the audience. The result was unfortunate. Herbert began with a nervous smile, "Hello, I'm Frank Herbert," and as he proceeded it became clear that his comprehension of what he was saying was less than complete. This was a pity, and Gould soon became more at home making his own spoken introductions. In his notes on Webern's Quartet, Opus 22, I recall, he quoted Adolfo Salazar's characterization of Webern's style as "parsimonious"—a witticism poor Frank Herbert could not appreciate at all.

(Personally I had reason to be grateful to Gould for introducing me to much of the modern Viennese repertoire; another recollection from one evening in 1953 or 1954 is listening with him, vocal score in hand, to the first recording of *Lulu*, and afterwards talking and playing over that exciting music with him. Following the broadcast of a very early orchestral work of mine, he phoned to say he had enjoyed it and found it "like Webern in spots"—which to me was a great compliment. The "influence" was less effective in the other direction. Although music was always at the center of our animated discussions, I found it impossible to persuade Gould to share my fascination with, for example, the Stravinsky pieces that were such an ear-opener to me at the time. In the much-reproduced news photo of Gould with Stravinsky and Bernstein, I notice that Gould is the one who is not smiling.)

The Guerreros and the Goulds had neighboring summer residences on Lake Simcoe. The leisure activities, in which everyone joined, included speedboat junkets with a crazed Glenn at the helm; ruthless rounds of Monopoly uncovering new meanings for the name of that game (which Glenn invariably won); and finally a similarly concentrated brand of croquet. I told Guerrero admiringly once that he played a shot as if he were absolutely sure he was going to win it. "Well," he asked, "isn't that the object of the game?" This was a shock to my "WASP" upbringing, in which one was urged to do his best and then lose gracefully. Glenn Gould had absorbed Guerrero's basic seriousness much better than I had. One could certainly observe its influence on him. By his "basic seriousness" I mean his total intellectual concentration on the object—whether croquet or Bach. (I do *not* mean that either he or Glenn was at all lacking in a sense of fun.)

I am told on good authority that on another occasion, a sweltering July day, Mrs. Gould refused to join in the game unless Glenn removed his muffler and gloves. It was Guerrero who acted as peacemaker, coming to Glenn's defense with a suggestion that a rheumatic condition might be the basis of his needing these evidently eccentric extra clothes. It was, by the way, Guerrero who advocated soaking the hands in hot water before a performance—and Gould was not the only pupil of his who adopted this sensible habit.

Altogether Guerrero and Gould had an unusually close teacher-student relationship spanning the decade between Glenn's tenth and twentieth years. Gradually, however, they had a falling-out. Myrtle Rose Guerrero says there were no angry words, no scenes, but while the two families continued to visit regularly, Glenn no longer joined them. Up to his death, Guerrero continued to follow Gould's international success, with an obvious pride. He could not, however, accept some of Gould's artistic decisions; above all Guerrero disliked to watch the "platform antics" as he called them. He wanted to attend Gould's triumphant Massey Hall concert in Toronto in April 1956, but decided he could not because the sight of those mannerisms would upset him. For his part, at some point in the mid-1950s, Gould found he no longer wanted to discuss his musical enthusiasms with Guerrero; the discussions devolved into arguments, and he found he could not convince his teacher. The process is a natural one in anyone's artistic maturation, but it is regrettable that they could not have remained friends with some sort of understanding that there were areas where they had to "agree to disagree." (I think that that kind of agreement was always hard for Gould.) It is even more regrettable, in my view, that he found he could refer to Guerrero only anonymously, or else not at all, when speaking of his own musical upbringing. This is the sense in which Gould himself helped foster Myth 3.

Gould and I later saw little of each other. I heard from him several times during the writing of his String Quartet, but when I attended the première at Stratford in 1956 I frankly could not appreciate it and had to tell him as diplomatically as I could that it was "not my kind of music." In a period when I was doing some critical writing, I came away from his sensational December 1960 performance of a Toronto Symphony double-bill (the Schoenberg and Mozart C minor concertos) feeling he was "the eighth wonder of the music world." I said so in my *Star* piece, and only regretted the headline-writer did not pick up this phrase. At Stratford in 1961, however, I had to disagree publicly with his way of championing Richard Strauss and it got back to me some years later that this had offended him. If he enjoyed success, he suffered through criticisms just as humanly.

As he was to say many times, after the mid-1960s he became of necessity "more and more of a private person." The brief chatty annual greeting became a printed card posted from Homburger's office. Probably the last occasion that we talked was in the early 1970s when I invited him to meet informally with the music students at the University of Toronto—to chat on any topic he liked. His answer was startling—"Oh, I'm afraid I don't do that sort of thing any more"— because I had not realized he had ever met with students to any extent; he did so at some U.S. colleges in the 1960s, but the Canadian instances were extremely rare, if in fact there were any.

Students asked me in wonder after the memorial to Glenn at St. Paul's Cathedral, "You mean you heard him play in person?" It is hard to realize that for the present younger generation this was simply not an available privilege as it was for us, his contemporaries.

INTERVIEW:
"YES, BUT WHAT'S HE
REALLY LIKE?"
Geoffrey Payzant

Explanatory Note:

I wrote the following little skit as an epilogue to my book *Glenn Gould, Music and Mind* (Toronto: Van Nostrand Reinhold, 1978). I wanted it to be a reminder that the book is not a biography of a piano player but a critical exposition of the works of a musical thinker.

With publishers it is a general rule that a book should not have too much to say about itself, so it was not possible for me to object very strenuously when my editor threw it out. But meanwhile I had shown it to Glenn Gould, who liked it and said that he and I ought to perform it on CBC radio just for fun: he would be Author's Friend and I would be Author. I thought this was a splendid suggestion.

"How would it be if I brought Myron along?" Gould asked. "Myron gets a big kick out of this sort of thing."

Glenn Gould's fertile and tireless imagination was inhabited by a repertory company of fictitious characters who turned up from time to time in his scripts for radio, television, and print. They were of various ethnic backgrounds and professions, were highly eccentric, and spoke their lines with (it had to be admitted) dreadful accents. A neurotic Viennese psychiatrist named Wolfgang von Krankmeister was one of them; Sir Nigel Twitt-Thornwaite ("the dean of British conductors"), modelled after the late Sir Adrian Boult, was another. Myron Chianti was, of course, the young Marlon Brando.

Satisfaction after an all-night recording session. (CBS Don Hunstein) 77

We miss the point of Glenn Gould as person and musician if we fail to see that these fictitious characters were entirely *real* to him. He was merely a fascinated observer of their goings-on.

In his writings Gould makes a distinction between "actuality" and "reality." Actuality is the totality of chance-bound events in the external, natural order, including human nature. Reality is the technologically mediated order of these same events, but under the control of the human spirit. Mankind has little or no control over actuality, but can elect to assume control over reality. Actuality includes what movie actors do in front of cameras, and what musicians do in front of microphones; reality is the edited, spliced, mixed output of the technology, an artificial order of events and relationships between events which are the product of human deliberation and choice, and which have their basis not in the world of space, time and causality, but in the world of the artist's imagination.

I believe that Glenn Gould's extraordinary ability to maintain the distinctness of polyphonic voices in his keyboard playing was related to his ability to keep track of the adventures and idiosyncracies of Sir Nigel, Dr. Krankmeister, Myron, and the others, as they swirled in his fantasy. Even if they were not immediate and real to some of us, their effects upon Gould's musical art are evident.

But to return to his suggestion that he should bring Myron to the studio when we recorded the skit: Myron was a special favourite of Gould's, and I confess that by the time of this conversation I had no difficulty regarding Myron as a person. Indeed I knew that the loudmouthed and tactless Myron would make mincemeat of my script, so after a brief hesitation I replied to Gould that Myron could come into the studio with us but he would have to sit quietly and not say a word. Gould got the point that I wasn't eager to rewrite the skit to include a part for Myron, and nothing more was said about it.

Half a year later Paul Robinson and I read it on CJRT-FM in Toronto as part of a special broadcast on Glenn Gould. Next day Gould telephoned to say that he had heard it and to congratulate me, with much cheerful punning and cackling, since of course he had known all along that the skit was itself a parody of his own radio-dialogue style. He ended his call with one of his little mock-formal speeches ("…you were in *top* form, sir!") and his usual salutation at that time: "Take care!"

We present the skit here exactly as it was heard on CJRT-FM on September 10, 1978.

Yes, but What's He *Really* Like?

The Characters:
Author
Author's Friend

Music: Bach-Gould, *Goldberg Variations*, the Fourth. First six bars, then voice-over quick fade.

Author's Friend: Yes, but what's he *really* like?

Author: What d'you mean, what's he *really* like? He's like a person who makes the kind of recordings he does and says the kinds of things he says in his articles and scripts.

AF: Don't be so stuffy. You know what I mean. What's he like to talk to in the flesh? How does he dress, what kind of car does he drive, who are his friends?

A (humbly): I don't know.

AF: You *don't know?* You must know if anyone does! You must have had meetings with him, lunches, sitting in on recording and taping sessions, coffee-breaks, hanging around generally….

A: Well, no. You see.…

AF: Stop. Let me get this straight. You and he live in the same city. You have written a book about him, but you didn't go to see him, is that how it was?

A (helpfully): Well, we talked on the telephone many times.

AF: You? Everyone knows you are an *idiot* on the telephone. You stammer and dither and always want to hand it to someone else. You must have driven him crazy on the telephone, just as you do the rest of us!

A (even more humbly): I mostly listened.

AF: I'm sure you did. But what was he like on the telephone?

A: That's a bit hard for me to say. I always got excited. I was afraid I would forget something I wanted to ask him. I sweated a lot, and usually after an hour or two of this....

AF: An hour or two? Are you telling me that he talked and you "mostly listened" for an hour or two at a time?

A (irritably)*:* I'm trying to tell you what he was like on the telephone. Yes, he talked sometimes for several hours, in that marvellous telephone voice which made my teenage daughter swoon whenever she answered his calls. This voice is a musical instrument, almost as astonishing as the mind which plays it. And many of his sentences are as elaborate and dense as the Regerian counterpoint with which he compares his radio documentaries, but more lucid.

AF: Sorry to interrupt. And I'll ask about the radio documentaries another time. But doesn't he get confused and lose track in those big sentences?

A: No, but *I* did, until I hit upon the bright idea of doodling a sort of graph of his sentences as he talked. Once when he was telling me about his music for the film *Slaughterhouse-Five* he plunged, in a single sentence, into fourteen levels of parentheses, subordinate clauses, qualifiers, asides, asides within other asides. My doodle showed that he closed each one of these in the correct sequence, and ended up at the level he started from, with the right verb.

AF: Wow! No wonder you sweated.

A: And gasped. But in spite of what you might be thinking, he wasn't showing off. This was sheer exuberance. He found the film project exciting, and he wanted me to get the feel of the excitement. His animatedness was more real and immediate to me on the telephone than almost anything I have known while talking to other people in person.

AF: What did you and he talk about on the telephone?

A: Mainly I asked for factual information, dates and places, and for clarification of things he has said and of things other people have said about him—that sort of thing. He was very candid and helpful, and always patient when I was being slow and stupid.

AF: Yes, that's you on the telephone, all right. But I find much of what you are telling me hard to believe. Didn't you come right out with it and *ask* if you might go to see him?

A: Yes, a couple of times, but....

AF: Well, what did he say?

A (wistfully): Well, sort of nothing. He seemed not to hear, or he slid gracefully into some other topic. He's always polite and considerate, and generous with his time. But I did ask him once about that baffle he puts between himself and the microphones, when he records at the piano, to limit the amount of his vocal noise that ends up on the disc. He said "Yes, of course, you've never been at one of our recording sessions..." and I jumped in with "No, but I'd like to sometime!" He went on with what he had been saying.

AF: So all this stuff about his privacy, about his need for solitude, is for real, and not just an affectation of his as I always thought. (Pause.) You're looking smug—that's what you tell us in the book, isn't it? And you approve of it, don't you?

A: What is there to approve or disapprove? A person works best under conditions that suit him best. As for me, I wouldn't be talking like this in front of all these people if I didn't want to. Neither would you.

AF: He has seen your book?

A: Yes, of course! At each crucial stage I sent him a copy of the latest version of the manuscript. This he read very quickly, and then he telephoned to talk about a few factual errors and misunderstandings.

AF (with exaggerated diffidence): Is it alright if I ask you how he liked it?

A: He spoke kindly of it. And when the time came for me to ask his formal permission to quote from his writings, many of them previously unpublished, he was very co-operative. Perhaps a fifth of the book is excerpts from these sources.

AF: Did he want you to make any changes in your quotations from his writings?

A: None at all, except for very minor editorial refinements, most of them in my own transcriptions from his radio and television shows, and the rest in some of his own magazine articles, printed in early days when he didn't quite feel at liberty to overrule his editors' so-called "improvements." Punctuation, word-order, things like that. He's a comma-freak. But he never suggested substantial changes in my text, or in my quotations from him.

AF: You write about him near the beginning of your book as having been a solitary boy with strong opinions and a hatred of cruelty. You elevate these to the position of central themes in what you call his musical philosophy. How has he turned out? Is he still like that?

A: You're trying to trick me into telling you what he's "really" like, aren't you? And like everyone else you think I'm holding something back. I'm not, and I can't help it if you refuse to be convinced. Anyway, the opinions are stronger than ever, and are the same opinions. But he has learned to modulate them and to express them more effectively. He has found in technology a way to make solitude work for him, and has fashioned this and his hatred of cruelty (or competitiveness) into a musical philosophy with a strong ethical slant.

AF: Since this is the only book about him up to now, I guess I'm going to have to take your word for all this.

A: Don't take *my* word for it. Take *his*. It's all in the book!

Music: Beethoven-Liszt-Gould, Symphony No. 5. First four notes.

At dawn in Toronto, 1979. (Roger Moride, John McGreevy Productions)

TORONTO
Glenn Gould

was born in Toronto, and it's been home base all my life. I'm not quite sure why; it's primarily a matter of convenience, I suppose. I'm not really cut out for city living and, given my druthers, I would avoid all cities and simply live in the country.

Toronto does belong on a very short list of cities I've visited that seem to offer to me, at any rate, peace of mind—cities which, for want of a better definition, do not impose their "cityness" upon you. Leningrad is probably the best example of the truly peaceful city. I think that, if I could come to grips with the language and the political system, I could live a very productive life in Leningrad. On the other hand, I'd have a crack-up for sure if I were compelled to live in Rome or New York—and of course, any Torontonian worthy of the name feels that way about Montreal, on principle.

The point is that, by design, I have very little contact with this city. In some respects, indeed, I think that the only Toronto I really know well is the one I carry about with me in memory. And most of the images in my memory-bank have to do with Toronto of the forties and early fifties when I was a teenager.

Toronto's had a remarkably good press in recent years. It has been called "the new, great city", or "a model of the alternative future", and not by Torontonians; these delightful epithets have come from American and European magazines and city planners. But then Toronto has traditionally garnered very favourable comments from visitors: Charles Dickens dropped by in 1842 and remarked that "the town is full of life, and motion, bustle, business and improvement". Canadians, by and large, are less complimentary; until very recently, "Hogtown" was the preferred description of Toronto by Canadians from other parts of the country, and it has been said that one of the few unifying factors, in this very divided land, is that all Canadians share a dislike — however perverse and irrational it may be — for Toronto.

When the St. Lawrence Seaway was completed in 1959, Toronto — though seven hundred miles up-lake and up-river from the Atlantic Ocean — became, in effect, a deep-sea port. I've always been an incorrigible boat-watcher, and I can still remember, when the Seaway had been completed, how exciting it was to prowl the Toronto waterfront and encounter ships that had brought Volkswagens from Germany or TV sets from Japan, and had names like *Wolfgang Russ* or *Munishima Maru*.

But well before the Seaway was completed, Toronto had already become international in another way. At the end of the Second World War, there was a great migration to Canada from all over the world — particularly from Europe and Asia — and a good percentage of those immigrants opted for Toronto. As a result of that the population of the city, which had been predominantly Anglo-Saxon, underwent a profound sea-change. The Anglo-Saxons were reduced to a minority, though still the largest minority to be sure, and the city began to reflect the cultural diversity of its new residents.

In 1793 Toronto's founder, Lieutenant-Governor John Graves Simcoe, predicted that the settlement would become a "palladium of British loyalty". And of his plans for the town, Simcoe wrote: "There was to be one church, one university to guard the Constitution, at every street corner a sentry, the very stones were to sing 'God Save The King'."

In Canadian political life, there's a saying, now almost cliché, that Canada is a "political mosaic". The point of this expression is to enable us to distinguish ourselves from the Americans, who are fond of describing their society as a "melting pot", and the implication is that in Canada (and nowhere better exemplified than in Toronto), however intense the heat, we do not melt.

Toronto is situated on the north shore of Lake Ontario, the most easterly and also the smallest of the Great Lakes. But it's a sizeable pond, nonetheless. As a matter of fact, a Dutch friend of mine never tires of telling his relatives back home that you could drop all of Holland into this lake and still have room for enough windmills to keep Don Quixote busy for a lifetime. Actually he's wrong: I looked it up and Holland is almost twice as large as Lake Ontario. So you could drop it into Lake Superior, or Lake Michigan, or Lake Huron and it would disappear without a trace, but if you tried it here there would be very serious flooding.

A series of small islands overlap with one another like a crossword puzzle and protect Toronto Bay. The islands are primarily a recreational area and, during the summer, ferryboats shuttle visitors and picnicking Torontonians back and forth across the harbour. But some hardy folks actually live on the islands all year round; in fact, there's been an island community of some sort for a century and a half.

Toronto's rationale as a city, indeed, is linked inevitably with its strategic location on Lake Ontario and, specifically, with its very fine harbour. After the American Revolution, the British were shopping around for likely spots to defend against the newly liberated colonists across the lake, and they elected to build a fort here. As an outpost of Empire, however, Fort York was by no means an unqualified success; the Americans sacked the town during the War of 1812.

Toronto's relationship with the American cities to the south, such as Buffalo which is forty miles across the lake, has often been the butt of local jokes. In my youth it was said that for a really lively weekend, what you had to do was drive to Buffalo. Nowadays Torontonians do not seem to feel that that migration serves any useful purpose, but we still seem to have some deep-seated psychological need to *look* at Buffalo every now and then. So, in 1976 we built a tower which, according to the tourist guides, is the tallest free-standing structure in the world. And they tell me that from up there, on a clear day, you can see—if not forever—at least to Buffalo.

There is no better example of the old Toronto versus the new than that shown by our two city halls, which stand on adjacent properties. The Old City Hall, which was finished in 1899, was built by a Canadian by the name of E. J. Lennox; he spent twelve years on the project and, by way of preliminary research, took a busman's holiday in Pennsylvania where he was apparently inspired by the then new jail in Pittsburgh. When I was in that city once on a concert tour (which is the musical equivalent of a penitentiary sentence), I happened to take a walk past that jail and, I must say, it looks not unlike our Old City Hall. Lennox maintained a remarkably consistent view of the appropriate enclosures for sinners and civil servants.

New City Hall was built in the early 1960s by the Finnish architect Viljo Revell. He died, very prematurely, just after his building was completed, and it was said at the time that his death might well have been hastened by the howls of outrage with which some of Toronto's elected officials greeted his remarkably imaginative design.

Toronto, at that time, was not exactly an hospitable place for contemporary art of any sort, and the decision to situate a large sculpture by Henry Moore in front of the New City Hall was the straw that broke the political camel's back. In fact, it was largely responsible for the electoral defeat of the mayor who supported its purchase. His chief opponent proclaimed that "Torontonians do not want abstract art shoved down their throats," and, of course, won the subsequent election handily.

Perhaps one indication of the remarkable change in Toronto's outlook during the last decade is that we now possess the largest collection of sculptures by Henry Moore in the western hemisphere; oddly enough, in view of all the earlier fuss, the collection was initiated by a gift from the sculptor himself. We Torontonians do have a way of ingratiating ourselves, I must say.

Beneath Toronto's towering bank buildings can be found underground shopping malls that one can follow throughout the better part of downtown, and it is similarly possible to walk through the city, out of doors, by following a network of ravines and river valleys, without once setting foot on concrete. Down the largest of these ravines runs the River Don, locally known as "the Muddy Don". It empties into Toronto Harbour and, if I were in marathon training, it would be possible for me to walk seventeen miles to its source without making direct contact with the city—although it would, of course, be all around me.

Another route to follow is Yonge Street, Toronto's original north-south artery, which demarcates east side from west side in much the same way that Fifth Avenue divides Manhattan. It was the trail by which settlers went north in the early years of the nineteenth century to homestead, and a favourite boast of local press agents is that it is, in fact, the longest street in the world. They arrive at this particular bit of propaganda by virtue of the fact that Yonge Street doesn't exactly end; it just sort of dissolves into the Ontario highway system, and it is possible to follow this road, north and west, for about twelve hundred miles (almost two thousand kilometres). Most of those miles traverse country that is absolutely haunting in its emptiness and bleakness and starkly magnificent beauty.

But the garish beginning of Yonge Street is not one of those miles. It's a bit of the street known as "The Strip"; I'm not sure who coined the name or whether he was aware of the *double entendre* involved. On a smaller scale, these few blocks pose for Toronto the same problems that 42nd Street and Broadway create in New York. Civil libertarians find "The Strip" an irresistible cause; most of us simply find it an embarrassment.

Perhaps the single most important influence on Toronto during the sixties was, in fact, something that took place over three hundred miles away, in Montreal. That city played host in 1967 to the World's Fair, which was called Expo '67. The two towns, Montreal and Toronto, have always had a sort of anything-you-can-build-I-can-build-better rivalry, and Toronto subsequently became determined to create its own Expo—if necessary, block by block. Perhaps our most Expo-like construction is a recreational area on the lakeshore, which is called Ontario Place.

Montreal's Expo was, of course, anything but an exercise in architectural consistency—it was actually a very eclectic assembly of buildings—and Toronto's substitute Expo has employed similar contrasts.

Toronto, by general consensus, is the financial capital of Canada. The contending office towers that dominate the downtown district house major banking institutions, and most of them are located on or near Bay Street, which is the Canadian equivalent of America's Wall

Street. People who are not particularly fond of Toronto insist that we go about the making of money with a religious devotion. I don't think that that's more true of this city than of most others, but if it is, then I suppose that other cliché—the one about such buildings being cathedrals of finance—would have to be given its due as well. In any case, most of us do our banking at very modest branch offices which, if the analogy must be pursued, are obviously parish churches.

A peculiar and important aspect of the Toronto mentality is a tendency to retain, even during times of radical change, a certain perspective, a certain detachment, a healthy scepticism about change for change's sake. I think it was probably that tendency which enabled Toronto to survive the sixties, when comparable cities south of the border were, quite literally, falling apart in both architectural and human terms. Toronto emerged from that turbulent decade as, arguably, one of the great cities of the world, certainly as an extraordinarily clean, safe, quiet, considerate sort of place in which to live.

Toronto's largest shopping concourse is called the Eaton Centre and some people say it is Toronto's answer to the Galleria in Milan; but whether that's true or not, it certainly is not your average Ma and Pa Kettle corner store. It is in fact the flagship of a vast retail empire which, despite its monumentality, has remained a family concern. The family concerned are the Eatons and they have been the leading lights of Toronto's, and indeed Canada's, merchandizing for the better part of a century.

Timothy Eaton, founder of the business—who sits in bronze at the entrance to the vast new store—was always willing to gamble on somewhat off-the-beaten-track locations; sometimes a move of only a few blocks was involved, but Timothy always had the feeling that if he located his stores where shoppers were, by the time he had finished building them (usually an expansive as well as expensive operation) that's where the shoppers wouldn't be. Well, perhaps the descendants who run his empire now know something we don't: the new Eaton Centre is located, improbably enough, kitty-corner from the Yonge Street "Strip". Having cost almost a quarter of a billion dollars, it could be that it will revitalize this rather seedy quarter of Toronto. We can only hope so.

When I was a child, and indeed until very recently, this city was referred to as "Toronto the Good". The reference was to the city's puritan traditions: one could not, for example, attend concerts on Sunday until the 1960s; it was not permissible to serve alcohol in any public place on the Sabbath until very recently; and now a furor has developed at City Hall over the issue of whether Torontonians should be permitted to drink beer at baseball games.

But you have to understand that, as an anti-athletic, non-concertgoing teetotaller, I approve all such restrictions. I, perhaps, rather than the hero of George Santayana's famous novel, am "The Last Puritan". So I always felt that "Toronto the Good" was a very nice nickname. On the other hand, a lot of my fellow citizens became very upset about it and tried to prove that we could be just as bad as any other place.

Toronto incorporates five boroughs which form a sort of satellite network around the original city. North York, which recently incorporated itself as a city, is the largest of these and houses about half a million people. It is my favourite area of the city by far, and although I live downtown, I keep a studio in North York. I think what attracts me to it is the fact that it offers a certain anonymity; it has a sort of improbable, Brasilia-like quality. In fact, it has much of the tensionless atmosphere of one of those capital cities where the only business is the business of government and which are deliberately located away from the geographical mainstream—Ottawa, say, or Canberra.

During the fifties and sixties, North York seemed to spring spontaneously from the soil; I can remember when the area was all farmland. And what developed was a community so carefully planned, so controlled in its density, in the structural and rhythmical regularity with which its homes, offices, shops and public buildings come together, that it doesn't seem like a city at all; which, needless to say, is the highest compliment I can pay it. To me it seems, as I have said, like a seat of government; or perhaps, rather better, like a vast company town, presided over by an autocratic but benevolent Chairman of the Board, whose only order of the day, every day, is—Tranquillity. It is fashionable to downgrade suburbia these days, of course. The march back to city centre, with all its zooty renovated row houses, is all the rage, I know; but this part of Toronto, I think, represents the North American suburban dream at its best. And I love it!

In my youth, Toronto was also called "The City of Churches" and, indeed, the most vivid of my childhood memories in connection with Toronto have to do with churches. They have to do with Sunday evening services, with evening light filtered through stained-glass windows, and with ministers who concluded their benediction with the phrase: "Lord, give us the peace that the earth cannot give." Monday mornings, you see, meant that one had to go back to school and encounter all sorts of terrifying situations out *there* in the city. So those moments of Sunday evening sanctuary became very special to me; they meant that one could find a certain tranquillity—even in the city—but only if one opted not to be part of it.

Well, I don't go to church these days, I must confess, but I do repeat that phrase to myself very often—the one about the peace that the earth cannot give—and find it a great comfort. What I've done, I think, while living here, is to concoct some sort of metaphoric stained-glass window, which allows me to survive what appear to me to be the perils of the city—much as I survived Monday mornings in the schoolroom. And the best thing I can say about Toronto is that it doesn't seem to intrude upon this hermit-like process.

It's been fascinating to get to know Toronto, after all these years, but not even this filmic exploration of it has made me a city convert, I'm afraid. I am more than ever convinced, though, that like Leningrad, Toronto is essentially a truly peaceful city.

But perhaps I see it through rose-coloured glasses; perhaps what I see is still so controlled by my memory that it's nothing more than a mirage. I hope not though, because if that mirage were ever to evaporate, I should have no alternative but to leave town.

Concertizing in Moscow. (Glenn Gould Estate)

APOLLONIAN
Joseph Roddy

Glenn Gould, a tall, lean, loose-limbed, long-jawed, blond-haired Canadian who, at twenty-seven, has already established a reputation as one of the world's finest pianists, is celebrated both for the austerity of the music he produces and the flamboyance of what he calls his side effects—the manner in which he comes onstage, sits down at the piano, and manipulates his body as he plays. A Gould recital begins with the recitalist loping in from the wings in an unpressed set of tails that fits him about as loosely as an overcoat. Bounding, bobbing, nodding vigorously, and throwing in a perfunctory bow, which the audience can scarcely detect in the general anarchy of his movements, Gould proceeds to plant himself on a low folding chair, and there he sits, with his long arms dangling almost to the floor. Moments pass and nothing happens; it begins to seem quite possible that Gould is never going to play anything or that he has forgotten what he came out to play. A shattering ten-finger fortissimo—out of Liszt's "Transcendental Etudes," say—would be just the thing to dispel the mystification that has by now settled over the audience, but Gould is no more likely to start with any such thing than with "Kitten on the Keys." His recital programs most often begin, when they finally do begin, with a Sweelinck fantasy or a Byrd pavan, or some other chaste sixteenth-century piece. What follows is apt to be Bach. Bach's is linear music, with concurrent melodies scampering off contrapuntally in all directions, and Gould follows each of them with a different part of his body, in a kind of hot pursuit.

While his right hand is engaged in stating the theme of a fugue, his left hand will conduct, sawing the air over the working member and providing it with orchestra-sized cues. A solo left-hand statement of a theme gets the same ministrations from the right hand. When both hands are on the keys, Gould uses his long jaw to conduct, and it nods the cues left and right while his lips meet and part on the beat, marking the tempo as mechanically as a metronome. Occasionally, in the softest passages, Gould gets his face so close to the keys that he could easily strike a pianissimo middle C with his nose. Now and then, playing fortissimo, he rears back so emphatically that his feet are lifted off the floor. Mostly, though, he plays in a deep slouch—the base of his spine on the forward edge of his low chair, his legs crossed and stretched out around the pedals, which he rarely uses, his shoulders hardly higher than the keyboard, his whole posture a scandal to the piano teachers in the audience, who, whatever their differences, agree that a pianist should sit up straight and sit still. Gould simply cannot sit still, and he can be counted on to straighten up only in climactic lyric passages, during which he rises from his slouch to almost a standing position and seems to hover over both the piano and the music coming from it. At such moments, he is likely to yield to another idiosyncrasy. For him, as for most good pianists, a performance is far more than a matter of giving sound and musical shape to a set of symbols that the composer has fixed on paper; it is an attempt to deliver a perfect copy of the ideal performance he can hear in his head at any time, even when his hands are in his pockets. When Gould talks about piano playing, he often illustrates his points by singing out sections of these ideal performances, and when he is giving a recital he sings along in an interior monologue, usually just sort of an audible mutter. On the stage, he conscientiously tries to keep the mutter inaudible, but sometimes—not as rarely as he would wish—in the middle of a recital he slips and breaks into full song, which can be heard loud and clear all the way to the back of the hall.

Ordinarily, abundant side effects of this sort are the by-products of a *con-molto-amore* performing style—a style that can easily tear any musical passion to tatters. This is not true of Gould. Frenzied as he appears to the eye, his music is essentially dispassionate, and in this respect he resembles most of his contemporaries—the bumper crop of excellent young pianists now performing in the United States and Europe. As a group, these youngsters—their average age is under thirty-five—differ as sharply from the older generation of pianists as Marlon Brando differs from Sir Laurence Olivier. In Friedrich Nietzsche's terms, the young pianists tend to perform in an Apollonian, or calm and classical, manner, as opposed to the Dionysiac, or romantic, style of many of their predecessors—Artur Rubinstein, the late Josef Hofmann, the late Sergei Rachmaninoff, and the earlier but still well-remembered Ignace Jan Paderewski, for instance. This distinction, though it is by no means hard and fast, is one that may be applied not only to the interpretation of music but to music itself. Generally speaking, the piano compositions of the eighteenth century, including the first three concertos of Beethoven, are Apollonian, adhering to classical formality and reserve; those of the nineteenth century are Dionysiac, being notable for poetic mood and emotional thunder; and those of this century, for all their involutions, have shown a tendency to return to the Apollonian ideal. In actual performance, of course, practically anything can happen. A pianist may play a Dionysiac composition in a Dionysiac style, and it is on this combination that the reputation of many a virtuoso of the older generation has been built. One striking example is Rubinstein's recorded performance, with Josef Krips and the RCA Victor Symphony Orchestra, of Brahms' Concerto No. 2, and another is Vladimir Horowitz's recording, with Toscanini and the NBC Symphony Orchestra, of the Tchaikovsky Concerto. The same works, though, have received Apollonian performances from Rudolf Serkin and Wilhelm Backhaus, who, being no longer young, may be regarded as precursors of the modern Apollonian style. On the other hand, Apollonian compositions, like the Mozart piano sonatas, may be put through powerfully Dionysiac performances, and have been—by, among others, Wanda Landowska. Nearly all the younger pianists—the most prominent of them, perhaps, being Gary Graffman, Byron Janis, Friedrich Gulda, Julius Katchen, Jacob Lateiner, John Browning, Eugene Istomin, Leon Fleisher, Claude Frank, Lilian Kallir, Daniel Barenboim, Paul Badura-Skoda, Seymour Lipkin, William Masselos, Philippe Entremont, Lee Luvisi, Malcolm

Frager, and Anton Kuerti—are predominantly Apollonian performers of both Apollonian and Dionysiac music, pianists made in the image of Mr. Serkin, with whom some of them studied. The conquering hero of the year before last, the twenty-five-year-old Van Cliburn, is a kind of throwback—a Dionysiac player of Dionysiac music in the grand old-fashioned manner, comparable in style to Artur Rubinstein. Cliburn's direct opposite is Gould, a rigorously Apollonian performer of rigorously Apollonian music, even though he puts more bodily motion into eight bars of a Bach partita than Cliburn uses in getting through an entire Liszt fantasia.

Fittingly, the composition that has done most to establish Gould as a top-ranking pianist is the highly Apollonian "Goldberg Variations" of Johann Sebastian Bach. In fact, the little air and its thirty masterly variations have contributed almost as much to Gould's fame as they have to that of Johann Gottlieb Goldberg—a clavier player, a student of Bach's, and a composer—who simply by playing the variations very well and very often won himself a durable niche in the history of music—a status his own preludes and fugues would never have earned him. For some years before Gould—a piano player, a student of Bach, and a composer—got around to offering the public his recorded version of the variations, they had been pretty much the property of Wanda Landowska, whose recording of them, on the harpsichord, was one of those circa-1945 prestige items that marked their few owners as extremely cultivated collectors of chamber-music esoterica. Gould's flight through the set—and it is a flight, consuming thirty-eight minutes and twenty-five seconds, or ten minutes and twenty-one seconds less than it took Mme. Landowska to cover the same distance—is as close to being a smash hit as a chamber-music record ever gets. The Landowska performance is an intensely Dionysiac one, played from inside the music, where the performer could not help but bend Bach's phrases to her own emotional involvement with them. Gould's recorded performance is a characteristically Apollonian one—lean, aloof, and fleet—as the young Canadian relates each part of the piece to the whole work in a way that leaves Bach scholars convinced that he knew in the most precise detail how he would play the last variation before he intoned the first one. Since its release four years ago, under the Columbia label, it has sold more than forty thousand copies, which is just about as astonishing in the record business as a big run on a new edition of the Enneads of Plotinus would be in the book trade. With it, Gould established a major musical reputation—perhaps the first such reputation ever to be built on one record. This reputation has since been solidly reinforced and enlarged at solo recitals and concert performances all over the world, and music critics everywhere have come to agree that Glenn Gould plays the piano with something more than ordinary mastery. "Mr. Gould, at his best, is a pianist of divine guidance," Jay S. Harrison wrote not long ago in the *Herald Tribune*, "and even at his worst is a musician so far in advance of most of his contemporaries that there is no legitimate basis for comparisons." In *High Fidelity*, the San Francisco critic Alfred Frankenstein has called Gould "the foremost pianist this continent has produced in recent decades," and in Moscow's *Culture and Life* Professor Heinrich Neuhaus has described the young pianist as "a tremendous talent, a great master, a lofty spirit, and a profound soul."

Among Gould's admirers, one of the most fervent—and it might seem least likely—is Artur Rubinstein, who has no use for the various approaches to the art of piano playing that lie between his own extreme Dionysiacism and Gould's equally uncompromising Apollonianism. "I, Rubinstein, am not yet forty," he said. "Glenn Gould is already sixty-five." According to Rubinstein, the only trouble with Gould is that he made the transition from prodigy to master without going through any of the tortures that the process normally involves. On the face of it, Rubinstein would appear to be right, for Gould's progress as a pianist has been swift and undeviating. In 1935, when he was a boy of three in Toronto, his mother, an amateur pianist, taught him to read music—he could not yet read words—and ever since he has gone from triumph to triumph, with only minor setbacks. At ten, having learned all that his mother could teach him, he began studying piano with Alberto Guerrero, a well-known Toronto teacher, who died a few months ago. Within a year or two, Gould was widely regarded as the best boy musician in the Dominion and was off to a

Four stages of Gould, circa 1960. (Glenn Gould Estate)

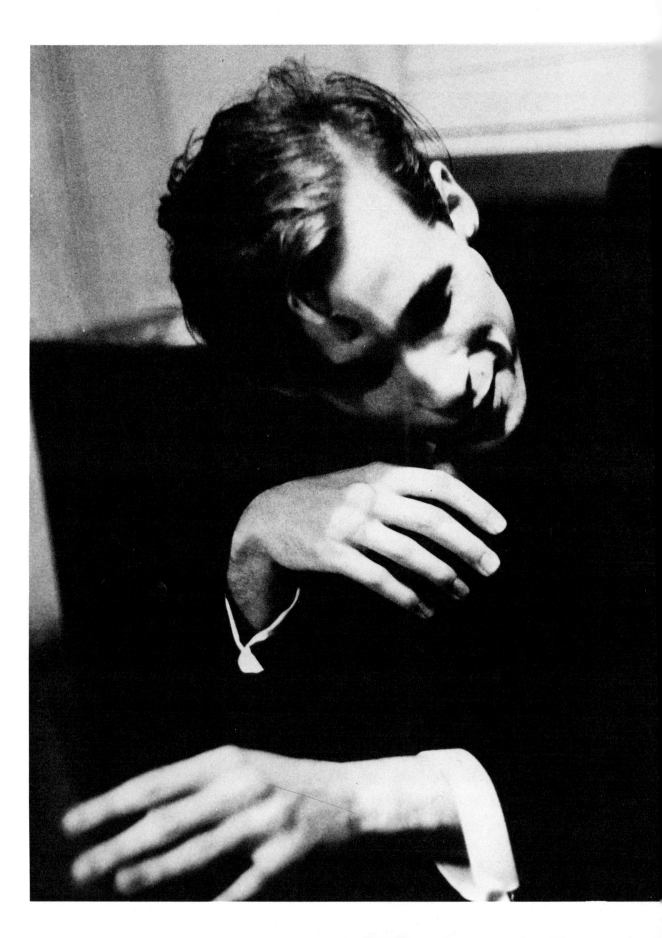

good start as one of the most promising of North American prodigies. At fourteen, he played Beethoven's non-Apollonian Fourth Piano Concerto with the Toronto Symphony—the first of his performances with a professional orchestra. The Toronto *Daily Star*'s critic, who was captivated both by his musicianship and his unaffected manner, wrote, "Every inch a boy, he sat waiting for his cue to come in as though he'd have enjoyed a whiz-bang at cops and robbers." The *Evening Telegram* reported, "He played Beethoven like a master." During these years, he was also engaged in a titanic struggle with Guerrero, a Chilean-born Dionysiac, who had devised what Gould remembers as ingeniously complex finger drills for him. While the boy played them, Guerrero would stand behind him and press down heavily on his shoulders. Gould would push up in self-defense, but the teacher would ordinarily win the match by driving the pupil into a slump. One result is that Gould now has a sturdier set of back and shoulder muscles than a good many practicing weight lifters. Another is his singular posture at the piano. After several years of vain efforts to sit up straight under the pressure from Guerrero, Gould came to the conclusion that he could play properly only in a slouch, with his elbows either pushed out from his sides practically parallel to the keyboard or dangling six or eight inches below the arch of his wrists. To accommodate the slouch, his father, a Toronto furrier, sawed down the legs of a high-backed wooden folding chair and tipped the feet with screws three inches long, enabling his son to adjust it exquisitely to the height and angle that suited him best, the height usually being about fourteen inches off the floor, a working level from four to seven inches lower than that of most professional pianists. The finished product, looking like a footstool with a back rest, was not a sightly object, but Gould soon found himself unable to do without it, and takes it with him to every concert hall he performs in. Of late, however, even this seat has seemed too high to him—he keeps trying to get lower and lower in relation to his instrument—and since he would appear to be sitting on the floor if the chair were shortened any further, he has resorted to raising the piano by putting blocks an inch and a half thick under each leg. The chair, which was only a makeshift to begin with, has practically fallen apart, and a few weeks ago Gould asked a Toronto cabinetmaker to build him a new and stronger one, even though he doubts whether he will ever feel right in it.

In 1952, when Gould was nineteen, he gave up his lessons with Guerrero, because, he has said, "Our outlooks on music were diametrically opposed. He was a 'heart' man and I wanted to be a 'head' kid. Besides, nine years is long enough for anyone to be a student of the same teacher. I decided it was time for me to set out on my own snowshoes, and I developed an insufferable amount of self-confidence, which has never left me." With no new teacher in mind, Gould withdrew to a summer cottage that his parents owned at Lake Simcoe, ninety miles north of Toronto, to consider his future. Alone there, he made some decisive agreements with himself about music. The piano, as he saw it, was an extremely limited instrument, inadequate to the expression of his musical ideas, and what he really wanted to be was a composer. However, the practical side of his nature asserted itself. As a composer of the sort of music he had in mind, he would not make much money, and he decided reluctantly that in order to afford the pleasures of composition he would have to earn his living as a concert pianist. For all his success in Toronto, he did not regard himself as a master of the piano, so he set out on a course of self-instruction to become one. Since then, he has spent more than half his time in solitude at the cottage, where he devotes himself single-mindedly to music. He plays for hours, thinks about how to play for just as many hours, studies scores, analyzes recordings by other pianists, and reads critical commentaries; everything he plays he records on tape, and he evaluates his own performances thoroughly and critically.

By dint of this routine, Gould has made himself into a pianist he can decently endure at Lake Simcoe. Away from there, it is not the same. Gould started making professional tours as a pianist in 1955, and though he has received ecstatic notices on every one of them, he has ended every one convinced that he is a much better pianist when playing alone at the cottage than he is in the concert hall. His explanation for that, arrived at after a lot of meditation and reel upon reel of tape recordings, is that he gives close to half his attention to the action of the piano whenever he plays practically any instrument other than the one he has at Lake Simcoe—a sixty-five-year-old Chickering. When the action of that piano agrees with him, as it almost always does, he can, by his own account, forget about the mechanics of playing and concentrate solely on matching the Bach that bounds off the piano's sounding board with the ideal Bach he hears in his head.

Five years on the concert circuits have had their mellowing effects on Gould, but when he first came on the scene it seemed he might have to leave immediately because there were no instruments he could bear to play. In this respect, he was only slightly more fussy than the run of concert pianists. To them, an instrument's action is "loose" when its keys fall and sound easily under the touch of the fingers, "tight" when an appreciable downward thrust is required. Between the extremes of tight and loose there are as many actions as there are shades of color between red and blue. And, in addition, the tone of pianos varies enormously in size and texture, from the big voices and luxuriant resonances of pianos that sound like full orchestras to the softness and juicelessness of pianos that might be described as puritan. Gould, with his austere attitude toward austere music, wanted his pianos to be tight and puritan. He wanted an assortment of other qualities, too, of course. As if to confound the firm of Steinway & Sons, which provides him with pianos wherever he plays, in exchange for his agreement to use only Steinways for his concerts, Gould has on occasion made some capricious demands. Usually, he could find a Steinway whose tone satisfied him, but during one period, starting in 1954, he was anything but content with the average Steinway's action. At the time, he was convinced that he needed wider gaps between the white keys, to enable him to wiggle them left and right when they were down in sounding position—a sort of body English that he felt somehow kept the piano strings vibrating. What this added up to was a piano that was vertically tight and laterally loose—a pair of characteristics that Steinway considered it impossible to combine but that Gould claimed were combined in his Chickering. For most of a year, he diligently searched for a Steinway with the requisite features, and he seldom saw a Steinway anywhere without giving it a try; between bouts of solitary study at Lake Simcoe, he spent hours in New York haggling with the company's technicians about how the Steinway he had in mind could be made to order. Various pianists who thought they knew what

Gould was looking for told him of Steinways they had run across here and there that were sure to make him perfectly happy. Gould followed up a few dozen such tips in towns all over the United States and Canada without finding his treasure at the end of the hunt. Casting about in one place and another, he came upon Baldwin pianos with the action he wanted but without the tone he wanted, and this led him to speculate on the possibility of fitting the action of a Baldwin into the body of a Steinway and designating the result a Baldstein or a Winway.

This project was never undertaken, for in January of 1955 Gould found the closest thing yet to the ideal piano he had been looking for. Strangely enough, the scene was the basement of the Steinway Building, on West Fifty-seventh Street, where the firm keeps a dozen or so instruments it reserves for artists giving recitals at Carnegie Hall or Town Hall. Naturally, Gould had visited the basement before and had tried out the instruments here, but this piano, a nine-foot concert grand built some four years before he was born, and given the number One Seventy-four in the artists' piano pool, had never, so far as he knows, been there when he was. Because Gould had dropped into the Steinway Building to talk pianos that day, not to play them, he had left his folding chair in his hotel room, and in order to take a quick sounding of the unknown One Seventy-four he got down on his knees—a position that he finds next best to his slouch and particularly well suited to Bach, because it combines an attitude of reverence with an immobilization of the feet that makes it impossible to touch the pedals, whose effect on Bach's music, he feels, would be a desecration. Gould played Bach for just a moment, stopped, began again in astonishment, and very shortly realized that this piano gave him everything he was after. He did his best to contain his exhilaration until he could get back to his hotel, collect his chair and try One Seventy-four once more, sitting down. It took only a few fugues and sarabands to show him that the instrument fully lived up to his expectations; it was tight and puritan, and the spaces between the keys were generous enough to allow all the wiggling he wanted. The width of Steinways is supposed to be as unvarying as the width of Fords, and when Gould claimed that One Seventy-four must be wider than the standard model, the company's technicians stoutly denied it. They were plainly nonplussed when he brought in a tape measure and proved that it was, by three-eighths of an inch. During the instrument's career, it had been favored at one time by Myra Hess and at another by Robert Casadesus, but Gould was the first pianist to claim that he could not work without it, and Steinway graciously did its best to keep One Seventy-four at his disposal. Over the next eight months, he carted it up and down the eastern seaboard, and the freight bills which, of course, he had to pay personally, came to just under four thousand dollars, not a cent of which Gould considered misspent.

When his tours took him farther afield—to Vancouver, say, or Moscow—Gould had to do without One Seventy-four. Then, like other Steinway artists on the road, he was reduced to choosing the best instrument he could find among the pianos the company has stocked in music stores and concert halls in almost every sizable city on earth. Most travellers, whatever their vocation, tend to rate cities according to a scale based on such indices as restaurants, fine arts, fleshpots, and sunlight; Gould goes about the earth concerned almost entirely with the supply of playable Steinways in the next town. During his tours in 1957 and 1958, he rated Moscow, Berlin, and Tel Aviv as fairly good places but was far more enthusiastic about St. Louis, Missouri. No city of its size anywhere could come up to St. Louis, Gould maintained, for it was the home of not one but two congenial Steinways. Salt Lake City was creditable, too, for it had a particularly good Steinway in the Mormon Tabernacle, and San Francisco ranked even higher, because of an instrument in the Municipal Opera House. Still, none of these instruments matched One Seventy-four, and Gould was always happy to get back to within reasonable piano-carting distance of Fifty-seventh Street. Unfortunately, like certain wines, pianos don't always travel well, and in March, 1957, One Seventy-four simply came apart. The Steinway people told Gould that it had been dropped at a freight depot on its way back from a concert he had given in Cleveland, and had to be retired to the factory for a complete overhaul. The collapse of the piano was not much of a surprise to the Steinway officials, who probably would have retired the elderly instrument earlier if Gould had not been so attached to it. It was a twenty-nine-year-old model, and, despite Gould's delight in it, the company felt that its tone was something less than representative of the Steinway product. When the piano went into the shop, it was deprived of its number and identity, and passed into a sort of limbo where its action would be rejuvenated, its strings replaced, its hammers reconditioned. It would someday be returned to active service, a standardized replacement in the artists' pool.

Gould was in despair. As far as he was concerned, the piano was simply lost. Even if he kept track of it through the workrooms and out again, the special characteristics that made it the perfect piano for him would never survive the assembly-line rebuilding it would undergo. At first, he felt completely off his form with music and out of sorts with himself—a depressive state for which the only therapy he knew was a fast flight home to the Chickering. Two or three concerts away from it were all he could take in one trek. Pianists usually arrange their tours by territories, but Gould was concerned not so much about getting successive dates in neighboring cities as about the flying time from any one of them back to Toronto. He knew that the strain showed. Gould thinks of his involuntary bursts of song in mid-performance as unconscious efforts to compensate vocally for the structural failings of the piano he is playing. He has noticed that the songs break out frequently when the piano is a stranger, and become downright disruptive when the piano turns out to be an enemy. "When I was playing One Seventy-four, I was practically unheard," he recalls. During his 1957 travels in Germany and his 1958 travels in Israel, Gould consulted piano technicians, who listened to his complaints and then adjusted pianos to his temporary satisfaction. An expert in Tel Aviv even persuaded him that his Chickering was the real source of his troubles—that, instead of trying to find a Steinway that played like it, he should try to make it play like a Steinway. Gould found this diagnosis so astonishingly original that he had the action of his dependable old Chickering completely altered as soon as he got back to Lake Simcoe. That turned out to be a mistake; until he grew accustomed to the instrument once more, it was almost useless to him, and he was left without a piano he could go home to. "Maybe there are no more pianos," Gould said sorrowfully at the time, brooding over his plight. "The Chickering's sick, and One Seventy-four is gone. I guess in a few years I'll retire, too."

Gould was shoeless and wearing a heavy muffler around his neck the first time I met him. It was a crisp spring morning, and the place was the Columbia recording studio on East Thirtieth Street. Gould was recording the Bach Partita No. 5, and he had the use of three Steinways—one to warm up on, another to record with, and a third to take refuge in when the second became intractable. This last was One Seventy-four, which the engineers always said did not record well. While he played, he kept a portable heater going full blast close to his left side, and a piece of Oriental carpeting under his feet; for a Canadian, he is extraordinarily sensitive to low temperatures—or even to what New Yorkers consider comfortable room temperatures —and he frequently carries the fragment of rug with him to the concert hall along with his chair. To his right, on the piano, he had laid out an assortment of pills, which he kept popping down, and during a break in the recording session he told me that they helped preserve the equilibrium he had established earlier in the morning by polishing off a hearty breakfast of arrowroot cookies and Poland Water. While he talked, he soaked his hands in a basin of hot water.

The break, it turned out, would last for some minutes, and Gould launched into an account of his childhood. "I went wrong early," he announced with mock portentousness. "When I was six, I managed to persuade my parents that mine was an uncommonly sensitive soul, which ought not to be exposed to the boorish vandalism I perceived among my contemporaries. Consequently, my 1939-40 season was made more agreeable by the improvisations of a private tutor. By one school of my biographers it is considered that this was my undoing." With this, he embarked on a narrative in which some of the events of his life were stirred together with some fantasized enlargements of them. At a guess, this pungent stew was one part fact, two parts invention, and three parts canny public relations. This talent for the embellishment of his own reputation was a bewildering one to find joined with his genius; it was rather like as if Albert Schweitzer should come out of the jungle for a thirteen-week stand as a TV pitchman for his own organ recordings. "My policy has long been to cut the cloth to fit the corner newsstand," Gould told me when I stopped him in the middle of his sixth-year reflections to ask if he always talked this way.

His pleasant association with the private tutor lasted only a year, I gathered, and then he went to public school in Toronto. "What the child psychologists would call the group spirit was found to be quite lacking in my personality," he said. "I suppose it was only natural that the fact that I was unable to come to terms with my associates forced me to take refuge ever more intently within the shelter of my own imagination. I clearly recall that in my first months at school the periods of the day I most abhorred were not those devoted to work but, rather, those devoted to organized relaxation. In those days—and, for all I know, it may be the same today—a favorite device of any schoolmarm with an ear for melody was the bi-weekly period of musical amusement, which usually dwelt at unnecessary length upon that hoary specimen of primordial polyphony, the round concerning the plight of the three sightless mice." Gould lifted his hands from the basin, and, dripping hot water on the floor, conducted the nursery song with great solemnity as he sang in a resounding baritone, "Three blind mice/ Three blind mice/See how they run!/See how they run!" Then he went on, "My first teacher was especially partial to the canonical implications of that round, probably under the misguided notion that the symmetry thus achieved was symbolic of the heroic achievements which were possible if we would *all pull together.*" The platitude had a rich overlay of British pluckiness. "Now, in the first place, my mind had already been trained in more intensive pursuits than the fulfillment of the rudimentary diatonicisms of that work. And since each entry of the round was upheld by one row of the class—all of them quite capable of holding their own against the ensuing stretti—I came to feel quite unimportant, and soon determined to contribute something of a more original nature. Hence, I became the one member of our class always to make a wrong entry in the round. In this fashion, our round-singing would take on a lustrous chromaticism, until the teacher brought the proceedings to an abrupt halt by breaking some chalk on my head," In case I had missed the significance of this narrative, Gould spelled it out for me: "It is a truly ironic gesture that the subject in which I first won unfavorable distinction was, indeed, music." I nodded, Gould nodded back, and one of the recording technicians approached to tell him that they were ready to get on with the job.

As Gould dried his hands, he said, "It has been my conviction for some time that my great interest in and enthusiasm for music is in large measure the result of my disagreements and dissatisfactions with my schoolmates. At any rate, by my tenth birthday I was absorbed not only in the acquiring of keyboard skills—both piano and organ—but in such pursuits in counterpoint as would have left my poor teacher speechless." He headed for the second Steinway, saying, "That should take care of the early-years bit," and I invited him to join me for lunch when he had finished the Bach.

Finishing the Bach proved to be no simple matter. Gould later told me that he had first played the Partita No. 5 when he was eighteen, and that in practice sessions, recitals, and pianoless run-throughs on airplanes and trains he had since, by his reckoning, played it more than five hundred times. In the studio that day, however, the second Steinway was not yielding anything to match his ideal version of the piece, and as a result he was moved to a lot of compensatory singing. To Howard Scott, the Columbia recording director, who was sitting in the studio control room, the performance came through more or less as a duet for voice and piano. Ever since Toscanini sang his way through a recorded broadcast of "La Bohème" and Pablo Casals grunted out an ad-lib self-accompaniment for an album of Bach suites for unaccompanied cello, the artist who can't help singing while he works has been turning up fairly regularly at recording sessions. With patriarchal elders of the stature of Toscanini and Casals, any suggestion from the control room that their lieder would have to go would constitute rank effrontery and probably detonate splendid bursts of Italian or Catalan invective. With Gould, no such response would be in character, and in the middle of a fugue passage Scott called out, "Glenn, we can hardly hear the piano because you're singing so loud."

"Look, Howard, it's the piano, not me," Gould replied, and for about a minute he looked hurt. Then he lighted up with a solution.

"Suppose I wear a gas mask while I play?" he said. "Then you won't hear me sing."

"Glenn," Scott answered wearily, "suppose we take a break for lunch now, and you start all over again on another piano this afternoon."

A few minutes later, Gould and I were on our way to a restaurant. It was not a cold day, but Gould was wearing a beret, ear muffs, a scarf, an overcoat, and a pair of sturdy leather mittens. In the restaurant, when he had peeled these off, he was still wearing a thick woollen shirt, a heavy sweater, a shaggy tweed sports jacket, woollen slacks, overshoes, and a pair of knit gloves from which the fingers had been cut. These last, he explained, would keep his hands moderately limber, and he probably would not have to soak them long to get them into playing shape. When a waitress came to take our order, Gould asked for scrambled eggs and a glass of Poland Water. She said tap water would have to do, but it wouldn't do for Gould. When he first ventured out of Toronto, I knew, he attributed many of the difficulties he encountered away from home—from bad digestion to bad pianos—to the inconstancies of city water. To eliminate that variable, he settled on Poland Water as the only water fit to drink. Its virtues, he feels, have been worth all the trouble of finding it on his travels—the trouble in this instance requiring Gould to rise from the table, get back into his overcoat, scarf, beret, ear muffs, and mittens, and go across the street to a delicatessen, from which he returned in a minute or two with a half-gallon of Poland Water and a bottle opener.

Over lunch, Gould talked about music and his plans for leaving an imprint on it. He learned many of the Haydn piano sonatas when he was eleven, he said ("That was my first Haydn period"), and many of the string quartets when he was nineteen ("That was my second Haydn period"). Mozart, he said, had so far held no interest for him. When I asked him if he knew why, he said he felt an obligation to resist that composer on snob grounds, because Mozart had become very fashionable. Before I could press him further on the point, he smiled wisely and said he was planning to have his first Mozart period fairly soon. The piano compositions of Chopin, Liszt, Schumann, Tchaikovsky, and Rachmaninoff were also of little interest to him, he added, because they attempted to make the piano behave like an orchestra—an attainment that, he said, very few orchestras could rise to. The music of the whole nineteenth century left him unmoved in fact, and, once past the "classical" era of composition, beginning with Bach and his forerunners and ending with Beethoven, his interest skipped to the present—to such "moderns" as Berg, Schönberg, and Webern, among the tone-row systematizers, and Hindemith and Křenek, among the slightly freer spirits. When I asked him if either Bach's manner or Berg's showed up in his own compositions, he said no—that friends who had heard his pieces told him they were more like Anton Bruckner or Richard Strauss than anyone else. "It seems," he continued, "that I perform in the eighteenth and twentieth centuries and compose in the nineteenth. That must be just jammed with psychoanalytic significance, but I have never paid to find out what it means."

By this time, Gould was having his second glass of Poland Water, and after finishing off his eggs, he recapped the bottle to take it along with him, and told me that if I would like to hear a string quartet he had written he would be performing it that night on the piano for his publishers; they were to meet with him at his hotel in order to check on the bowing and phrasing marks in his score. "Barger & Barclay. Very British publishers I landed, eh?" he said. "They are a couple of guys out in Great Neck, Long Island." I said I would like very much to come along.

That night, when I arrived at Gould's hotel suite, he said, "Welcome to the workroom of the Marquis de Sade." There were two double beds in the bedroom, and an extra mattress on the floor, and there was a Steinway in the living room. "I couldn't sleep last night," he went on. "Bad action in the mattress. So I got the manager to send up another bed at about four in the morning. That didn't help, so I asked for a new mattress." I asked him how the Bach recording had gone in the afternoon, and he told me he *had* worn a gas mask for a while (one of the technicians had brought it in) but later found the piano in such good spirits that there was no need for it. The performance was probably the best Bach he had ever heard, he added. After completing the record, he had spent a few hours working on a long-standing project he has since abandoned—an opera based on Kafka's "Metamorphosis," the story of the man who turns into a cockroach. "This quartet of mine that you'll hear is a work of my early period," he said. "It's my equivalent of No. 1 of Beethoven's Opus 18, a series of six quartets, so that leaves me five to go. Anyway, it was performed last year at the Stratford Festival. But not very well. I can play the whole thing on the piano, except that in a few spots I need another piano player to handle the cello part. It's so exhausting, though, that I have to go to bed for two days after I do it." He played a few bars for me on the piano, singing and conducting at the same time, but then the publishers—William Barger, who, Gould told me, was a working psychiatrist, and Robert Barclay, an athletic-looking man—knocked at the door, and after the introductions were over, Gould hunched himself on the couch with a proof of the quartet score they had brought. Page by page, he answered their questions—whether certain consecutive notes should be slurred or detached, whether the tremolo passages should be played at the center of the bow or at its tip, how the dynamic markings should be changed in one place or another. Every now and then, to illustrate what he meant, he would sing one of the violin parts in a hooty falsetto using a yellow pencil for a bow and scraping it over his left forearm. There were so many interruptions that he never did get to play the piece straight through on the piano, but from the snatches that he sang and from what I saw of the score, it was, as he had told me, composed in the nineteenth-century style— ripe, romantic, Dionysiac. As Gould's only published composition, it was given its first public hearing in this country last winter, played by a string quartet made up of members of the Cleveland Orchestra. It was roundly admired, and the same group has since recorded it for a fall release by Columbia Records.

Some months later, Gould was back in New York to appear with the New York Philharmonic. He was to play Beethoven's Second Piano Concerto, and Leonard Bernstein was to be the conductor. A morning rehearsal was scheduled for the day of the concert, and a few minutes before it began I sought Gould out in his Carnegie Hall dressing room, where I found him munching arrowroot cookies and worrying about an oncoming cold. "I was at Bernstein's house yesterday afternoon," he said, "and we played through the Beethoven on his two pianos. The really wonderful thing I learned is that Lenny is a Chickering, too. He's a Baldwin now, but he had a Chickering up in Boston when he was a child." Gould was toying with a miniature score of the concerto as he talked, rolling it into a cylinder and peering through it as if it were a telescope. Finally, he put it in his hip pocket and began soaking his hands in a washbasin.

Bernstein walked in.

"Glenn, baby!" he called. "In your heart of hearts, do you feel the first movement in a fast four today, or *alla breve?*"

"Oh, a fast four, by all means," Gould answered. "Like this," he went on, drying his hands and heading for the dressing-room piano to illustrate the tempo he liked. "I feel it conducts in a fast four."

"I've never conducted it in four before, because I've never conducted it before," Bernstein said. "This is a Bernstein première."

"Good," Gould said. "I have an idea—thought of it last night. Let's walk out there together, and you play the piano part and I'll conduct the orchestra. It will be the surprise act of the season."

"Oh, no!" Bernstein said, and went on, affecting a pompous manner, "The Beethoven Second is not one of the five glorious concertos in my solo repertoire this season."

"It's been in mine, sir, since I was thirteen," Gould said, bowing low to the conductor.

Onstage that morning, Gould still had the score stuffed into his pants pocket, like a handkerchief. Once he was settled in his folding chair in front of the piano, he slipped out of his shoes, put his feet on his piece of carpet, and braced his knees on the front of the keyboard; while Bernstein led the orchestra through the eighty-nine bars of the concerto preceding the solo piano's entrance, Gould slumped down and seemed to take no interest whatever in the music swelling up around him. With one bar to go, he turned his head and leaned forward until his cheek was a few inches above the keys, and, on a cue from Bernstein, he began playing.

After the rehearsal, I walked with Gould to his hotel, and on the way he told me that he did not plan to get to the hall that night until nearly nine-thirty—a few minutes before he was scheduled to play.

He did not want to attend the earlier part of the concert, he said, because when he was to play Beethoven with an orchestra, he never liked to hear the orchestra play anything else beforehand. "Before Bach I can listen to Strauss, Franck, Sibelius, jukeboxes—anything," he added. "But nothing before Beethoven. I have to wind myself into a kind of cocoon before playing him. I go in like a horse with blinders. This afternoon I'm going to spend in bed. I think I may be coming down with the flu."

At seven-thirty, in his room, Gould got out of bed, slipped off the two pairs of mittens he had been wearing, and proceeded to perform the concerto twice. There was a piano in the room, but he didn't touch it. Instead, he paced about, playing the solo part with his fingers, conducting the orchestra part with his chin, and singing both at the top of his voice. The hand-soaking rite, a quieter activity, started at about eight-thirty and lasted almost an hour. A bare minute or two before Gould was due to perform, he arrived at Carnegie Hall, dressed as if for a long hike across the polar icecap. When he came out from under three or four layers of fabrics and hides, he was wearing his usual over-size formal dress suit. Under its white vest, Gould wore a baggy cable-stitch sweater. "You're not going to take that sweater off, are you?" Bernstein came in and asked, with the hopeful air of a man warming to the idea of introducing the Philharmonic's audience to a new twist in evening wear. Because Bernstein had raised the question, Gould decided that he had better take off the sweater, and in pulling it over his head he upset his indifferently arranged long hair, which then fell over his face. Without asking for a comb or trying to push it back with his hands, Gould headed for the stage. "When he passed me," one of the back-row violinists later said, "he looked like an old sheepdog. I was even thinking of getting up and leading him to the piano. I didn't see how he could find it."

Gould was in fine form. He played the first movement of the concerto in a kind of sidesaddle address to the piano, with his knees crossed and his back half turned to the audience. Throughout the second, the slow movement, he was evidently in the grip of rapture, gazing openmouthed at the ceiling of the stage. For most of the finale, he was in full slouch—an attitude of repose, with his head so far back that he seemed to be watching his hands as if they were somebody else's. At the end, the applause poured out. One of the profoundest tributes Gould received, however, came from Bernstein, who said, "He gives me a whole new interest in music."

Backstage after the performance, it was suggested to Gould that he and Bernstein record the concerto as soon as possible. "Bernstein isn't ready," Gould answered—or so the critic Abram Chasins, author of "Speaking of Pianists...," has written. The remark has a persuasive touch of Gould cheek, but Gould denies having made it; a few weeks after the concert, he did record the Beethoven Second with Bernstein, and since then the Bach D-Minor Concerto and the Beethoven Third. He says that he will take care of Chasins when he gets around to writing *his* book, "Speaking of Critics." It is conceivable that he will get around to writing such a book, for he has shown no shyness about committing himself to print. He has written the album notes for some of his recordings, and these prose creations are as fanciful and foppish as his disquisitions on his elementary-school days. For instance, in the album notes for his recording of Beethoven's First Piano Concerto, with the Columbia Symphony Orchestra, under Vladimir Golschmann, Gould looks down on his subject with a supremely weary air. "The second movement," he writes, "is a rather lethargic nocturne with an overly repetitive main theme possessed of the typically nocturnal habit of pleading the case once too often." The cadenzas he plays in the recording are of his own invention, but he notes that they give their performer little chance to show his finger skills, "thereby, of course, denying the original purpose of cadenza writing as a virtuoso display"—a show of humility that Gould could not let pass without discreetly pointing to it. "At any event," he goes on, clarifying nothing, "I have not yet requested the orchestra to file to the balcony while for three glorious minutes the piano is hung decorously from the chandelier."

Gould's album notes have been known to infuriate music critics, and on one occasion he came in for abuse from practically all sides, both for what he had to say about some pieces and for how he translated his ideas into actual performance. The compositions in question were the last three piano sonatas of Beethoven, and it was audacious of Gould to tackle them at all, either in prose or in a recording, for, just as the "Goldberg Variations" had been Mme. Landowska's private preserve until he came along, the Beethoven sonatas had been the domain of Artur Schnabel, who recorded nearly all of Beethoven's piano music before he died, in 1951. While Gould's performance of the Bach had won almost universal praise, his handling of the Beethoven was widely condemned. A pianist, and especially a young pianist, playing the sonatas is supposed to emulate Schnabel reverently, and, in the view of many observers, Gould was not nearly reverent enough. It is impossible to say what a "definitive" performance a Beethoven sonata would be like—or, for that matter, a "definitive" performance of any other composition written before its composer had the advantage of recording it himself. Owing to the imprecision of music's symbols, there are often half a dozen quite reasonable ways out of a single problem of interpretation, and this is especially true of the compositions of Beethoven, who didn't always use all the symbols that were available to him. Of his thirty-two sonatas, only one—Opus 106, the satanically difficult "Hammerklavier"—has its tempos set exactly, in metronome markings computed by Beethoven himself. Moreover, in all his piano sonatas—and the total runs to nearly a thousand printed pages—the composer did not take the trouble to mark more than about thirty pedalling indications, and in many passages even the notes are in dispute. Back in 1935, Schnabel edited a two-volume edition of Beethoven's sonatas, in which he had inserted metronome settings and pedal instructions, and this work, littered with supplementary footnotes, which attempt to explain the musical profundities wrapped in Beethoven's inadequate notation, has long been accepted as the canonical text of the sonatas. On the whole, Gould accepted it, too—the points of similarity between his interpretations and Schnabel's far exceeded the points of difference—but he also had some ideas of his own, and these the critics pounced on. For instance, Gould plays the first movement of Opus 110 with more expansiveness than Schnabel, the second at a slower tempo, the third with less passion, and the final fugue with clearer definition of each of its polyphonic lines. And

Gould compounded this irreverence by some of the things he had to say in his album notes. He pointed out that the sonatas had been subjected to far too many unenlightened analyses, and charged head-long at the sensibilities of many critics. "The giddy heights to which these absurdities [the analyses] can wing have been realized by several contemporary novelists, notable offenders being Thomas Mann and Aldous Huxley," he wrote, and, arguing that the pieces were basically simple, went on to say, "Perhaps they do not yield the apocalyptic disclosures that have been so graphically ascribed to them." In commenting on this, Abram Chasins, for one, resorted to heavy sarcasm. "There was a time," he wrote, "when we were deluded into believing that these sonatas were full of profound and inspiring ideas. I blush to remember how hoodwinked we were in our youth, especially by a wily old fox named Schnabel, and we are no end grateful to Mr. Gould for awakening us to Schnabel's sharp practices."

Gould's reaction to the denunciations has been mild but firm. Chasins notwithstanding, he considers himself a Beethoven player of the Schnabel school, and he has done most of his studying of the pieces from Schnabel's texts. Some Gould devotees have pointed out other similarities between the Old Master and this disciple, who never met him. Long before Gould's father rigged up the short-legged folding chair for his son, Schnabel was doing all his playing from a low-slung bench with a back rest. And, like Schnabel, Gould plays recital programs scrupulously free of any flashy *Schlagobers*—the easy-appeal showpieces that traditionally wind up an evening's recital. Schnabel, referring to his uncompromising stand on program planning, once said that the principal difference between his recitals and those of other pianists was that his were boring not only in the first half but also in the second. In that sense, Gould's are just as boring. Even apart from his natural aversion to Chopin, Liszt, and Rachmaninoff, Gould is determined to play only substantial music—the kind that Schnabel characterized as music composed better than it can be played.

As for the contested Beethoven recordings, Gould sticks by them, and demonstrates that fact at almost every recital he gives, by performing one of the sonatas just as he played it on the record. Schnabel himself was less consistent; after his massive edition of the sonatas was published, he frequently found altogether different ways of playing certain passages. Gould, though he still has most of a lifetime in which to change his approach to them, has so far shown no inclination to play them differently. He has, however, shown an inclination to record them differently. Once, to the despair of the audio engineers at Columbia, who applied the latest high-fidelity techniques to the recording of the sonatas, Gould said that he wished his rich-toned record had, instead, the constricted sound quality he hears in the low-fidelity Schnabel records made nearly thirty years ago. To this the recording director retorted, "All you have to do is listen to the record on a long-distance telephone."

One year before Van Cliburn won the international competition in Moscow, Gould turned up in Russia for a series of recitals and concerts. He found the Union of Soviet Socialist Republics a splendid place for it was studded with relatively fine German-made Steinways. When he played them, the Russians were easily as impressed by the young Canadian's Bach as they were later to be by the young American's Tchaikovsky. After Gould played the "Goldberg Variations" in Moscow's Tchaikovsky Hall, one critic concluded that the only possible explanation for such excellence was that the pianist must be more than two hundred years old and an ex-pupil of Bach himself. Between performances, Gould gave a lecture on Berg and Schönberg at the Moscow Conservatory, where, as a heavy token of appreciation, his admirers loaded him down with the complete piano works of Miaskovsky to take back to Toronto with him. On the way home, he whipped through the Beethoven Third Piano Concerto with the Berlin Philharmonic, under Herbert von Karajan, and his mastery of its content was so arresting that H. H. Stuckenschmidt, Germany's most respected music critic, was moved to call Gould the greatest pianist since Ferruccio Busoni, the Italian-born virtuoso who made his reputation in Berlin in the early nineteen-hundreds as the greatest pianist since Franz Liszt.

Shortly after that encomium appeared, a young woman Gould knows at Columbia Records received a picture postcard from him urging her to stir up some wild celebrations in honor of his return to New York. "Trust plans are going nicely for the Welcome-Home-Gould Banquet," he wrote. "Suggest $50-a-plate dinner and compulsory attendance for all Steinway executives and Columbia A. & R. [Artist and Repertoire] men. For lobby display, a collection of photographs of Busoni and Gould at comparative ages. For souvenir booklet, 'The Grand Manner, from Busoni to Gould,' prepared by the music staff of the Library of Congress." The New York reception that Gould proposed in broad jest was very much on the order of the one Van Cliburn was actually accorded, with great civic seriousness, a year later.

Since his return from this tour, Gould has spent much of his time between performances brooding about all the composing he is not getting around to, and deriving only meagre consolation from various arresting evidences of his celebrity as a pianist. Roger Dettmer, of the Chicago *American*, wrote that his recent Beethoven concerto recording was "the most sensitive and musicianly reading of the solo part since Schnabel made the C-Minor his own." The Chinese restaurant he depends on when he is at Lake Simcoe now stocks Poland Water for him, and while he dines, the proprietor plays the Gould recording of the Křenek sonata. He recently appeared in two half-hour documentary shows the Canadian Broadcasting Corporation devoted to his career, and he enjoyed doing them because they enable him to confirm a suspicion he (and some of his friends) have long held—that he could make a living as an actor if he gave up the piano. The network's producers want him to stay with music, however, and have been trying to persuade him to be a television teacher, commentator, and performer, in the manner of his friend Leonard Bernstein, and he may very well do it. Bernstein has been trying lately to get him to look a little less unkempt. A few hours before their last Philharmonic concert together, Gould was invited to the conductor's apartment and found himself having his hair trimmed by Bernstein's wife and his shoes polished by Bernstein's children. The producers at the C.B.C. hope that Bernstein will take him to his tailor, too.

Gould and Bernstein were last seen together early this year, on one of Bernstein's Sunday-afternoon shows with the New York Philharmonic, and since then Gould has taped a lecture on Beethoven, which will be shown on C.B.C. next year. He plans to do more lectures, and if all goes well he will probably confine himself in the future to one concert tour a year, lasting two or three months and including time out in New York to make a few records. He often complains that the trials of the itinerant piano player have become too much for him, and recently he has been turning over some of his concert fees to New York investment brokers, trusting that they will earn him a fortune and eventually make concert tours unnecessary. However, a few recent reverses on the big board have intruded on his dream of living on a portfolio of blue-chip stocks and a repertoire of austere pieces. "Another bad week like that," he said, "and I'll have to record Grieg and Tchaikovsky to recoup."

Outside of the financial district, New York has improved a great deal lately in his estimation. For one thing, he has installed in a recording studio here a Hamburg-built Steinway he came upon in Berlin last winter and found so satisfying that he bought it on the spot, happily convinced that at last he had discovered the replacement for One Seventy-four. It wasn't quite all that, he realized when it was uncrated, but it was still much closer to what he wanted than any of the domestic Steinways, and its presence here has saved him a lot of restorative trips home to the Chickering. Then, too, a friend of his, drifting around one of the small auditoriums in Carnegie Hall a few weeks ago, came upon a concert grand with the number One seventy-four stencilled on its plate, and called him at Lake Simcoe to report the find. Gould is eager to see what kind of piano has drawn his favorite number, and as soon as he can spare the time he'll come to New York and try it out. He will bring his new chair with him.

The artist as technocrat. (CBS Don Hunstein)

GLENN GOULD: BACH IN THE ELECTRONIC AGE
Richard Kostelanetz

Always dream and shoot higher than you know you can do. Don't bother just to be better than your contemporaries and predecessors. Try to be better than yourself.

WILLIAM FAULKNER

"Okay, I'd like to help you," Glenn Gould told me over the telephone, "but I have two stipulations. You shan't interview any of my family or friends. They won't honor your request. Second, that we do as much of this as possible over the phone." That was the beginning of a friendship that promises to be telephonically mine for years to come. Though an impatient man, Gould is remarkably generous about time spent on the phone, even returning as soon as possible the calls his answering service collects; but he is reluctant to make face-to-face contact. We have spoken at all times of the day and night, between distances as various as a few miles across New York City to New York-Toronto (his home), from a few minutes to over two hours. "Let's talk again soon. All the best."

Gould takes the cue of Marshall McLuhan, a local acquaintance, and makes the telephone an extension of himself; and he not only does as much business as possible by phone but he would sooner telephone his family and friends—extend himself literally into their ears—than visit them or even have them visit him. His parents, who live some hundred miles away, receive his calls often; but he sees them only a few times a year, mostly for brief vacations. He has a secretary whom he meets once a year for a ritual drink; but in the evening he dictates letters and essays to her over the phone, and the following afternoon she sends the

125

carbons to him by taxicab. A telephone conversation before bedtime in tandem with Nembutal helps him get to sleep. Gould lives alone, spends most of his day at home, sees few people; nevertheless, he is constantly in touch with everyone important to him, at once, with minimum fuss.

His exploitation of the telephone is only one facet of a technologically sophisticated existence, for Gould takes McLuhan's ideas about the electronic media more seriously than McLuhan himself. Some years ago, Gould deduced that not only was concert-giving a real pain but the performances he offered were not as perfect as those available on record. "One was forced to compete with oneself," he remembers. "Because I couldn't do as well, those futile concerts reduced my inclination to practice to nil." So, in 1964, he confirmed a decision made four years earlier and completely gave up the old-fashioned custom of concert-giving in order to channel his performing primarily into the new technologies of recording machines, radio transmission, and television. He frankly sees no justification for playing compromised performances before mere thousands of people when records extend his best rendition into millions of living rooms. Moreover, the act of putting a certain piece on record "frees you to go on to something else," particularly pieces unfamiliar to the conservative concert-hall audience. Beyond that, the benefits for Gould are as much psychological as esthetic; for where he was once a notorious hypochondriac, now, he says, "Since I stopped giving concerts, I've scarcely had so much as a sniffle. Most of my earlier illnesses were psychosomatic—a sheer protest against my regimen. These past four years have been the best of my life."

Gould used to give live lecture-demonstrations; but since the Canadian and British Broadcasting Corporations both let him do the same on television—extend his pedagogy across two countries—he has reduced his appearances before live audiences to a bare minimum, regarding the few that he now gives each year as an excuse to travel to places he has not visited before and to keep the habit of facing live audiences, "just in case." Whereas he once taught classes at the University of Toronto, more recently he has been expressing his "irrepressible hamminess" over the weekly, hour-long Canadian radio program *The Art of Glenn Gould*, on which he is liable to give a lecture, let the producer play his records, or even dramatize a parody he wrote of a music critics' conference, where he mimicked many of the voices, sometimes doing two at once. (He rehearsed this one for me over the long-distance phone.)

If his output is, by his design, as electronic as possible, so is his intake; for he simply connects himself into a variety of inputs and they feed into him. "I'm not interested in gadgets per se, but what they can do for me." Gould watches a lot of television, exploits his hi-fi set, reads several newspapers (products of wire services), carries a radio with him all the time, and at home sometimes listens to both the AM and FM simultaneously. "Quite mysteriously, I discovered that I could better learn Schoenberg's difficult piano score, Opus 23, if I listened to them both at once, the FM to hear music and the AM to hear the news. I want to stay in touch." Gould can learn a Beethoven score while carrying on a conversation; and he often reads one of the many magazines to which he subscribes while listening attentively to someone on the telephone. Afterward, he will remember details from both inputs for Gould appears to be, as McLuhan puts it, omniattentive. Subscribing to his own preachments, he attends live concerts only to hear compositions unavailable on radio or record.

His cultural intake is various and enormous; so is his output. In our conversations, he talked knowledgeably about contemporary literature (particularly the intricate, ironic techniques of Jorge Luis Borges), theology (Kierkegaard and Tillich), electronic machinery, music both pop and classical, world problems, Canadian politics and patriotism, theories of the female orgasm, the stock market (especially Canadian mining properties), movies, the business of music, and research into extrasensory perception. More professionally, his output includes records: recent and current projects being the complete Bach keyboard works, Mozart's piano sonatas, Beethoven's sonatas, and all the Schoenberg pieces involving the piano, as well as his present radio shows. Like Bach before him, this noted performer also composes, so far a String Quartet and several choral pieces, most of them curiously romantic in ambience; and he plans to do more compositions in a wholly different mode. He contributes articles and reviews regularly to *High Fidelity* and other magazines, sometimes under the outrageous pseudonym of Dr. Herbert von Hockmeister; and everything he publishes reveals his enthusiasm for the literary craft, the musician's ear for intricate cadences; and the ham's desire for a good laugh. "This curious attitude of affection for the errors of the past secures for the teaching of music more quack educators per square faculty than are the lot of any other major discipline."

The fact that he performs in a multiplicity of ways makes him a "musical personality," but his reluctance to make any scene keeps his name out of the gossip columns. Everything he does is informed by such diverse qualities as a great eccentricity, a broad comedy, an unself-conscious informality, and a high level of intellectual concern. Gould is always working on a brace of projects; and like all people passionately involved with their work, he endlessly exudes his love of everything he does—he personally conducts a relentless promotional campaign on behalf of his recent outputs. He is able to produce so much, I suspect, precisely because his intake is so high; and as a result, he functions like a revved-up machine, continually digesting all experience around him and transforming it into several kinds of manufacture. Indeed, his predominant interest is neither music nor writing but that machine, which is, after all, his primary instrument and, perhaps, his most extraordinary work of art. Its operation seems to provide his greatest visceral pleasure; and upon it he lavishes especially tender care and scrupulous attention.

We have actually met, briefly several times, mostly because I insisted that we do; and Gould has been cordial, though more reserved than usual, probably because human contact is not his most congenial medium and I once made the mistake of warmly embracing his right hand just after a recording session. (He screamed, I heard something crack; he ran off to soak it in hot water, returned in a few minutes, apologized for his rude departure, accepted my regrets, and then sent the piano tuner home.) He is more polite than most of the world's eminent—he would sooner direct his attention elsewhere than tell an intruder to get lost—and young enough to treat an even younger interviewer as an equal; and he is among the few members of the serious musical profession, where nastiness seems cultivated, to make a habit of saying nice words about everyone, even the most popular targets of fashionable scorn. Paradoxically, although he is an acerbic critic of intellectual attitudes and professional positions, toward individuals he is scrupulously generous, "perhaps because I am continually amazed that anything gets done at all."

Gould is average in height, glassy-eyed in demeanor, and now stockier and tougher-looking than the delicate, skinny young man whose picture graced the legendary, best-selling recording of Bach's *Goldberg Variations* that established his reputation. He has a well-formed face, with a broad forehead and a heavy jaw, all topped by slightly receding and rampantly thinning brown hair. As most frontal pictures of him show, he is essentially good-looking; but a few eccentric details will keep him from being a male beauty—his stooped shoulders, which join the large jaw in creating a faintly primitive appearance; his reluctance to shave or get haircuts regularly creates the impression that he might need a dime; and his clothes, which are informal and ill-matching; and every time we have met, he has managed to remove his shoes and expose the holes in his socks. He tolerates little quarrel with his impulses toward immediate personal comfort.

He moves spryly in an idiosyncratic manner that combines ungainly swagger with a certain grace; and instead of entirely refusing to shake hands, as he used to do, he now raises his wrist and turns his fingers down as you reach forward, so all you generally clutch are a few fingers which quickly pull themselves away. He seems as self-entrenched as he actually is; and even when revealing his most idiosyncratic foibles, he communicates the clear impression that he knows exactly what he is doing all the time (as well as what impressions he might be creating) and that, as a romantic, he absolutely insists upon his will. "The only thing Glenn likes to do more than perform is talk," at least two acquaintances told me; and he is, indeed, a sparkling and interminable talker. Gould regards all the world outside his house as a stage: and wherever he goes, he performs with glittering words, often clowning, invariably humorous, and usually dominant. His mind is as quick as his speech, and he remembers clearly miscellaneous youthful experiences (some of which haunt him) and conversations held weeks, if not months, before. Any scene with him develops a rapid rhythm which he can single-handedly sustain.

He comes to New York for a few days every few weeks, primarily to make records which still provide about one half of his income (radio, television and stocks making the rest). He takes the night train from Toronto, arriving in New York early in the morning. As he memorizes the scores on the train and puts himself to sleep with Nembutal, he is able to go straight to work. In one hand is his suitcase, and in the other a slender wooden box about three feet by two and a few inches thick. It contains a few tapes, miscellaneous junk, and, folded up, the dilapidated chair that has been Gould's constant musical companion for fifteen years. Gould discovered some years ago that he could play far better from a very low chair that happened to be in the Gould home, and his father designed its seat to be raised and lowered like a swivel stool. Since Gould is sensitive about such delicate matters, he has made the chair such an integral part of his essential equipment that he has spurned offers to build him a substitute. Some years ago, the hazards of airplane travel smashed its seat; and he expended considerable effort finding pieces of green cloth and mattress rag that, he judges, "lend precisely the same tension and support as the chair originally had." When he finishes a recording session, he folds the chair into its case and lugs it back to Toronto.

His New York piano he customized from a pre-War Steinway chassis, largely to simulate aural aspects of a harpsichord; and where he once made records with several instruments—one piano for Bach, another for Beethoven, a third for Brahms—now he is so devoted to this hybrid that he occasionally ships it to Toronto. "It is as close to the ideal instrument as I'll ever be able to find." Before recording, he relaxes his hands and elbows by soaking them in water he runs from warm to hot. Whenever he plays, he hums and chants, sometimes quite audibly; and although the engineers put a wall of baffle around his chair, the superfluous sound still creeps onto the final product. "It's a terrible distraction that I don't like either. I wish I could get rid of it," he says, "and I would if I could, believe me; but I can't." This is perhaps his sole confession of inexcusable weakness. Whether on the piano or not, his performances of Beethoven generally strike critics as less distinguished and even less inventive than his Bach, while some Schoenbergians regard his recording of the master as distinctly sloppy and perversely romantic.

The hum is another symptom of his intense involvement with performing; for at the instrument, Gould is a coiled dynamo of rampant visceral energy. Nearly ever part of his body moves as he plays—his large head sways from side to side, and as his right foot operates the piano's pedals, his left shifts to preserve his balance. Only his broad hips are stable and relaxed. His fingers, neither long nor stubby, are well-muscled; and his famous trills are as spectacular to see as they are to hear—his fingernails literally flutter over the keys. Although he sits considerably lower than most pianists—only fourteen, rather than the usual twenty, inches off the floor—he seems to bear down on the piano; and everything he plays conveys a sense of highly tempered but incipiently overwhelming energy.

The paradox is that out of such Dionysian activity come rather Apollonian interpretations of the music. At baroque counterpoint technique—the ability to articulate two or more melodies at once without subordinating one to the other—Gould is spectacularly masterful; no one else can perform this dimension of Bach, say, so brilliantly. "In purely pianistic terms, he has an extraordinary ability to keep the texture clear at all points," writes Robert P. Morgan in *High Fidelity*. "He is able to bring everything out, not just the most important line but the subsidiary lines as well. The subject of the fugue, for example, is rarely louder than the parts accompanying it, yet is always clearly articulated." He also exhibits particular genius for phrasing—for articulating both the precise notes and the subliminal character of every passage of notes (rather than building a climax)— but as a natural original, he also radically reinterprets the tempo of familiar pieces, rendering them in ways unheard before but often heard since—in rhythmic measures so original they offend, if not infuriate, before they persuade. As a result, even in Bach's superficially repetitious *Well-Tempered Clavier*, Gould amazingly manages to bestow on each prelude and fugue an individual identity. Achieving such precise musical articulation involves incredibly exacting rapport between the head and the hand—between the sounds the mind wants to hear and those the fingers can produce; and it is precisely by playing from the fingers that he adapts harpsichord technique to the piano. Indeed, so extraordinary and compelling is Gould's tactile dexterity that every time I watch him play I "see" thousands of synapses connecting every second, propelling dozens of signals across his circuits.

At the recording session, as soon as he finishes a complete rendition, he comments excitedly and specifically on his performance; and if these remarks are negative, the recording engineer whispers "take two" into the tape and Gould plays the deficient section again. ("I resent," he once remarked, "the onetimeness, or the non-taketwoness, of the live concert experience.") Skipping lunch and other pleasantries, he comes to the control room and goes over the tape with the record's producer. While listening to the playback, Gould watches the score, humming one of the melodies and conducting himself with a pencil-baton in his left hand; from time to time, he jots down editorial notes on the manuscript or sips from a cup of tea. A perfectionist by personal taste, he rejects a section merely because an eighth note has slipped from a line; and he often instructs the tape editor that a few bars from the third take of a certain section should be spliced into an entire section of the second take, which should in turn be integrated in place of similar material in the original. Sometimes Gould will record several distinctly different interpretations of the same score and then pick judiciously among the available results, even splicing two originally contrary renditions into his final integral version. In the end, therefore, the record of a Gould performance that we hear is really a carefully patched collection of segments. Some performers and critics think that fiddling with bits and pieces represents a kind of artistic "cheating," particularly when incisive editing produces the kind of inspired performance unlikely, if not impossible, in a sustained recital; but more concerned with ends (the record) than means (how he made it), Gould believes that the performer is obliged not only to play as well as possible but also to edit his rendition exactly to his conception of excellence. "A performer should treat tape as a film director treats his rushes." Actually, he splices considerably less than many performers, for when he put down his editing notes for a medium-length Beethoven sonata, the engineer who looked at them remarked, "That's minimal splicing around here. Someone else recently did fifty-two cuts in a ten-minute piece." After he finishes preparing instructions for the technician who actually reworks the tape, Gould will hear the definitive edited version of a previous recording session; and then he will either stay for another day of recording or take the night train home. He dislikes New York City and sees as little of it as possible.

His attitude to recordings is an intrinsic dimension of his enormous technological bias and sophistication; and as a writer he is, appropriately, best known as the philosopher of the recording. Indeed, his essays on the prospects and influence of recordings comprise as thorough and imaginative an exploration of this issue as has ever been done. Here Gould flatly suggests, "the habit of concert-going and concert-giving, both as a social institution and as chief symbol of musical mercantilism, will be...dormant in the twenty-first century. ('For Rent: Complex of Six Acoustically Charming Auditoria. Apply, J. Rockefeller.')" More specifically, Gould argues that the development of recordings, a product of electronic technology, has thoroughly changed the musical situation in various ways. Our generation values a sound style characterized by a great degree of "clarity, immediacy, and indeed almost tactile proximity," a sound that was neither available to nor wanted by the musical profession or public two generations ago. For instance, where orchestras once attempted to create a sound splendid enough to fill a concert hall, now the desired sound, even in concert, is more appropriate to the scale of a living room. Indeed, in his own record-listening, Gould is particularly sensitive to the effects produced by various strategies of microphone placement. Second, records make continually available to the musical audience certain kinds of esoteric music, particularly preclassic and highly contemporary, that would otherwise be heard only on rare occasions, if at all. Third, records do for music what the art book did for art; for where the latter is, in André Malraux's famous phrase, a museum without walls, so recordings create in every man's library both a concert without halls and a musical museum whose curator is the record owner; therefore, all known musical styles—indeed, all kinds of music—are, thanks to records, available to the record owner at once.

(This may explain why Gould's own enthusiasms embrace such contrary figures as Strauss and Schoenberg.) Fourth, the performer shares responsibility for the final product with the record's producer and his editors and technicians. Fifth, all the available recordings of a particular piece create a living "tradition" that forces the work's next performer to offer something distinctly original. "If there is any excuse to make a recording," Gould has said elsewhere, "it is to do it differently—as it has never been done before. If one can't quite do that, abandon the project and move on to something else." Finally, "Within the last few decades...music has ceased to be an occasion, requiring an excuse and a tuxedo and accorded, when encountered, an almost religious devotion; music has become a pervasive influence in our lives, and as our dependence upon it has increased, our reverence for it has in a certain sense declined."

Conjecturing about the impact of future technologies upon music, Gould not only suspects that by the time he finishes putting all his current projects on records he will need to redo them for video-tape cartridge, but he also declares, "I'd love to issue a kit of variant performances and let the listener assemble his own performance. It would draw the audience into the re-creative process." Beyond that, he envisions a machine that will literally allow every man to become his own conductor. As it "eliminates the pitch/speed equation," it would enable the listener to draw from "the felicities which appeal to him as among varying performances of a musical composition" and then combine those most felicitous versions into a single, personal interpretation. The machine would have the capability of allowing the listener to become, Gould writes, "a master editor," choosing phrases "from any number of performances of the same work which may have totally different tempo predilections and dynamic relations. This would make it physically possible for the listener to produce his own Fifth Beethoven Symphony as a compote of the, to his mind, preferable features of a Mr. Karajan, Mr. Bernstein, or any other combination of interpreters that he would like to supervise." When that machine becomes generally available, Gould, I am sure, will be among the first to purchase one.

In background, the cosmopolite is indubitably a provincial; yet this isolation from cultural fashion probably endowed him with that eccentric individualism that, once the world accepted it, made him extremely cosmopolitan. He was born in Toronto, Ontario, in 1932, of prosperous Presbyterian parents; and though he is no longer a church-goer, Protestant ideas still haunt his consciousness. His entire education took place in his hometown, much of it literally at home. His first piano teacher was, prosaically enough, his mother; and thanks to tutoring, he combined his musical education with sporadic attendance at the public schools. He entered Toronto's Royal Conservatory of Music at nine, precociously graduating at twelve, but continued to study there until his late teens. To this day his accent retains that Toronto mixture of elegant diction and anglicisms overlaid with Midwestern intonations. An autodidact by inclination and a shaper of his own destiny by insistence, Gould as a teen-ager discovered Schoenberg and other contemporary composers, even though his teachers had not championed them; and he now considers twelve-tone technique "the only really valid linguistic innovation in the twentieth century." Around this time, he also worked out wholly on his own that stunningly original interpretation of Bach's *Goldberg Variations* in which he successfully appropriated a harpsichord piece for the piano. Yet he was not a child prodigy in the conventional Menuhin sense; and when he first attracted public notice, at the age of twelve, his instrument of virtuosity was not the piano but the organ.

He gave two or three concerts a year in and around Toronto all through his teens; and although he was then cocky enough to send tapes of his Schoenberg performances to certain avant-garde New York composers, they denied him a precocious New York debut. (These pieces, in New York at least, were generally the domain of the late pianist Edward Steuermann, who had been part of Schoenberg's Viennese circle.) "That was the only period of my life when I enjoyed giving concerts," Gould now judges. "Performing before an audience gave me a glorious sense of power at fifteen." Few pianists made such auspicious American debuts as Gould did in 1955, first in Washington and then at New York's Town Hall. Never one to compromise with the going pianistic fashion, in the latter concert he showed his eccentric versatility with a piece (originally for harpsichord) by the esoteric sixteenth-century Dutch composer Jan Pieterszoon Sweelinck, an Orlando Gibbons pavane, five Bach *Sinfonias*, Bach's *Partita No. 5 in G major*, a sonata by Alban Berg, one other Viennese atonal piece, and the Beethoven for which he received so much praise—*Sonata in E Major, Op. 109*; back then, as well as today, he eschewed the pianists' standard romantic repertoire of Schumann, Schubert, Chopin and Liszt. Not only did Gould's subsequent success establish a new style in piano performance but he also instituted a taste in programming that has affected younger musicians: "Ever since Gould, every young pianist feels obliged to include some 'intellectual' pieces in his recital," said the pianist Christopher Sager, then aged twenty-six, "difficult works such as Bach's *Goldberg*, Beethoven's *Diabelli Variations* and Schoenberg's later piano pieces."

Those opening concerts persuaded nearly all the newspaper critics to chime their superlatives together; and before long magazine articles appeared which devoted as much space to Gould's eccentricities as to his artistry. Not only did Gould use a weird-looking and oddly low chair which, shockingly, had a back, put glasses of water on the piano, and sometimes assume a posture resembling the Australian crawl, audibly hum through a performance as well as "play some passages far too fast and others outrageously slow," look incorrigibly unkempt and wear formal dress that was noticeably oversized, but he also carried both his favorite brand of bottled spring water and an opulent cache of drugs wherever he went, ate only arrowroot cookies for breakfast, wore mittens and a coat all the time, refused to shake hands, and even publicly quarreled with his elders over standards of interpretation and competence. "I think he is an absolutely inexplicable musician," another young pianist charged. "There are only two ways of doing things, very fast and very slow." "He would come," his former record producer Howard Scott remembers, "with one suitcase containing his chair, the other with scores, some clothes, and a toilet kit of pills. He had a pill for everything." On tour, he established a notorious reputation for canceling concerts—one in five on the average—and for demanding a gamut of special considerations. His behavior in those days convinced everyone he was surely out of his mind; but as he has never subscribed to a psychiatrist, he was probably more foxy than crazy, more uncomfortable than disturbed. In short, Gould exhibited none of the ingredients that make for musical success except sheer genius (and an ability for fomenting journalistic copy); and his artistry was at once so radical and excellent, although uneven, that the musical audience generously reclassified his excesses as artistic privileges.

Gould currently resides in a six-room penthouse that tops a late-thirties Toronto apartment building. In the living room are two pianos—one an 1895 Chickering—as well as an attractive painting by a Chinese now living in Paris, and miscellaneous disarray. As Gould neither cooks nor cleans, an occasional housekeeper fights a losing battle with the mess as well as supplies him some evenings with the one big meal he eats each day. Since he generally practices the piano less than an hour a day (touching it longer only before a recording session) and often goes for days without playing at all, he currently devotes most of his time to other activities, particularly writing and broadcasting. He entertains at home infrequently and leaves the house as little as possible, usually either to perform work or dine with friends, "most of whom are in communications—with the press or the networks. They have that synoptic view of things I like."

Although a slave to his commitments, most of which he fulfills responsibly, Gould also has the instincts of a bohemian, as well as the income to finance his several-hundred-dollar monthly telephone bill; and what probably saved him from the conventions that shackle even the most adventurous of us is the fact that only once did he hold a regular job. At eleven, during the war, he was the organist at a local "Anglican" (Canadian for Episcopal) church; but since he would often lose his place whenever the congregation sang, his forgetfulness led to an embarrassing mistake which brought his rapid dismissal. Perhaps because he has been famous his entire adult life, he now carries himself in some respects, especially in his desperate quest for privacy, more like a movie star than an artist or intellectual.

At home, Gould does first drafts of his writing in longhand (this and his preference for trains are his two major technologically archaic habits); and when he has a lot of work to do, and his parents are away, he disappears into their home near Toronto, or he drives up into

Northern Ontario, where he will check into a motel or one of the older hotels in the area and work there. His favorite method for "cooling off" his machinery is driving alone through the lumber towns along the Lake Superior shore while listening to rock music on the radio. He prefers northern climates to tepid ones—London being the only city that might woo him away from Toronto; and in general, he would like to spend more time in the country. "I've got to have hills, water and leaden sky," he says. "My ability to work varies inversely with the niceness of the weather." His most enjoyable recent visits were spent in Canada's northernmost territories, and in 1967 he produced a radio show about this region—his first extended venture into non-musical reportage. Indeed, "The Idea of North," in which he superimposed contrapuntally various conversations and phrases into an essay on the effects of isolation, was so well received that the C.B.C. gave Gould a five-year contract solely to produce radio specials. "It's now my favorite medium."

In the past few years Gould has literally redesigned his style of life, just as he transformed his piano exactly to the specifications he wanted—rearranged his environment and ultimately himself as his own most thoughtfully created and favorite work of art. This involves not only his choices of inclusions and exclusions but also sufficient discipline to act on his plan. He claims that he can understand and judge other people far better by talking to them on the phone than seeing them in the flesh. "My eyes are always deceived," he explains. His major exclusion in his design appears to be intimate personal relationships; he lives with no one, never has (since he left his parental home) and probably never will. Nonetheless, he feels intimately involved with many public personalities, most of whom he knows largely, if not exclusively, through radio and television, simply because they are his constant companions; and his aquaintance with the pop singer Petula Clark, a favorite subject in his conversations, has been entirely electronic. Gould speaks excitedly about her, softly cackling at his own jokes. "Actually, I did want to meet her when she was in Toronto for some concerts, but I was taping at the time. I discovered her when I was driving alone on one of my northern trips; I heard "My Love" before I heard "Downtown." I think she's been made to represent something enormously significant and I'm writing an essay called "The Search for 'Pet' Clark." It's significant, in a quasi-sociological way, that there is such a dichotomy between what she's saying and the music she's given to sing it to. I'm not one, you see, who thinks the Beatles are writing great music for our time; I think it's atrocious—and atrociously produced. But Pet Clark—for one thing there's the voice, which I've called 'fiercely loyal to its one great octave,' and then her presence—what I call the Gidget syndrome. There's a detachment, a sexual circumspection; she can express the agonies of adolescence and yet demonstrate a pressing on to adulthood. She can put the adults at ease, yet get through to the teen-age audience. And the thing is, she's *my age.*" When Gould had finished his Petula Clark essay, he called up to read a longish section of it to me on the telephone. He read fast, acting it out, the phrasing seemingly rehearsed; and just after its final words, he sighed, "I *like* it."

The paradox is that Gould is a reclusively private person who lives, via the media, an extremely public life, in constant "touch" with the world community; for not only do his records become the intimate possessions of millions of people but the world's activities are also immediately present to him. This explains why Gould feels himself related more to the mass than the elite; for where a truly private person loves and is loved by some*one*, Gould loves everyone and everyone in turn loves him. He writes for a public of readers, broadcasts for a mass of listeners; and even over such a functionally private medium as the telephone, he is performing—behaving as he would in public. He simply knows and has known no other way. Indicatively, the "individuals" that appear in his parodies and satires are invariably drawn upon either public figures or media stereotypes. Gould has, by a series of choices, set up a certain mode of life; and he is as much the victim as the beneficiary of his system.

Gould's eccentric procedures are far from mere gimmickry, because all of them serve particular functions in his life; beneath all the diffuse eccentricity is a consistent wisdom. He still carries several medicines, for instance, because he is accident-prone; and given his awareness of that condition, he would be foolish if he went anywhere without them. To deal with such information as he has acquired about himself, he has developed a series of strategies; and how he treats such information exemplifies the idea of a human being as a kind of cybernetic system with several dimensions of apparatus, all of which can be organized to achieve certain ends. Like all cybernetic systems, man continually adjusts to new information, called feedback, that results from his actions. For instance, say you discover that staying out in the noonday tropical sun usually produces severe sunburn; then, thanks to feedback, you realize that if you go out into the noonday sun again, another sunburn will be your fate. Every time a cybernetic system acts, it gets to consider the result of its actions and modify its behavior accordingly; and many of Gould's unusual habits and precautions are based upon informational feedback he learned in previous experiences.

Indeed, everyone continually adjusts his systems to new information he acquires about both himself and external situations; but what distinguishes Gould from most of us is a distinct difference of degree. He suffers no boss except himself and has so few social obligations, that he is free enough to be wholly responsible to himself for nearly every hour of his waking day. Therefore, unlike the rest of us, he gathers more subtle kinds of information, attempts more unconventional experiments with himself, makes so many more readjustments, and then makes himself systematically adhere to these new ways. He dislikes shaking hands with people, primarily because his hands are delicate and they earn much of his livelihood. He used to put a glass of water on the piano when he performed in public, because the tension of playing a live concert sometimes made him gag. He takes trains because he discovered that planes make him ill, and drinks no alcohol because a swimming head some years ago nearly caused an accident. If Marcel Duchamp decided that he could not "work" more than two hours a day and did not, Gould recognizes that he can labor many more and since his interests and ambitions are various, he does so. He plays the piano from an unusual angle, because that odd position is more effective for him. He purchased a new Chevrolet Impala, because that is the only brand that has seats his sensitive back finds comfortable. If extrasensory information either he or a certain friend perceives warns him that a projected trip might bring misfortune, he cancels it. For every eccentric gesture, there is invariably a legitimate reason. Gould is adventurous enough to act on his new knowledge, intelligent enough to regard his experience disinterestedly, and wealthy enough to exploit the extensions the new technologies offer him; and these procedures, indeed, explain why he is such a highly individualized, extremely contented, enormously productive, and maximally efficient system.

MEMORIES:
GLENN GOULD 1932-1982
Robert J. Silverman

am diminished. I shall never again hear a certain voice inquiring if he had called at an awkward time and then, after hearing a vigorous no—the house might be filled with visitors—launching into an enthusiastic exposition about his latest interest.

One did not have to be very perceptive to sense the remarkable way he shaped his thoughts nor the tautness of his imagery. He spoke, extemporaneously, the way I shall never be able to write, though I attempt a hundred drafts.

We talked about many things over the years: mysticism (he was a strong believer in telepathy and "coincidence"), hunting (he abhorred the concept), music, Shakespeare, the game called Monopoly, technology, Jack Benny, growing up, getting old, pianos, recording techniques, books, his new film, politics, an article or interview...always with humor, sans malice or cynicism and rarely with negative comments about other musicians—Horowitz was the exception.

He was a political conservative and financially well off, yet he lived the life of a monk. Money represented a means to achieve goals, not to acquire creature comforts.

He was a pacifist. Mx missiles, underground silos, fall-out shelters, and the men involved with all of that, frightened him. He understood, only too well, man's ability to comprehend the road toward self-survival.

He wrote 14 or so articles for *The Piano Quarterly* and met every deadline. The manuscripts arrived in pristine condition. And if he'd say

143

he'd call at 9 on Wednesday, that's when the call would come through. In making arrangements to try out a new piano, or to rehearse an orchestra he would arrive on time and fully prepared.

His bathroom sink was littered with bottles of pills and tablets. He took uppers or downers as well as vitamin pills. He made ridiculous efforts to avoid catching a cold. He could drive technicians up the wall with his search for perfection. But, I ask, "Who among us doesn't have a nutty corner or two?"

While he had a marvelous sense of humor he never asked if I'd heard the latest one about...

Sometimes we would improvise on a situation both of us found ludicrous. For sure he was a frustrated actor (listen to the record) and I remember our playing "Margaret Thatcher Ordering Her Admirals to Capture the Falklands, or Don't Come Back."

Mrs. Thatcher: It all must be done just so. We must make sure to have some nice patriotic symbols. Throw the passengers off the *QE 2* and fill it with our boys.
War minister: How about Prince Charlie?
Mrs. Thatcher: Delightful idea! And let's not forget to give him a medal for valor.
Weak voice: It's likely to be a bit expensive.
Mrs. Thatcher: Britannia must rule the waves. British sheep are now in the hands of filthy foreigners. We must free them, whatever the cost!

Sometimes he'd call on an evening when I was very tired. As the hours of talk wore on I would get wearier and wearier. One night after two or three hours of chatter, and with Glenn showing no signs of weakened energy (after all, he only began his workday toward evening, so nighttime was his daytime), anyway, at some point that night I fell fast asleep while stretched out on the floor. I awoke when I felt a sharp kick on the sole of my foot. I heard my son asking, "Are you awake? Are you talking to someone?" My eyes popped open *fast* and I heard a voice cheerfully chatting away. I'll never know how long I dozed or what I missed.

He'd planned two future articles for *The Piano Quarterly*. One concerned the lack of interest in the piano shown by the post-romantics—Mahler, Wagner, Strauss. The other was to be an expansion of the liner notes he was going to write for a new CBS album containing early music of Richard Strauss. The new article was typical of something he liked to do, namely: recycle material.

It was the practice of recycling that got him into awkward situations more than once. As an outgrowth of a series that he did for the Canadian Broadcasting Corporation, he wrote an extensive article for *The Piano Quarterly* relating his experiences with Leopold Stokowski.

Because of its length, 13,000 words, I decided to break up the article and run it in three parts. The first article appeared on schedule. Meanwhile, he had shown the piece to other people and one day, to my surprise, it showed up in *The New York Times* magazine section in a slightly shortened version. I thought, "Wow, *The New York Times* is now reprinting from *The Piano Quarterly!*" Little did I know what was happening.

A few days later came a call from Glenn. "We're in trouble!" "WE'RE in trouble? What did I do?" I wondered.

It seemed that certain key people at the *Times* didn't know that the Stokowski article was already running in *The Piano Quarterly.* "They are furious because this is the first time in their history that they've run a reprint. Further, the Sunday *Times* is a separate entity from the daily paper and there is terrific infighting between the two staffs for control of the music articles that appear in the magazine section."

Not being filled with any bright ideas I played it cool and advised an attitude of calmness, suggesting we wait to see if anything further developed. He later reported that the *Times* people said that they would never again accept an article from him.

They paid him $10,000, I think it was, for the reprint. *The Piano Quarterly* paid him $0000.00.

On another occasion he announced that he had reached an impasse with Steinway regarding his piano (his beloved 318). Steinway had rebuilt the action but it had come back worse than before. He remembered that I had mentioned, with some favor, playing upon a Yamaha and he asked if I could make arrangements for him to try one in New York City. He also said that he wanted to try a Bechstein and that he had heard that a number of the leading pianists in New York, including Brendel and Watts, were now playing the German Steinway.

Well, while I didn't have positive feelings toward the Steinway company—read Schnabel's or Rubinstein's books, or recall Garrick Ohlsson's tale of travail with that company—Steinway's pianos are still superior instruments. This is an era where few American products can be trusted for quality. So I made strenuous efforts for him to try every available Steinway in New York City and at the Long Island factory and for a while it looked as though he'd found his replacement for 318. But, alas, the Steinway search ended in failure.

Eventually he tried a new Yamaha that sat in the window of the showroom of the Ostrovsky Piano Company. The showroom is located in New York City on West 56th Street, just opposite the back end of Carnegie Hall. In order to ensure his privacy, Mrs. Ostrovsky had sheets hung over the front picture windows. I wonder what people walking along that busy street must have thought as Glenn played—with just some plate glass acting as a sound barrier. Did a crowd form?

The new piano failed the test. But a used Yamaha, in the back of the store, even though out of tune, turned out to be just the instrument he'd been searching for. He called to report that the long search was at last over. Later he recorded most of the new Goldberg and the Haydn sonatas on the Yamaha.

Even though we had spoken on the phone for many years, I first met him *in person* in 1981. We had set the date earlier in the summer and so I called him the night before our appointment, from Cleveland, in mid-July, to tell him that I would be arriving at the hotel (he had made the arrangements) sometime the following afternoon.

As I drove up to the entrance, I noticed that there were parking attendants. Being penurious by nature, I decided to park the car myself, so I drove past the hotel entrance into the parking lot. As I sat collecting my wits after the long drive, I became aware of a black shadow obscuring the left window. Turning my head I saw what appeared to be black raincoat. Then the door opened and I stared up at a broadly grinning face, in dire need of a shave and with a wool cap perched on the top of his head. He said (and, I have to admit, my heart filled with joy), "Oh, Bob, I've been waiting for you all afternoon."

The next three days were filled with endless talk, listening to music, and viewing video tapes. It was both stimulating and exhausting because we went at it for stretches of upward of 16 hours. When I finally had to call it quits he asked if I was *sure* I had to leave. Now, given a little stimulation I love to talk and share ideas, but I realized I'd more than met my match. What unrelenting energy!

I paid him a second visit last summer, this time accompanied by my wife. We could only stay for one day because of previous commitments. But what a day! It commenced at 4 in the afternoon and by 10 Ingrid was ready to collapse. We were staying at the hotel where he also had a studio. The studio was located in a cave-like room in the hotel's lower reaches. Ingrid started to say her "good-byes" but Glenn insisted we accompany her to her room. Now to go from one place to another inside a hotel should be a simple matter. But with Glenn it was a production. On went the black raincoat and the cap. I guess that he considered the hat and raincoat important, either because of his fear of colds, or whatever. Anyway, that night I lasted until 5 A.M.

I remember we talked about conducting. I had suggested, some time in the past, that he would make a fine conductor. At that time, he said that he had done some conducting earlier in his career but that he had feared that it might affect his playing because it employed different muscles. So he had abandoned the effort.

But he decided to try again. He had hired some musicians and begun to rehearse with them. He thought that it should be possible to record the piano and the orchestra parts separately. The idea is not really unique because it is often used by the pop record people and it is not too much different from the technique employed in the making of films. There, the sound track is written and laid in after the visual has been completed. Glenn thought it might be possible to record concertos with different orchestras throughout the world. "Wouldn't it be fun to try out this process with Von Karajan?"

For purposes of a test he hired 26 musicians from the Hamilton Philharmonic ("I can go about my business with relative anonymity in Hamilton") and he wondered if I could find a young pianist who knew the Beethoven Second Piano Concerto and who would be willing to forego his own interpretation and play the part exactly the way he was asked. I put through a call to Martin Canin at Juilliard and in a short time all the pieces fit together. A student of Martin's knew the concerto, was willing to go to Toronto (for a small honorarium) and perform under Glenn's direction. He must have played well because Glenn said that the young man was extremely talented. He wondered what factors determined a career, because he could not understand why Mr. Klibonoff was not already an established artist.

Only two movements were recorded before time ran out. He said that he had taken the second movement at half its usual tempo and that this had thrown the musicians.

"I would beat in 12 and every bar or two the concertmaster would stand up and say to the players, 'He means this.'"

"Maybe they don't speak Music," I suggested.

Later he recorded the Siegfried Idyll and at the time of our visit insisted upon singing and conducting the entire work to us. It was amusing to watch my wife's face as he sang and gyrated, trying his best to bring out all the lines at the same time. Perhaps the recorded version is good enough to release. If so, CBS Masterworks could couple it with the transcription that he made for piano many years ago.

Geoffrey Payzant has written a brilliant book describing Glenn Gould's attitudes toward many matters. It is Payzant's opinion, and I agree, that Gould will be remembered, not only for his musical skills, but also as one of the 20th century's outstanding philosophers.

One particular concept stays with me. He suggested that technology might yet save man from self-destruction. "Computers can store so much information that the day may come when our national leaders will first read a computer printout before arriving at a decision. Since the printout would contain masses of factual information, the decision-maker might be guided by its message rather than 'gut feelings' or advice from 'experts.' Thus, man would more likely be guided by reason than emotion."

The stroke occurred on Monday. On the Saturday night before, he called, mostly to report that he was the subject of a feature story that was going to appear in the Sunday *Times*. Would I read it and could he check back on Sunday night to discuss it? On Sunday we talked for the last time about the article and about the number of young music critics of unusual talent and knowledge. Names that were mentioned included Edward Rothstein (author of the article), Tim Page, Glenn Plaskin and Nicholas Kenyon. That night he could not have been more cheerful...

Some weeks ago I went to Toronto to attend a memorial service in Glenn's honor. As I passed through customs I asked a customs officer for directions to the cathedral. Still displaying my penuriousness I decided to take the cheapest form of transportation.

As I sat down in the bus a hand tapped my shoulder. A gentleman sitting behind said that he had heard me asking for directions and said that he assumed we were both going to the same place for the same reason. After the usual introductions, my curiosity aroused, I began to question my new-found companion. Was he a musician? "No." Was he an amateur pianist? "No." What did he do for a living? "I'm a lawyer." What kind of law? He then described the kind of work he did and talked about a case that he was presenting to the Supreme Court in two days. He said that even then he was working on the final details of the brief.

I thought, with considerable wonder, that here was a man who had come all the way from Washington to attend a memorial service, not knowing a soul, and never having known Glenn and with an important case coming up. "Why?" I asked.

"For me there are two men who represent the best that the 20th century has offered us to date. One is T.S. Eliot. The other, Glenn Gould."

I sat there and began to feel better than I had all day. I thought that if Mr. Wesley Caine had his priorities straight, so must others.

STOKOWSKI
IN SIX SCENES
Glenn Gould

am not by nature a stage door John. Though never reluctant to leap into print with a declaration of enthusiasm—indeed, advocacy-journalism is the only critical yardstick I recognize—I have rarely been anxious to meet the artists I admire. Sometimes, needless to say, a confrontation has been inevitable—professional circumstances being what they are—and from most such encounters, I have managed to escape with my illusions more or less intact. But, by and large, and given my druthers, I have all my life avoided the company of musicians.

I have done this not because of any conviction that musicians as a breed are inevitably frivolous, or worldly, or consumed by the need to chatter on about their own most recent triumphs; some are, to be sure, and these one would seek to avoid in any case. And I'm well aware, moreover, that there are, in our profession, colleagues with whom one can talk of theology, or politics, or the psychology of the soap-opera or, alternatively, in whose presence one can dare to be alone with one's own thoughts and share that unembarrassed silence which is the true mark of friendship.

But, generally speaking, musicians tend to talk of music—it is, after all, the obvious conversational ice-breaker. They tend to talk about the analytic theories, or the emotional revelations, or the tactile experiments which have accrued by virtue of their recent study of a score, or attendance at a lecture, or exposure to a colleague's performance. And even if such talk is motivated by infinite charity, and fraternal goodwill (and all too often it is not) it virtually necessitates some response, some comment or counter-argument, at least in a conversational context. In print, or via the electronic media, the same data has quite a different impact; it can be edited to suit one's mood, to fit one's experience, to protect one's vulnerability. As a last resort, a dial can be twiddled, a set tuned out, a page turned. But, in conversation, courtesy demands that the addressee react and, in so doing, relate his own experience to the analytical, emotional, or tactile propositions under discussion.

And it is, in my view, a dangerous exercise. Artists, I think, work best in isolation—in an environment where their knowledge of the world outside is always under editorial control, and never permitted to intrude upon the indivisibility of that unit formed by the artist's idea and its execution.

So, I have never been a stage door John—except in the case of one colleague: Leopold Stokowski. And when we met, one Sunday evening in June 1957, my lack of fan-club expertise was showing.

I

The locale was improbable enough—the railway station platform at Frankfurt am Main. We had both been on tour in Europe—though neither of us had been working in Frankfurt—and were both waiting for the call to board the sleeper on the Amsterdam-Vienna express. I turned suddenly to check out the whereabouts of the porter and my luggage, and sighted, just down the track, the century's most celebrated podium profile. The Maestro appeared to be taking a constitutional, pacing back and forth over a course that, at its closest point, put him within about eight feet of the post I had staked out just beyond the sleeper's steps. I watched while he measured off the same, short, triangular circuit three or four times. On each occasion, he tacked right toward the train, right again toward the station, then started back down the homestretch toward my post. Each time he did this, I worked out a breezy, sure-fire, introductory line: "Good evening, Maestro, lovely weather, isn't it. By the way, my name is..." or— "Maestro Stokowski, permit me to introduce myself. I'm one of your greatest admirers and I..." Impossible; you can't hit a moving target with a cliché like that. Besides, he never did close that eight-foot gap, and there was something about his slow, firm tread with its relentless pursuit of the same patch of concrete—rather like a priest at exercise in the courtyard of a seminary, scriptures in hand—that made any move of mine seem an intolerable intrusion on his person.

On the other hand, I had not relinquished my post, and it was an advantageous one. Sooner or later, the boarding call would come and then *he* would have to make the approach; *he* would be, however briefly, on *my* territory.

The call came, and so did he. And so did other passengers. And so did porters and luggage racks, and not one of my snappy lines fit the occasion. "Good evening, Maestro, quite a crowded Pullman, isn't it."—"How do you do, Sir. These Germans certainly do make the trains run on time, don't they?" I had no more time to think. He was only three steps away—two—one. I did the only thing possible: I dropped my ticket. Right beneath his nose. Accidentally, of course. Casually, almost. He had to stop while I bent to pick it up. "Damn it," I said, in a just barely audible tone which was intended to lend the ploy some credibility. I took my time retrieving the ticket and, as I looked around, ostensibly to apologize to whichever good burgher might have been momentarily inconvenienced by my mishap, I did manage (or at least, I like to think I did) a look of genuine incredulity. "Why it's— it's   it's Maestro Stokowski, isn't it?" I was still in the process of straightening up as I offered this perceptive observation; Stokowski looked down at me, and in a benignly weary voice which had been developed from decades of dealing with pesky press types and dumb questions about what Greta Garbo was really like, replied: "It is, young man."

I straightened up, I introduced myself (I decided on the moment to leave out the part about being a fan) and Stokowski, with that impeccably paced and punctuated delivery, said: "I have read that you were recently in Leningrad." (It was incredible: he knew who I was; he knew what I'd been doing.) "Yes, indeed, Maestro, just two weeks ago, in fact." "Perhaps, then, later in the evening, I will visit with you. I would be interested to learn your impressions of Leningrad today, and perhaps you might have some interest in my impressions of Leningrad many years ago." I assured him I would; I would have been interested in his impressions of Mickey Mouse if it had made a visit with him possible.

But he had said "perhaps"; "perhaps" he would come and visit. He wouldn't—I was sure of it; besides, he probably hadn't noticed which compartment I was in. Perhaps, I reasoned, I should ask the porter to let him know where I was. I resolved to wait for an hour and, if he hadn't come by then, to try my luck with the porter.

The knock came within half an hour.

Music, per se, was discussed only once. By way of opening pleasantries, we checked out itineraries (we were both taking part in the Vienna Festival the following week) and I mentioned that I was enroute from Berlin. "What did you play there?" Stokowski inquired politely. "The Beethoven Third" I responded, then added, rather proudly, "with Karajan." "The Beethoven Third," Stokowski mused, as though attempting to recollect a web of motives that, on one or two occasions, he might possibly have encountered under lesser hands than his own; "the Beethoven Third," he said again, "is that not the lovely concerto in G major?" It was a superb gambit, and my first experience of the harmless games Stokowski liked to play while putting the world, as he would have it, in perspective for his interlocutors. Lovely or otherwise, the Beethoven Third is in the key of C minor, as Stokowski knew all too well; but in one seemingly innocuous, skillfully indirect sentence, he had let me know that he was not in awe of the 'Generalmusikdirektor of Europe,' that soloists, as a breed, were to be shunned on principle, and that concertos, as a symphonic subspecies, were quite beneath his notice.

Otherwise, as scheduled, we talked of Leningrad—of the city then and now, of the buildings rebuilt on Nevsky Prospekt, of the Bolshoi Hall, of the Philharmonic and Mravinsky, of the tea at the Hotel Europa, of the mood of the city and the mood of the country. (It was the era of 'the thaw,' of 'B. & K.,' an era when relatively few visits from North America were permitted.) We talked for an hour, or perhaps a little less and then, in that same, deliberate, courtly manner with which he had announced his intention to visit, he took his leave. "We will meet in the Vienna station in the morning," he declared.

I am not, and was not, starstruck—as I have already twice protested—but nonetheless a dream had come true.

II

In the beginning, the dream was more like a nightmare. I was eight when 'Fantasia' hit Toronto, and I hated every minute of it. It played at a long-since-demolished theatre called Shea's Hippodrome where each run of a feature was preceded by a twenty-minute organ concert. These interludes were a showcase for what was referred to on the marquee as the 'Mighty Wurlitzer'—an electronic mammoth which was disgorged from beneath the stage, and lit so that each manual and row of couplers appeared in a different color. I took a dim view of colors as a child and, in fact, I still do. Battleship grey and midnight blue are at the top of my personal color chart, I can neither work productively nor think clearly in a room painted with primaries, and my moods bear an inverse relationship to the degree of sunlight on any given day. ('Behind every silver lining, there's a cloud,' I tell myself, when things threaten to get bright.)

In addition, at the age of eight, my idea of a movie was something with a plot—preferably a plot with a war theme. My favorites featured shots of German battle-cruisers, emerging grim and grey from fog banks in Norwegian fjords, and with cuts to the blacked-out bridge of some hapless British destroyer where Clive Brook or John Clements or Jack Hawkins might say something like: "Men, we are about to engage Scharnhorst and Gneisenau. I need not tell you that their range exceeds ours. But the First Lord has ordered us to hold the beasts at bay and that we shall do at any cost."

In any event, my parents informed me that I was going to see 'Fantasia,' that it was in color, all about music, and that I would get to hear one of the world's greatest conductors. At the time, I had only seen one movie in color—'Snow White'—and I hadn't been too thrilled with that; besides, everybody knew that the really good movies—the ones with plots, and enemy agents, and German battle-cruisers—were in black and white. The 'all about music' part didn't please me either; I went, though, because I figured that maybe this great conductor would be taking his orchestra to entertain the troops at Dunkirk and that they would all be blown to smithereens by some nice, black Stukas that would come out of the clouds all of a sudden and drop their 500-pounders while the Messerschmidt 109's strafed the beach.

I did not, however, figure on pink hippos, or green dinosaurs, or scarlet volcanoes, and it began to seem less and less likely that Jack Hawkins, or John Clements or Clive Brook or any other self-respecting destroyer captain would ever agree to turn up in a movie like that. I went home depressed, feeling faintly nauseous, and with the first headache I can remember; the images of the 'Mighty Wurlitzer' and of the Disney creations had all run together in my head. I told my parents I couldn't eat any dinner, and went to bed hoping that I could rid my mind of that awful riot of color. I tried to imagine that I'd just closed down the conning-tower hatch on some cool, grey submarine and that I would soon submerge beneath the midnight blue waters of the North Atlantic.

III

Stokowski was at the height of his fame when 'Fantasia' was released but, for a young music student, growing up at that time, it was not quite 'done' to admire him. In fact, if one frequented conservatory halls and was wary of peer-group pressure, it was best to keep an interest in Stokowski to oneself. He was, or so my colleagues insisted, a 'sellout'—a man who had given up a 'serious' career in order to cash in on his popularity and profile. No one denied that his tenure in Philadelphia had altered the course of symphonic music in America; no one denied that he had created, in his own image, an orchestra that could stand comparison with the greatest in the world—that, by the time he left it, indeed, may have been the greatest in the world; no one denied that he had put his reputation and his box-office on the line, time and again, in the interests of new music; and, of course, no one denied that, for some mysterious reason, his innumerable recordings tended to *sound* better than those of most of his colleagues—no one denied it but, at the time, no one was much interested in thinking about why that might be, either.

For he was, after all, a 'sellout.' He had left Philadelphia, succumbed to the blandishments of Hollywood, and offered what seemed like a lame and fatuous excuse for this heresy. "I go to a higher calling," he was reported to have said to the press conference which was called to announce his departure. (His appearances on the silver screen had been with the likes of Deanna Durbin and Donald Duck; "some higher calling," my colleagues might well have snorted in response.)

Besides, there was another conductor as famous as Stokowski and who, in academic circles, was considered more respectable. In the American context, Toscanini related to Stokowski much as Weingartner related to Mengelberg overseas. Toscanini was, or so it was said, a 'literalist'; for him, the composer's instructions were gospel. Whichever notes, tempo marks, dynamic indications, were set before him in the score were, to the best of his and his orchestra's ability, what you heard. And that orchestra—the NBC Symphony—was a fixture of American broadcasting in the 30s and 40s; it could be heard every Saturday at 5 from Studio 8H, and those weekend music specials were much discussed and much admired by my conservatory confrères. To my ears, it seemed that the sound was edgy and unbalanced, that Toscanini's interpretations did not carry one forward with the visionary sweep of his fellow 'literalist'—Weingartner—and that the playing, by and large, born of terror rather than conviction, was sloppy. But the time was right for Toscanini. It was the age of the artist as artisan—of craftmanship, of Gebrauchsmusik, of reaction against the giddy wilfulness of the 20s, of preparation for the rigor of compositional choice which the 50s would bring.

Above all, it was an age which paid homage to the spirit of Sebastian Bach. One hundred fifty years of campaigns waged by such luminaries as Baron van Swieten and Felix Mendelssohn had finally paid off: the name of Bach was now synonymous with musical integrity. Bach, of course, had always been regarded as a technical whiz, but his spirit had never before dominated an era as it did the 30s and 40s. Virtually every major musician was determined to follow *his* example, to work as it was deemed *he* had worked—as an artisan—a sober, conscientious craftsman in whom diligence and inspiration were inextricably intertwined. Stravinsky, for example, claimed that his 'Dunbarton Oaks Concerto' was written in 'the spirit of the Brandenburgs.' Heitor Villa-Lobos began his celebrated series of 'Bachianas Brasilieras'—latin tunes ecumenically merged with Lutheran harmonies. Alfredo Casella wrote 'Ricercari' on the name B-A-C-H. Schönberg used the same motive—B-flat, A, C, B natural—in his first twelve-tone row. "You play the organ, and you claim to like Bach," said one of my teachers—a Toscanini advocate— "how can you possibly approve of Stokowski?" (We all knew of the transcription travesties for which he'd been responsible in the name of the cantor of Leipzig.)

It was, to be sure, the Achilles' heel in the anatomy of my admiration, for I had already wasted long hours of practice in a futile attempt to make diapason-heavy church organs simulate E. Power Biggs' Sunday morning sound from the 'Germanic Museum' at Harvard. I thought of myself as a purist and I scoffed at the Stokowski transcriptions; nowadays, strange to say, they hardly bother me at all.

I was not, however, prepared to let my views on Bach determine my reaction to Stokowski's work in general. My first encounter with masterpieces I'd read about and wondered about—Schönberg's 'Gurre-Lieder,' for example, or Mahler's 'Eighth'—were via his broadcasts and recordings and, after such radio or phonograph exposures, I invariably found myself in a state that I can only call exalted. It didn't matter that my colleagues rambled on about Stokowski's eccentricities and deviations from the text, and then segued to an account of Toscanini's latest metronome steeplechase; for me, Stokowski had already redefined the role of the interpreter.

Stokowski was, for want of a better word, an ecstatic. He was involved with the notes, the tempo marks, the dynamics in a score to the same extent that a film-maker is involved with the original book or source which supplies the impetus, the idea, for his film. "Black marks on paper," he would say to me a quarter century later; "we write black marks on white paper—the mere facts of frequency; but music is a communication much more subtle than mere facts. The best a composer can do when within him he hears a great melody is to put it on paper. We call it music, but that is not music; that is only paper. Some believe that one should merely mechanically reproduce the marks on the paper, but I do not believe in that. One must go much further than that. We must defend the composer against the mechanical conception of life which is becoming more and more strong today."

IV

That quote was featured in a Canadian Broadcasting Corporation radio documentary which I produced in 1970. The subject was Stokowski's life and times and the program was based upon the last, and most successful, of three interviews which he granted me during the preceding five years. From the first of these—my first 'professional' contact with the Maestro, indeed—I learned a valuable lesson: Though an easy man to talk to, Stokowski was difficult to interview; never less than courteous and rarely impatient, he was, rather frequently, bored. Perhaps it was simply that, at his age, virtually all the questions that could be asked, had been. To be sure, he still thought, and spoke, paragraphically, but the paragraphs, as time went on, were short, designed primarily for efficiency and despatch, and their sentences, though superbly manicured—often, indeed even seemingly rehearsed —functioned on occasion like interchangeable modules.

It was still possible to get a great interview from him—an interview with lines that soared and caught the ear, and ideas that flirted with, then triumphed over, the clichés they sometimes mimicked—but for that, as has been said of an anecdotally celebrated donkey, one had first to get his attention. And, on the occasion of our initial interview in November 1965, this was a trick that I had not yet mastered.

At the time, I was working for *High Fidelity* magazine on an essay called 'The Prospects of Recording' and, as a counterpoint to my text, the margins were to be given over to corroborative or contradictory testimony from a variety of expert musical witnesses. Everyone agreed that Stokowski's comments were a 'must'. By the time that first interview took place, he had spent 48 years in the recording studio; and there were to be 12 more—12 incredibly productive years—which would bring forth his finest work since the 1930s. No musician of our time had given so much thought to the prospects of recording or had better exemplified, through his major career decisions, the practical and philosophical consequences of technology.

At about eight one evening, I arrived with Leonard Marcus (the current Editor, then Special Projects Editor of *High Fidelity*) at Stokowski's Fifth Avenue apartment. The Maestro met us at the door, invited us to settle in before the fireplace, offered a drink, made a waspish comment in response to my profession to teetotalism, and shuffled off to the kitchen to attend to our orders in person. While he was gone, Leonard checked out the cassette he'd brought along, then drifted over to the window which looked out toward the lights of the Central Park reservoir. I fidgeted with a question-outline I'd stowed in my jacket pocket; somehow, that fireplace demanded conversation rather than interrogation—I thought that the use of notes might seem premeditated, even unprofessional—but I was sure I'd forget some of the great lead-ins I'd jotted down before leaving my hotel. In the end, I opted for the impromptu approach, consigned the notes to my pocket, and joined Leonard at the window.

"That is a view," he observed; Leonard tolerates New York but lives in the country. "Right," I responded; I can't tolerate New York with or without the Central Park reservoir. "I mean, if you've got to live in this town, that is the view to have," Leonard insisted. "Sure is," I conceded; I kept hoping that Leonard would keep his admiration under wraps so that I could keep at least some of those great lead-in lines in my head until the Maestro returned.

(I knew exactly what I wanted from Stokowski. I wanted him to describe to me, as he would do four years later, how he had begun in the studio—reluctantly, intimidated by the limitations of the recording process and by the necessity for compromise which it imposed.

> "I remember, I think it was in the year 1917, that a recording company asked me to make records and I said: 'May I listen to some of your records?' and they permitted me to do that. They were so terrible, I said, 'No, I cannot distort music; sorry, but no, I will not do it'. Then, a little after that, I realized how stupid I

had been to refuse. I should try to make the records and, if they were bad, try to discover why they were bad and do something about improving the quality. I thought to myself, 'You're a fool; you shouldn't have said no'. So, I then said to them, 'Please forgive me, but may I try?' We did try, and the records were not good."

I wanted him to relate the excitement he experienced with the advent of electronic recording.

"I thought I must try to understand how it could be done electronically, so I asked the Bell Laboratories: 'Could I come to you and study electricity as regards recording music?' They permitted it and soon after that, they said, 'We would like to create a laboratory underneath the stage of the Academy of Music in Philadelphia'. (At that time, I was the conductor of the Philadelphia Orchestra.) Bell made a laboratory underneath the stage from which they listened to all our concerts and all our rehearsals and used that as material for the betterment of recording techniques."

I wanted him to establish, as he would in that later interview, that a recording should not attempt to duplicate a concert experience on disc.

"Of course, the concert hall is something we have known from our ancestors. Our grandfathers always heard music from the stage, but I believe the time will come when we shall make records in the open air, where every instrument has its particular pick-up and is amplified to the right extent. All those sounds are then brought together into one composite, with the right intensity of amplification for each instrument at each moment, because sometimes the woodwinds should be louder than the strings, or the brass should be louder than everybody, or a certain percussion instrument should be louder than any other instrument. Or it could be done in a large enclosed space, but the point is that I should like to have one hundred different results from each individual instrument and give them their due intensity or volume of sound according to that moment in the music."

I knew exactly what I wanted but, at that time, did not know how to get it.)

Stokowski rejoined us, handed Leonard his drink, and poured my tea. "Ready?" he asked; I was not, but Leonard turned on the cassette and the interview began regardless.

I asked questions that were reasonable and, in other company, might even have been appropriate. I asked whether composer-recorded testaments rendered conventional 'interpretation' obsolete. Stokowski, obviously, thought not. I asked whether he modified his studio inter- pretations to suit the acoustic conditions of living-room playback; indeed he did. I asked whether one might not find something to say in favor of the omnipresence of music in our lives—the much-criticized Muzakian environment. I've always felt one might; Stokowski disagreed.

Background music has been attacked from many quarters—by Europeans as a symptom of the decadence of North American society, by North Americans as a product of megalopolitan conformity. Indeed it is, perhaps, accepted at face value only in those societies where no continuing tradition of Occidental music is to be found.

Background music, of course, confirms all the argumentative criteria by which the opponents of musical technology determine their judgments. It has no sense of historic date—the fact that it is studio-produced and the stylistic compote of its musical substance prevents this; the personnel involved are almost always anony- mous; a great deal of overtracking and other electronic wizardry is involved in its making—hence such arguments as those of automation, aesthetic morality, and the Van Meegeren syndrome find in background music a tempting target. This target, however, protected at present by commercial rather than aesthetic consid- erations, is immune to attack.

Those who see in background music a sinister fulfillment of the Orwellian environment control assume that it is capable of enlisting all who are exposed to it as proponents of its own vast cliché. But this is precisely the point! Because it can infiltrate our lives from so many different angles, the cliché residue of all the idioms employed in background becomes an intuitive part of our musical vocabulary. Consequently, in order to gain our attention any musical experience must be of a quite exceptional nature. And, meanwhile, through this ingenious glossary, the listener achieves a direct associative experience of the post-Renaissance vocabulary, something that not even the most inventive music appreciation course would be able to afford him.

Such questions might well have been appropriate for a d.j. or an A&R man, perhaps, but they did not take advantage of the Stokowskian presence; they were all wrong for this particular interview-guest, and I think we both knew it. Nevertheless, he answered each thoughtfully, precisely, and with those perfectly formed sentences which were a tape-editor's delight. (Stokowski's rare interview fluffs were invariably deliberate—another aspect of his game strategy. At one point in the later, radio documentary interview, while referring to music education, he said: "We must give it geschmeidig—no, souplesse—no, that's not good—what's a good English word?—'subtlety?'—we must give it subtlety; we must give it elasticity." 'Subtlety' and 'elasticity' were, of course, where he was heading all along; 'geschmeidig' and 'souplesse' were international calling-cards intended to emphasize the universality of the concept he was attempting to articulate as well as the cosmopolitan nature of his own experience. It was a typical Stokowskian touch and, in the radio program, I left the 'fluff' intact in the master voice-track.)

As he neared the end of each answer, Stokowski would signal a cut-off with his right hand. These gestures were usually set six or seven words back into the final sentence and put the interviewer on notice that the answer was about to conclude and that supplementary questions, if any, should follow forthwith. On the occasion of our first interview, I found this mannerism exceedingly unnerving; several times, indeed, I went blank on a follow-up question and had to fight back the impulse to reach for my lead-in sheet. As a consequence, after about thirty minutes of ill-conceived questions, truncated answers, and disconcerting cut-offs, I gave my own signal to Leonard; short of reaching for my notes, I could think of nothing more to ask the Maestro—the interview was over.

Leonard looked disappointed, but turned off the cassette and we both thanked Stokowski for his cooperation. Then, as we prepared to leave, Stokowski suddenly turned to me and said: "May I ask why we have never been invited to make records together?" I was stunned—after all, he hated soloists, he disapproved of concertos, he associated the Beethoven Third with the key of G major!—but I ad-libbed something about thinking he was committed elsewhere contractually. He responded with a brief lecture on the virtues of being a free-lance. ("I am able to record with you for your company," he pointed out, "but you are not able to record with me for mine.") I continued my improvisation by observing that, were it not for this misconception, CBS would naturally have sought him out as a concerto collaborator years before. (In truth, there was nothing 'natural' about it; Stokowski and the concerto repertoire were deemed mutually exclusive, and no such thought, to the best of my knowledge, had occurred to anyone.) Then, donning an A&R hat which I was by no means entitled to wear, I asked if he would consider recording the 'Emperor' Concerto that very season. This time, there were no key-association games. "With pleasure," he responded, "but I would wish to use my own orchestra—the 'American Symphony'." "Naturally," I agreed; I had now promoted myself to Vice-President in charge of Marketing and was not about to be deterred by such trifling matters as Columbia's contractual commitments to the New York Philharmonic. Notwithstanding the bargaining power my new office conferred, I stopped short of discussing royalty-splits, album-titling and photo credits, told him I was sure CBS would be in touch within a day or two, thanked him again for the interview, and said goodnight.

Once in the cab, I told Leonard about the visit on the train and the Maestro's 'recollection' of the Beethoven Third; we tried to remember if he had recorded any piano concertos since his association with Rachmaninoff in the 30s. "He was probably just being polite," I said. "I don't think so," Leonard replied; "I got the impression he meant it."

"But I played several concerts with the Houston Symphony while he was music director there, and he was never around; there were always guest-conductors." "I still think he meant it," Leonard affirmed. "Well, I'll get on the phone in the morning," I added, "but I'll bet you it will never come off."

And, indeed, as I thought about it that evening, it did seem an improbable piece of casting; on the other hand, eight years before, on the train to Vienna, the knock came on time.

V

The studio dates with the American Symphony were scheduled for the first week of March, 1966. CBS was counting on a late-spring release, post-production—editing and mixing—had to follow immediately, and five days prior to the recording sessions, I had a piano run-through with Stokowski, during which I functioned as both soloist and sideman.

"What is your tempo?" the Maestro inquired, as I settled in at the instrument. "My tempo is your tempo," I responded in a bad imitation of Rudy Vallee. "I hope, however," I continued, rather cautiously, "that, whatever the tempo, we can make this piece into a symphony with piano obbligato; I really don't think it ought to be a virtuoso vehicle." I did not expect Stokowski to argue against that proposition, but I was not attempting to buy his interpretive vote; rather, I wanted to indicate to him my willingness to accentuate the positive in a musical genre toward which, in general, I have a profoundly negative attitude, and to enlist his aid in an attempt to demythologize the virtuoso traditions which have gathered round this particular work.

Some years earlier, during my concert-giving days, I had developed various strategies designed to sabotage the intrusions of solo exhibitionism upon concerto architecture. On occasion, these amounted to rather obvious metaphors and were confined to matters of platform presentation: I had no difficulty at all, for example, persuading Herbert von Karajan to conduct a performance of Bach's D minor Concerto from the lip of the stage so that the piano could be surrounded by, and integrated with the strings of the Philharmonia Orchestra. More frequently, however, they involved tempo ratios which were intended to undercut the you-play-your-theme-then-watch-me-do-it-slower-softer-subtler-than-you-can dichotomy which characterizes the conventional relationship between soloist and tutti force, between heroic individual and subservient mass. Josef Krips had been a willing accomplice in a cycle of Beethoven Concerto performances in which we gave short shrift to the competitive absurdities of the form; Leonard Bernstein, on the other hand, was a reluctant collaborator when the same approach was applied to Brahms' D minor Concerto.

After a preamble in which I outlined my views on these matters, Stokowski asked again, rather warily this time: "May I hear your tempo?" I explained that I had, in fact, two tempi at the ready and demonstrated with a few sentences from the opening movement's tutti and from the beginning of the finale. Exhibits A were up-tempo versions—brusque, businesslike and, I thought, rather lacking in character; Exhibits B were, or so I hoped, possessed of a certain martial melancholy. Neither, however, were comfortable, middle-of-the-road tempo choices, and both were designed to encourage continuity rather than pace variation. To my delight, the Maestro expressed his preference for the slow set and, with that decision taken, I turned back to the piano and began at the beginning.

I played the orchestra's opening tonic chord, held it with the pedal, and beat a broad 2-3-4 with my left hand. I did this without looking at Stokowski—who would, I felt sure, begin his own countdown immediately—because this gesture was intended to prepare him for a measured, metrically unyielding statement of the piano's first introductory cadenza, and it would not have surprised me had he called a halt at that very moment. In earlier years, startled glances were frequently directed my way from the podium while this passage was being rehearsed. Tradition has it that, during the first movement's three prefatory cadenzas, the soloist is entitled to wing forth like a bat out of hell; I preferred to insert a series of relatively earthbound interpolations in order to link the measured beat of those opening orchestral chords to whichever tempo was to govern the movement proper. To be sure, one could not sustain these harmonically static, Czerny-like roulades without the intercession of *some* rubato but, in my view, all scales, arpeggios, trills, and other decorative materials, to which so much of the piano's attention is directed in this work, should be treated as supportive elements of the texture—rather like continuo passages in a baroque concerto grosso. In any event, Stokowski made no comment as I introduced him to my reined-in interpretation of the first cadenza and, during the two subsequent orchestral chords, I relaxed my left hand gestures when I noticed, out of the corner of my eye, that his beat appeared firmly in accord; the in-tempo cadenzas, apparently, had passed the test.

Like most of Beethoven's middle-period blockbusters, the 'Emperor' Concerto is a rather simple-minded work, harmonically. It concentrates on primary chord materials, modulatory subtleties are at a premium, and nowhere this side of the Grand Ol'Opry can one encounter more unadorned II-V-I progressions. A role of some psychological importance, however, is assigned to one rather off-the-beaten-track harmonic region—the major key relation based on the minor sixth degree of the scale. The second movement of this E flat major work is set in the key of B major—no precedents are shattered; a similar inter-movement relationship, C major to A flat major, exists in the First Piano Concerto—and, in the first movement, the tonic chord of this key—frequently altered enharmonically in deference to its attachment to the nominal minor region and notated with the rather arcane signature of C flat major—serves as the pivot point of the exposition and the climax of the development.

In the first of these segments, which occurs immediately prior to the orchestra's march-like second theme, the piano contributes two related sentences: a subdued, quasi-syncopated anticipation in B minor, and eight a-thematic bars' worth of the tonic and dominant chords of C flat major. And, at this point, one encounters yet another venerable convention. For since the orchestra is about to annunciate its theme with fortissimo vengeance, metrical persistence and, predictably, in the dominant key, B flat major, the soloist is invited to emphasize his own so-close-and-yet-so-far semitone's separation from that secondary key; he's expected to surround the quite conventional outlines of the C flat major passage with a halo of pedal, allow the pulse of the movement to relax almost to the point of extinction and, for twenty seconds or so, to wander footloose in a world of unrestrained rubato. Such gestures, of course, are intended to characterize the concerto's *dramatis personnae*: The orchestra, obviously, depicts worldly necessity, hard-nosed practicality, the constraints of the collective—the soloist, infinite refinement, imperturbable self-reliance, the triumph of the individual. That there are no instructions in the score to justify these mood and tempo demarcation points is not, I think, a proper argument to use against them; at any rate, given my own record of textual infidelities, it is not an argument on which I would choose to make a stand. Perhaps, however, there is, in human nature, some intuitive perception of coherent formal patterns which individuality *per se* cannot bestow, and collectivity *per se* cannot deny; if so, it renders the hierarchical divisions and competitive impulses of the virtuoso concerto psychologically naive, and architecturally destructive.

In any case, I knew that this passage would provide the acid test. I wanted to inflect it primarily through variations of touch rather than of tempo and I felt that, if Stokowski could accept that concept here, there could be few disagreements elsewhere. As I played it, I emphasized the left hand crotchets, made few concessions in the direction of rubato, reestablished tempo primo a bar before the orchestral tutti, then continued with a few bars of the second theme, and stopped. "Okay so far?" I ventured. "Please proceed," Stokowski replied. "There's one thing about this tempo," I added, getting carried away—"it makes all these themes work within the same perspective." "Yes, that is true," the Maestro conceded: "but do you not think there are a few moments which should perhaps go a little faster and a few which might go a little slower?" It was, of course, a masterpiece of understatement as well as of tact and, as so often with Stokowski, I felt that he had read my mind; I made a mental note to broaden the equivalent passage in the recapitulation just a bit. "Yes, of course, Maestro, I quite agree," I lied; "but I'll tell you another thing about this tempo: Given the acoustics of Manhattan Center, it's the only way to go."

Manhattan Center is a late-19th century complex of meeting rooms, banquet halls, and auditoria located near 34th Street and 8th Avenue in the borough whose name it bears. Its seventh and eighth floors house a shaggily elegant ballroom that appears to have given up on its grooming after the last debutante chose it for a first curtsy to society. It has a high ceiling, a mezzanine which encroaches on three sides and, as a recording studio, only one natural blessing—a generous decay which adds ambient interest to music that is neither contrapuntally complex nor intellectually challenging. For many years, this room was CBS Records' prime full-orchestra hall in New York City—smaller ensembles being accommodated in the more refined and specific acoustics of their studio at 30th Street and 3rd Avenue.

I had worked in Manhattan Center only once before—a session with Leonard Bernstein and the New York Philharmonic—and had found that, despite the undeniable glamor of the sound it afforded, it was almost impossible to keep in ensemble touch with the more distant reaches of the band. One's natural tendency while playing there, I felt, was to surrender to the Center's 'wet' sound and settle for a diffused and generalized approximation of ensemble—sometimes referred to in jacket notes as 'sweep and grandeur'. I had, in fact, vowed never to work there again and, in the weeks preceding the 'Emperor' recording, had moved, without success, for a change of venue.

When I arrived some twenty minutes into the first session, Stokowski was busy rehearsing the major tuttis. I took my place unseen at the as yet unpositioned piano and, as the orchestra approached the end of the first movement's central episode, appended, by way of a greeting to the Maestro, the sequence of chromatic scale, trills, and arpeggios which completes the transition from exposition to development. Stokowski's first words to me—"I cannot hear you well"—came as no surprise at all; the stage was set for another battle with the acoustics of Manhattan Center.

Or rather, it was being set: Producer Andrew Kazdin approached from the booth and guided the stage crew as they maneuvered the piano from a position adjacent to the back desk of the fiddles where it had been parked, to within hailing distance of the podium. "Do you think that will give you enough eye contact?" he asked. "I can *see* the Maestro—that's not the problem," I responded. "It's just that I can't hear anything in this bloody place." Andy shrugged; he has an abiding affection for the Center and, by devising improbable seating plans, has frequently succeeded in wedding its cathedral-like resonance to precise, detailed, even pop-style pick-ups. "Come, please, let us try—letter C," Stokowski commanded. The crew dispersed, Andy returned to the booth, and we began to rehearse the interludes which follow the opening tutti.

The 'Emperor' poses fewer problems of togetherness than any of Beethoven's other concerted works—it's virtually devoid of the stickly ensemble wickets which are scattered throughout the Third and Fourth concertos, for example—and I was confident, indeed, that with the approach we'd agreed on at the run-through, it would all but play itself. I had, of course, managed to overlook the fact that, in order to accommodate my continuo-style figurations which played so large a part in our grand design for this interpretation, the orchestral volume would have to be reduced accordingly and that, in lightly scored sections, this would simply compound the acoustic problems of the Center.

We came to grief a few bars after letter D where solo passages for woodwinds are mated to triadic figurations in the piano part, and Stokowski signalled a halt. "Mr. Kazdin," he called to no mike in particular, "it will be necessary for me to see Mr. Gould's hands." (The Maestro was in the unenviable position of having to coordinate this inarticulate swirl of sound with a solo instrument that had been stationed so as to allow for maximum separation and minimum inter-track leakage.) "I'm coming out," Kazdin responded. While the piano was repositioned—angled so that Stokowski could practice the digital equivalent of lip-reading—I took Kazdin aside. "Andy," I said, "I can't hear the winds at all; you're really going to have to be our ears. There's simply no way for us to tell whether we're covered on anything out here."

The way to tell that is to retreat to the booth for playbacks, but the economics of orchestral recording rarely allow for a perusal of any material other than 'basic takes'—and most of those are encountered while the orchestra members enjoy their obligatory union breaks. The supplemental inserts which provide the indispensable mortar for the construction of any well-edited tape-product are, of course, overheard by the producer during the session, but not even the most experienced studio hand can guarantee his artists that every insert will mate successfully in terms of tempo, dynamics, and instrumental balance, with the material it's intended to cover. Indeed, Stokowski and I were both so apprehensive about a number of the wind and piano dialogues in the first movement that a special listening session was hastily arranged for the following morning.

As it turned out, Andy Kazdin had, indeed, listened well: We were covered, though in some cases, by the skin of our teeth. The Maestro joined me, somewhat to Andy's annoyance, in a denunciation of the ballroom as a recording site, but both of us were convinced that the second and third movements would benefit by this additional listening experience—as, indeed, they did.

In the meantime, Donald Hunstein, a veteran Columbia photographer, arrived to take cover shots. It was decided that we could not afford to waste time at the Center and should adjourn to Columbia's photo studio where a pint-size Steinway was being prepped to resemble its concert-grand cousin.

Hunstein wanted a rehearsal-style shot; I was to sit at the piano, apparently poised for action, while Stokowski, standing in the bend of the instrument, was to offer a grandfatherly gaze to me and an appropriately thoughtful right profile to the camera. Each time Hunstein began to shoot, however, Stokowski would turn his head to the right and begin to scrutinize the bass strings; on occasion, by way of variety, he would raise his eyes to the ceiling, as though communing with the ghost of Hans Richter, but, at best, our glances were intersecting at a 90 degree angle. Stokowski never did explain these curious maneuvers and, though Hunstein repositioned him time and again, the photographer continued to encounter new and ingenious variations on the same strategy. I suddenly realized that I had rarely seen anything but a left profile shot of Leopold Stokowski and, in the end, Hunstein had to settle for the right-angle intersect. This, was, I thought, a prudent choice, for the only lay-out which would have satisfied both conductor and photographer would have necessitated a 180 degree turn of the piano with Stokowski, left profile exposed, looking on from the bass end of the keyboard. This, of course, would have involved an unwarranted waste of studio time and—worse—

placed the camera to *my* right—a notoriously disadvantageous angle.

The day following the second session was devoted to a definitive splice-point selection; the first movement was reviewed, the second and third surveyed for the first time, and Stokowski worked tirelessly from early afternoon till late in the evening. His concentration was total, focused as much on the piano part as on the orchestral material—although I have been known to look out for my own interests on such occasions—and appeared to render him immune to compliments. During the session the day before, I had found his interpretation of the second movement quite overwhelming and, now that we were able to listen to it at leisure, was tempted to indulge myself with requests for repeated, and unnecessary, playbacks. In particular, I was unable to let one two-bar orchestral interlude pass by without comment. The Maestro had moulded this passage with an intensity which I had never before encountered—introducing an impassioned crescendo to the center of the phrase and a plaintive diminuendo thereafter—and created, in the process, one of those patented Stokowskian moments. To this day—twelve years after the event—it produces an involuntary shudder whenever I hear it and, at the editing session, I was simply unable to control myself. Each time this segment passed over the tape heads, I would say something like: "Oh my God, that's so beautiful—let's hear it again." Stokowski invariably fussed with his score and pretended not to notice—rather like a child embarrassed in the presence of his schoolmates when given too good a grade—but I think he, too, was pleased.

Toward the end of this session, Engineer Ed Michalski returned from a coffee-break and announced that the pop sounds which had occasionally penetrated our listening-space from the booth next door, were produced by, for, and in the presence of—Barbra Streisand. "You mean, Streisand's next door?" I said. "Yeah, they're mixing her new album," Michalski replied. "Um, Andy, if you don't mind, since we're stopped anyway, I think I'll just wander down the hall for a moment," I announced. "Fine," Kazdin replied.

I am not, as I believe I have mentioned elsewhere, a stage door John. I am, however, a confessed Streisand addict and, as I headed for the water cooler, I had occasion to lament the fact that the editing cubicle doors at CBS are atrociously designed. It's one thing to discourage sidewalk superintendents—no windows at all would do that very effectively; it's quite another to inset into each cubicle entrance a piece of glass approximately 8 inches by 12 inches, which prompts and, at the same time, prohibits proper surveillance.

During the recording session, Stokowski and Kazdin had had a protracted discussion about the penultimate passage of the finale—the duo for timpani and piano. Stokowski had at first insisted that the timpani should be moved closer to the piano for a separate insert on this passage; Kazdin, himself a percussionist, argued that the intensity Stokowski wanted could be better attained by leaving the timpani alone and moving the mikes instead. Next evening, when we had worked our way through to the finale, the Maestro asked Ed Michalski for repeated playbacks of this passage, each time requesting more volume and more intensity from the timpani. Kazdin's miking had indeed produced the sound he was after and Stokowski, turning to Michalski, said: "How is it that when I ask you to do something, I hear the result immediately? When I ask my orchestra for such a result, I am not always so rewarded." It was a charming, though typically indirect, gesture of concession.

As we were working through this passage, with frequent tape-rewinds to satisfy the Maestro's demands, someone commented on what sounded like a light knock at the door. We waited for a moment, it did not reoccur, no nose appeared at the eight by twelve inch glass, and nobody bothered to do anything about it. Stokowski began to discuss the closing measures. For the six-bar solo piano scale-sequence which follows the timpani passage, I had made one relatively strict take and one considerably more unbuttoned version which was virtually oblivious of bar-lines. "I like very much the wildness of that version," Stokowski said. "I think it is necessary to introduce such a mood at this moment."

As we were discussing the pros and cons of this inclusion, the knock came again, rather more firmly this time, and a nose could most definitely be seen in the glass inset. Kazdin went to the door and discovered two visitors. "Hi," said their spokeswoman, "I just wanted to say hello, because I'm a fan and since we were leaving, I thought I'd

just stop by and tell you that, and I…" Unfortunately, I do not remember most of what followed. I do remember that Andy appeared uncertain as to whether "Won't you come in?" or "How nice of you to drop by" would be the appropriate thing to say. I remember that Elliott Gould was grinning from the right side of the door-frame, and I remember that, since none of us did or said anything decisive, the lady was finally reduced to adding, "I'm Barbra Streisand." And I remember, to my eternal embarrassment, contributing the most maladroit moment of that or any other conversation by saying "I know."

Mostly, though, I remember noticing that Leopold Stokowski, sitting beside me, appeared vaguely annoyed about the whole thing—about the interruption of his discourse on the importance of that penultimate moment, about the appearance of this talkative young woman whose name he either did not catch or did not know, and that he drummed his fingers on the arm of his chair—more or less in the rhythm of the timpani solo—to indicate his displeasure. And I remember realizing, as I started to stand up, that, this time, I had no train ticket to drop. You win some, you lose some.

VI

My last interview with Stokowski took place on a December afternoon in 1969. The scene was once again his New York apartment but, this time, for the benefit of a camera crew, I sat next to the window that looked out towards Central Park and Stokowski sat opposite, across a desk, and with a score of one of Haydn's 'Paris' symphonies opened before him. He had been instructed by the director, Peter Moseley, to speak directly to the camera—my questions were to be deleted from both audio-tape and film—and to ignore me; once again, our glances intersected at 90 degrees.

The project was initiated earlier that year by John Roberts, then Director of Music for CBC radio, who had written to ask whether I would be interested in producing a documentary about Stokowski. At that time, and for many months prior, I was at work on a complicated, fourteen-character documentary-drama on the subject of outport life

Preparing for "Stokowski: A Portrait for Radio," December 1969. (CBC)

in Newfoundland and I replied that, when the last of our downeasters was securely in the 'can', I would welcome a rest, a change of pace, and a much simpler assignment. I conceded that something on a musical subject would provide the change of pace, but indicated that I was not at all sure about Stokowski as a 'simple assignment.' Roberts suggested that the program could be pretty much what I wanted to make of it and that, if the Stokowski interview did not pan out too well, we could supplement it with any amount of testimony about his career. I said that a conventional documentary—the sort of program that would rely on the reminiscences of elderly parishioners who could remember him in the organ loft of St. Bartholomew's in 1905—would not interest me at all. I could visualize only a program in which Stokowski, supered upon a non-stop musical montage—largely drawn from his own recordings—would serve as subject and narrator. What I had in mind was a sort of seamless soliloquy and for that, I pointed out, I would need a superb basic interview. I suggested that we contact Stokowski, do the interview at his convenience, and that, if we came up with material which could sustain such a concept, I would sign a contract and proceed with the production; if we did not, I would donate my interview services, and the tapes could be donated to CBC Archives.

In the meantime, Curtis Davis, then Director of Cultural Programming for National Educational Television, told me that he had commissioned a film portrait of Stokowski and that, as one of its sequences, he would like to include some footage which dealt with the making of *my* documentary. I replied that I wasn't sure there was going to *be* a documentary and Curtis countered with the offer of a semi-collaborative effort: N.E.T. would be allowed to film my interview in its entirety, use one on-camera sequence in their production, and have access to my audio 'outs' for voice-over material; in exchange, if my interview did not meet expectations and if I still intended to proceed with the project, N.E.T.'s substantial Stokowski archive would be at my disposal. This, of course, would necessitate quite a different sort of production than I had in mind but it shortened the odds somewhat and, as I sat drinking tea with Stokowski, while the N.E.T. crew checked out their equipment, I told myself that, if this did not become a masterpiece, it would at least be a solidly professional piece of work.

For, in the meantime, during the years since our chat for *High Fidelity*, I had become a 'pro'. In addition to Newfoundland outporters, I had logged radio interviews with politicians, academics, theologians, artists, psychiatrists, bureaucrats; I had interviewed a Northern Service nurse, and Canada's 13th Prime Minister; I had learned to cope with reticent interview-guests (film-maker Norman McLaren, Mrs. Arnold Schoenberg) and garrulous ones (The Right Honorable John Diefenbaker, composer Milton Babbitt); I had encountered some, like Marshall McLuhan, who were reticent and garrulous by turn. No, I said to myself, his cuts-off are not going to throw me this time.

I even felt that, as a pro, I could afford to appear unprofessional; I took several pages of notes from my jacket pocket and set them on the desk in front of me. This gesture was not lost on Stokowski who looked up from the Haydn to ask: "May I know your questions?" "Certainly, Maestro," I replied. "Let's see, now"—I began to study the notes as though I couldn't quite remember them myself. "Oh, yes, I'd like to ask you about the music of all the late-romantic composers, but particularly Mahler and Schoenberg (the so-called "Romantic revival" was in full swing at the time); also, I'd like to have your views on Charles Ives (I had attended, and reviewed, the world premiere of Ives' Fourth Symphony which Stokowski conducted in 1965); and then I thought we might talk about the meaning of 'tradition' in music and of 'fidelity' to the score—of the composer-performer relationship, generally; and, of course, I wanted to ask you for your recollections of early experiences in the recording studio and for your predictions about future contacts between music and technology." Stokowski nodded and appeared satisfied. I put the sheets back on the desk. "Of course," I smiled, "I really shouldn't tell you my questions in advance—I should try to surprise you." (I could afford to smile—I still intended to surprise him.)

"I think we're finally ready to go," Peter Moseley said. "Right," I responded. "I'll just check on *our* equipment." I walked across the living-room and spoke to Del McKenzie, then CBC's New York Office Manager, who was subbing as a technician. "We've already wasted an awful lot of time while they set up," I said; "I want to ask a very important question right at the top of the interview—and I won't be able to ask it twice—so if you're having any problems, this is the time to say so." "I'm miking him as tightly as I can," Del replied, "but it's not going to be as clean as an audio product should be unless we can keep the camera crew quiet. Maybe you could speak to Moseley." I did so, and then returned to my seat by the window. Stokowski was now becoming impatient and had begun to tap on the desk with the pencil he'd been using to mark the Haydn score. "Speed," the N.E.T. audioman called out. "Whenever you're ready," Peter Moseley whispered.

I waited for eight to ten seconds by way of dramatic pause, squirmed in my seat as though I'd forgotten what I'd come for, and then took the biggest gamble of my career as an interviewer. "Maestro," I said, "I have this recurring dream. In it, I appear to be on some other planet, perhaps in some other solar system and, at first, it seems as though I am the only earthman there. And I have a tremendous sense of exhilaration because I seem to believe, in the dream, that I have been given the opportunity—and the authority—to impart my value-systems to whatever form of life there might be on that planet; I have the feeling that I can create a whole planetary value-system in my own image." (Stokowski, anticipating a short question, had been looking at the camera, as instructed, but he was now looking directly at me, and with a look that seemed to say: "Whose interview is this, anyway?" I could sense that Peter Moseley and the crew were stirring uneasily, as though wondering whether they should save film until my preamble had come to an end. But I was now well past the point of no return and plunged on.) "In any event," I continued, "my dream always ends badly; I usually sight some other earthman on this planet and realize that I am not alone and will not have the opportunity to proceed, uncontradicted, with my project. But now, let us suppose that, by some technological miracle, we could transport you to such a planet and give you the power that I do not have in my dream; and let us suppose also that, on this planet, there is a race of highly-developed beings who, to all appearances, have achieved a state of peaceful coexistence—a state of civilization higher than our own—and have done this, moreover, without reference to the notion we call 'art'—firstly, would you want them to know about the 'artistic' manifestations of our world and, secondly, if you did, how much would you want them to know?"

Stokowski continued to stare at me, moving his lips without uttering a word and, for some moments, I thought that he was not going to answer at all. Then, very slowly, he returned his gaze to the camera and began to speak.

"Think of our solar system, its colossal size. I have the impression that there are many solar systems, that ours is a very big one, but that there are others which are much larger. And that their distance from other solid bodies floating in the atmosphere, this distance is enormous. I have also the impression that not only is there endless space and the endless mass of the solar systems that are in that space, but there is endless time and endless mental power, that there are great masses of mind of which ours, in this little earth that we live on, is only a small part. We all live on this same planet. We breathe the same air and we are under the power of the light which the sun gives. No sunlight, no existence on this earth. We are all under the same conditions and it is our privilege to make the best of those conditions—of the air we breathe, of the light we receive from the sun, that life-giving light."

(It was perfect, it was poetry, it was exactly what I'd come for; if he could keep it up, I had a program.)

"At present all over the world is war—so much destruction and so little, compared with that destruction, that is creative. Many minds who are in what we call 'war', those minds might have enormous creative power. But they are killed, smashed by the destruction. If one studies history, one sees a series of wars. One sees clearly that nobody wins any of those wars. Everybody loses. They are madness. They are the lowest form of intelligence. The men who control things at the top, they have this low form of intelligence. They create these wars. It is time all humanity understood."

(Vietnam was at its height in December 1969; Stokowski had no answers and no pretentions as a historian, but he had that special gift which old age frequently enhances: the ability to state the obvious without embarrassment. And it lent to his conversation, as so often to his music-making, two paradoxical qualities—an improvisatory freedom which could absorb and transcend even the most hackneyed cliché, and a sense of the inevitable. An "inevitable" improvisation ought to be a contradiction in terms; but Stokowski, in words and in music, gave it meaning.)

"The artist, then, is living under the same conditions, making the best of those conditions, realizing that no matter how much effort he gives to improve his art, no matter how great an effort, there is no limit upwards, no limit. No matter how much a great artist improves his art, develops it, there is no limit to further improvement, further reaching upward."

(He had now gone non-stop for 3 minutes and 20 seconds—already the all-time longest Stokowski answer on record. I risked intruding upon the frame of the shot by leaning towards him, nodding supportively in consort with each prospective comma, and gesturing with particular enthusiasm when any cadential period threatened. At all costs, I had to keep him going.)

"Art is like the deep roots of a great oak tree, and out of those roots grow many branches, many kinds of art: the dance, architecture, painting, music, the art of words, the art that Shakespeare had. In a marvelous way he understood those things—our faults, our strengths, how we struggle to live. I travel in many countries and I notice that Shakespeare is translated into the language of that country, is performed in that country, his poetry is read, and he is not merely the artist of one country, but the artist of the world. What a wonderful solution to life! The artist of the world."

(He had a film editor's sense of rhythm. His soliloquy, beginning with a shot of the cosmos, had tightened its frame of reference as he contemplated our planet, then dissolved to a close-up of the artist as prototype. In my final mix, this portion of his commentary would be supered upon three musical sequences—excerpts from Schönberg's 'Verklärte Nacht', Holst's 'Planets', and Scriabin's 'Poem of Ecstasy'.)

"I find that every day come new possibilities and new ideas and they must not be ignored, they must be examined. For example, there are many kinds of sounds—don't be shocked at what I'm going to say, but I like the sound of street noises; taxicabs are blowing their horns and all kinds of sounds are going on—they have a rhythm, they have a blending of life in the streets, and it is a kind of music. Some people would say that it is just a horrible noise, and they have a right to their opinion, too. To their ears, it *is* a horrible noise. To my ears, it is interesting, because it is life. Those who think it is nonsense will either not listen at all or they will listen with prejudice, and prejudice is a very dangerous disease. The others will listen and perhaps will receive that mysterious message which is in all music, which words cannot express. Shakespeare used the word for dramatic reasons, but he also used the word for poetic reasons. He selected language which sounds to me like music. The words and the rhythms of the words are just like music to my ears."

(Later, by correspondence, we would play out one last Stokowskian game. I wrote to tell him of the musical process which I intended to use in the documentary—that I planned to employ no less than 22 musical selections and that the great majority of these would be segued via dissolves—gradual harmonic overlaps—with hard cuts confined to a monaural sequence which illustrated his early studio experiences. He replied: "Dear friend: I have never believed in 'montage.' Do you agree? Are you willing to remix?" I applied to Curtis Davis, the most astute Stokowski-watcher I knew, for advice. "When you write him, be sure to define your process as a 'symphonic synthesis.' I think that term will not be lost on him," Curtis replied. It was not; Stokowski could hardly disown *his* symphonic syntheses of Wagner, and I proceeded with my mix as planned; hard cuts might have been appropriate for a radio portrait of Toscanini or George Szell, but they were emphatically not suited to the character, life-style, or musical proclivities of my subject.)

"It is quite possible that the so-called cave man had such ideas too, on his level, in his way, according to his ideas of the best life of that time. There have always been persons on this earth who love beauty and order. It is so important to know what we really do know definitely, and to realize the immense mass of possibilities there are to life that we do not know. There may be corresponding forms of life on other planets. It is difficult to know what they are feeling and what they are thinking. Their life might be quite different from our human life or our animal life. Also, there would be the question of language, the question of how we communicate. So it would be very difficult. Yet I would think it a great privilege if I could know their ideas of what is orderly and what is beautiful. That would be the first step, I think, to try and understand *their* life, to find out what *they* think and feel and desire."

(In the end, this soliloquy ran to 8 minutes, 38 seconds. It would later be divided so as to provide book-ends for the one-hour program—the division occurring after the first Shakespeare reference, and the concluding phrase would be regenerated from his first sentence. For, with his film-editor's gift, he had already sensed the need for a process-reversal, for a mirror-image of his opening thoughts. Beginning with the second Shakespeare reference, he had begun to move inexorably from the particular to the universal.)

"If I did have that possibility, I would do my best to give a clear impression to what other form of life there might be on that planet, of what I think is beautiful and orderly, what I think is creative and what I think is destructive. It would be possible, I hope, to let them see what is happening on this Earth—so much destruction, so little that is creative."

(His original answer ended with those words, but I could not bear to take my leave of Stokowski while he mused upon man's capacity for self-destruction. I felt that his mirror-image must be completed. I had deleted two words from his first sentence so that something could be held in reserve for the end—and now, in its regenerated repetition, that sentence was restored to its original form. After all, Stokowski himself refused to regard the score, or the material with which he had to work, as Holy Writ; for him, it was rather like a collection of newly discovered parchments for a gospel yet to be transcribed. Besides, it seemed to me that to perfect a structure through creative deception— to cheat with the help of the technological resource in the interest of a more satisfying form—was a particularly Stokowskian thing to do. In his life-time, he had witnessed the triumph, and confirmed the essential humanity, of those technological ideas which had inspired his activity as a musician; for him, technology had indeed become a "higher calling." He had understood that, through its mediation, one could transcend the frailty of nature and concentrate on a vision of the ideal. His life and work had testified to our ability to remove ourselves from ourselves and achieve a state of ecstasy.)

"Think of our solar system, its colossal size, its possibility."

ECSTASY OF GLENN GOULD
I
John Dann

The sculptured portrait in its most ambitious form seeks to go beyond mere verisimilitude to an inner human reality. Through the sculptural interpretation of a person's unique physiognomy, gradually tempered by life's experience, it attempts to communicate evidence of man's perennial striving for self-understanding and for a mastery over his physical and material limitations. The merit of such work is not that it glorifies the individual, but that it can reveal through his aspirations and achievements that which is relevant to all.

Considering the great influence Glenn Gould has had on my life, it seems altogether fitting that my first encounter with him occurred under what (as I was later to learn) were typical Gouldian conditions. I was fourteen or fifteen years old when, with immutable resolve, I decreed that I should leave school as soon as possible, to devote my life to the study and creation of sculpture. No one around me at the time, either at home or at school, knew very much about sculpture (I had discovered its existence only recently myself), so there was a good deal of tension in the air and talk of throwing life away and of mental instability and so forth. Nonetheless, imagining myself in the agreeably heroic position of the ostracized artist, I was quite happy. At that time, about the only one to concur in every respect with my plans was my dog. So I arranged whenever possible to be driven to the family cottage where, with him as my sole companion, I would spend a week or so in glorious isolation. Here, in what was for me Canada's

Sculptural portrait by John Dann. (Robert Lynch)

wilderness, I took long walks, thought thoughts with all the resource-fulness of youth and, for the first time, listened to the music of Glenn Gould.

During those sheltered days, spent beyond time and place, as I came to terms with my recent sculptural awakening, I was not aware of the many implications of the impact that this music had on me. Without my being aware, it communicated with that entity deep within me which was directly responsible for my fledgling sculptural aspirations. Of course I was euphoric, for I perceived within the music that eternal quality which was central to my own youthful artistic credo. But I was experiencing, for the first time, something the great value and unique-ness of which I did not yet realize. I was experiencing something I would grow to cherish and which would provide me with constant inspiration—the ecstasy of Glenn Gould.

At that time my ignorance was nowhere more apparent than in regard to music, although my happiest moments, when not reducing large blocks of air-blown cement to rubble, were spent sitting before the phonograph absorbing all I could of the magical world of structured sound. As I listened to more and more music, I found myself formulat-ing passionate convictions, at extreme opposites on the like-dislike scale, about both composers and performers. My admiration for Glenn Gould grew with each addition to my collection of his recordings. I came to believe that my enthusiasm, which I had understood simply as a predilection for the music of Bach, could be explained only in terms of Gould's profound insight into the nature of mankind, expressed through an intense personal relationship with his music.

It became apparent, as I learned more about the man behind the music, that every aspect of his life contributed in some way to developing a central philosophical tenet. His music, his many writings and radio and television work, his love and need of solitude, and his admiration for those who in their lifetime gave up or avoided the well-trodden path of worldly ambition and who, at the beckoning of an inner voice, followed more obscure and quiet ways, all point collectively and separately to a belief in the underlying spirituality of artistic expression. Obviously he was aware of this spirituality and its artistic potential early in life; the pursuit of its realization was the inevitable result of his insight. His withdrawal into a private world of solitude and introspection became an essential element in that pursuit, for Gould, like the Cistercian hermit Thomas Merton, realized that solitude enhanced his ability to communicate with a world in which he felt so out of place.

Communication on the most intimate level was of the highest importance to Glenn Gould. He gave of himself unreservedly. His recordings reveal the vulnerable, trusting, joyous, eternal nature of man's soul, and we, perceiving the invisible through that which is made, are drawn into this wonderfully mystical realm of ecstasy. But ecstatic expression and the contemplation of one's own divinity do not find easy reception or ready acceptance in the quotidian habits of our society. That Gould abandoned the proffered honours and public adulation of that society, shedding its reality for a deeper and invisible reality, must have been irksome to many.

That he did so, that he cherished to the exclusion of all else a personal artistic development, perceiving the artist as an individual involved in an independent creative process beyond the reach of contemporary considerations was, for me, of particular importance. I derived immense encouragement in my own pursuits from my experience of Glenn Gould. For him, the justification of art was that it enabled man to become aware of his inner self and it was ecstasy, nurtured in solitary contemplation, that infused the creative process, endowing art with the power of universal communication. This ecstatic experience was for Gould a bridge over the abyss which lies between man's mundane and his spiritual existence. He believed that it was the necessary element in the creation and appreciation of art.

Thus, having made sculptured portraits of several people of outstanding character and substance, attempting in these works to express the inner essence of the subject, I was inevitably led by my esteem for Gould to a desire to make a sculpture of him.

My usual practice when making a piece of this kind is to work at length in the presence of the individual represented. This process, more than merely permitting a close study of the subject's physical features, allows one to gradually absorb the hidden characteristics and to give them life through sculptural form. With Gould, this approach was out of the question. Not only did his aversion to face-to-face contact make it so, but also the fact that he did not reveal himself at that level of human interaction. However, the essential Gould was readily available through his own highly personal communications with the world, and since it seemed to me that he was nowhere more accessible than through his music, I began, for the first time, a portrait of someone I had never seen, and did so by delving into the intimate world of his work. This was the basis for the sculpture which is photographically reproduced in these pages. In it I attempted to express what I perceived to be the most important aspect of Gould's life: his ability, through ecstasy, to unite with our spiritual essence.

Glenn Gould's life was one which, behind the elaborate smoke screens of eccentricity and light-hearted exuberance, delved into the most profound questions of human existence. Born with an extraordinary and unsettling musical ability and perceptive nature, he was intensely aware of forces within himself that would not conform to any convenient mundane explanation, and he must have felt the longing to connect with the omnipotent source of his being. This instinctive insight was refined by an acute intellect which understood the relationships between man, art and divinity. He viewed man as a solitary being. His own need for solitude was derived, in part, from a mistrust of the fragility and superficiality of conventional forms of communication, which tend to obscure this fact of human solitude. Gould knew that solitude was essential if one wished to enter the realm of the inner self; and he saw artistic expression, in its highest form, as the manifestation of, and ultimately the expendable means towards, a state of sublime inner awareness. Glenn Gould sought that state, but not for himself alone. He did not bury his talents for fear of failure, but used them with courage, love and compassion to reveal for all a universal harmony and lasting peace.

Recording the Goldberg Variations in New York, 1955. (CBS)

ECSTASY OF
GLENN GOULD
II
Denis Dutton

Though the world of music and art has always been thought to thrive on novelty, history teaches us that it often rejects the imaginatively new simply because it is too new. Examples are limitless, but I have in mind something which concerned me back in the late 1950s. There was a considerable period then when it was common to complain that virtually all of the younger generation of pianists (and not only pianists, but musicians in general) were practically indistinguishable from one another. All very fine technically, so the story went, but what of spirit? They all played "like machines," devoid of temperament, of individual personality.

Generally speaking, I agreed. A child of the LP era, I nevertheless lurked in dusty record shops searching out the 78 discs of de Pachmann, Rosenthal, Friedman, Lhevinne, Godowsky, and my pianistic idols, Rachmaninoff and Hofmann. However remote or scratchy the sound of those recordings, the performances they transcribed were full of musical life; they were the deeply personal testaments of musicians of character. But I soon learned that many who shared my interest in pianists of generations past seemed motivated more by nostalgia than by a simple desire to hear the consummate artistry of these great musicians. For most 78 enthusiasts, I came to see then and still believe today, a musician could only be of interest if he was at least retired, and preferably dead. In short, the attitude of many record collectors, though it involved the continued veneration of some of history's most admirable performing musicians, was—and still is—based more in a sentimental longing for a lost Golden Age of performance than it was in a continuing search for musical greatness.

The acid test which revealed to my satisfaction the narrow mentality of my fellow 78 enthusiasts was Glenn Gould. Against all the dull, mechanical technicians, here was a pianist whose interpretations were at once imaginative, coherent, and utterly unlike anything heard before. The young Gould was dismissed as an eccentric, though I had noticed that eccentricity was apparently a virtue when heard in the recordings of the old de Pachmann. How I wished I had possessed the apparatus to add 78 clicks and surface noise to, say, Gould's Beethoven Opus 109 and present it as a lost Friedman or Godowsky recording. I could only imagine the reaction: *No one can play Beethoven like that anymore!* (This would have been a variation on Gould's concept of "creative cheating," put to the task of rooting out a form of what he called the "Van Meegeren syndrome.")

Now, as fate would have it, it falls to us to be nostalgic about the artistry of Glenn Gould. And while I hope the brilliance of Gould never inspires the sort of narrow enthusiasm which blinded some to his genius, and which might impede the recognition of other young performers in the future, we cannot fail to see that Glenn Gould was a phenomenon so compelling, so unlike anything else in music in our time or any other time, that he will not be forgotten. In fact, I would hazard that if there is any twentieth-century performing musician who is still listened to five hundred years from now, it will be Glenn Gould. His recorded legacy is as close as I can imagine to being a permanent contribution to the history of musical art as any performer has produced since the invention of the phonograph.

I want to argue that the artistry of Gould cannot be thought about in quite the same way as we commonly think about the work of most performers. In doing so, I will, however, apply to Gould two terms which, since they are these days applied to everything from opera singers to sports cars, have practically lost all meaning. I claim that in a fundamental sense Gould's art is *inimitable* and significantly *unique.* Of course, carried to some ultimate point of analysis, every musical performance is inimitable, and in a trivial sense, every snowflake is unique. But I wish nonetheless to defend these as significant characterizations of Gould's genius.

That something is great in art does not always mean that it cannot in some respects be imitated. Beethoven and Wagner pioneered forms and techniques of expression which were great in their own right and which could yet serve as models or patterns for other composers. Naturally, most of the followers of such great artists produced merely derivative music. Many other composers, however, influenced by such figures as Beethoven or Wagner, did wondrous things themselves, while still working within forms inherited from their forebears. Sometimes music which is modeled on some prior form will be better than that in which the form itself was originated. Chopin, as is well known, did not originate the form of the nocturne, but took it over from its inventor, John Field, whose relatively uninteresting nocturnes sound superficially like Chopin's.

In this sense, there are inventive and original figures in music from whom we can *learn*, because they pioneered techniques or styles which can inform future generations. Their work stands as a foundation upon which can be built further creative efforts. The word "pioneer" is used here advisedly because such artists explore territory which others may further exploit later on. Thus they contribute to musical progress.

When I say that Glenn Gould is "inimitable" I mean to claim that his genius is *not* of this sort. His art offers no techniques, methods, or patterns which could be utilized by other musicians to attain their own artistic ends. There is not, in my view, even a Gouldian style of playing which could profitably serve as a pattern for another artist. This, of course, may sound like a strange thing to say: when the art of a pianist is so distinctive, so instantly recognizable as Glenn Gould's, it seems natural to suppose that he would offer a model for others. But while Gould has inspired and will continue to inspire other musicians (just as the very different art of Artur Schnabel inspired the young Gould), he offers no pattern or blueprint for Gouldian interpretation. Consider what such a blueprint would look like if we could ever determine it: it might call for us to stress inner voices, roll a chord or two, or choose odd tempi.

But that in itself would not make one's playing truly Gouldian. The problem would be *which* inner voices to bring out and *where*, or which odd tempi to choose. One thing that I have always found very striking about Gould's approach to music, from the 1955 *Goldberg Variations* to his most recent posthumous releases, is how ineffectual I have been in trying to anticipate even the superficial external features of his performances. One might expect that over twenty-five years of listening to the recordings of an artist would finally give one some small ability to predict how he would "handle" a piece of the standard repertoire. Yet right up to his latest release at the time of this writing, a Brahms recording, I find myself powerless to predict even roughly Gould's approach. The *Rhapsodies*, Opus 79, are my most current case in point: those astonishing performances are unmistakably and indelibly the work of Glenn Gould, but never could I have guessed how he has interpreted these pieces. Gould is in this respect so very unlike any of a dozen fine and famous virtuosos I could name. With the others I am certain I could, with fair probability, predict how their recordings of the Opus 79 *Rhapsodies* would sound.

Again, this is not to deny that there is something sharply distinct and instantly recognizable about the pianism of Glenn Gould. The profoundly personal character of his music making and of the "Gouldian style" is not analysable into a set of rules which might be applied by another artist. In this sense, Gould's playing is not playing of a *certain kind*, playing which could be attempted by another pianist who might bring it off as well as, or probably worse than, Gould. The best I can imagine another artist doing with a Gouldian approach is to produce a *parody* of it, replete with atonal humming, no doubt. In fact, the greatness of the art of Glenn Gould does not lie in any sort of replicable technique or method, but in a noumenal, indefinable substrate which underlies the external constraints of style and technique.

Glenn Gould had a word for this: it was "ecstasy." Ecstasy for him did not denote a special euphoric emotion which might be produced in the performance—or in listening to the performance—of a piece of music. Ecstasy is a state achieved when the performer goes beyond himself, beyond his technique, beyond the mechanical means of producing the performance, to attain a sublime, integrated view of the musical work of art. Gouldian ecstasy, as Geoffrey Payzant describes it, is a merging of "self with the innerness of the music." Strictly speaking, ecstasy is a solitary condition, available to a performer and perhaps through him to an audience; for Gould, the solitary listening to recordings of music could make it accessible. But to the individual performer or listener, ecstasy is achieved when one stands outside of oneself, experiencing a uniquely coherent vision—which at the ecstatic moment must seem the only possible vision—of the music at hand.

There is an aspect of Gould's conception of ecstasy which is remarkably consistent with his whole artistic personality. Glenn Gould was in certain respects both a romantic and an idealist. He was always dissatisfied with present possibilities, with the here-and-now and the ordinary and conventional. He gave up live concerts because he thought more life was possible beyond the confines of the concert hall, something attainable only through recording. He gave up ordinary recording because there were things that were possible only by taking over the actual production work, the splicing and editing, himself. He often played the piano as though he thought it a clavichord, or an organ, or a symphony orchestra. He could play transcriptions of the *Pastoral Symphony* or the *Siegfried Idyll* as though they were Bach, and play a Bach prelude as though it were a Brahms intermezzo. He took some of the most emotional music ever written and revealed to us its purely rational inner logic, and he took what had hitherto been regarded as some of the coolest and most academic of musical works and demonstrated that they too had a core of burning passion. In whatever he did, he shared with romantic idealism the desire to transcend present possibilities, to reach out to some ideal conception which had never entered the more circumscribed musical imaginations of the rest of us.

This brings me to my claim that Gould's art was not only inimitable—for he did nothing to establish a style which others might adopt—but that it was significantly unique as well. Let me explain. Glenn Gould despised musical competitions. As Payzant has shown, he was deeply anti-competitive in spirit; in music, the only competition was with himself to evoke a clear conception of the music. But there is more. Gould was an interpretative pluralist. He recognized that any number of equally valid interpretations of a musical score were possible. If such pluralism is taken seriously in critical practice, it follows that we must judge performances, or in any event Gould's performances as he conceived them, according to their own implicit internal standards of meaning and coherence, and not according to some external, perhaps historically established, tradition or paradigm. This view is not devised with an eye toward insulating Gould from criticism; if we adopt it toward his work, we will not always be required to praise. We may now and then find his playing awful. However if, say, his interpretation of a Mozart sonata is judged atrocious, it will not be found wanting because it fails to live up to some external convention of proper Mozart. It will be atrocious because it falls to pieces of its own accord, because it makes no coherent sense, because, in the last analysis, it does not achieve the ecstatic inner unity of self and music.

It is an unhappy fact that over the years a great deal of the criticism directed at Gould has been undertaken in a very different spirit from this. Critics—I have done it myself—will compare, say, nine different recordings of a Chopin nocturne and grade them from best to worst. Now if you have nine different Chopinists all playing within an established tradition, it can make good sense to "grade" performances in this way; in fact, a lot can be learned from doing it. But it has its pitfalls. Of course, at its worst, in this sort of competition the "best" recording may turn out to be that which most closely approximates what the critic was once taught was the "right" way to play the piece, or it may be the reading which is most similar to the first recording of the nocturne which the critic owned. These would be easily condemned cases of prejudice. But the problem is much more insidious when we are confronting performances which have as their point the ecstatic inner coherence which Glenn Gould invariably tried to attain, especially when this involved deliberately ignoring established traditions of performance. This was a problem whenever Gould recorded works from the standard repertoire. Lucky, in a way, that his first Columbia disc was the *Goldberg Variations*. In 1955 so few music lovers had ever heard them that there was little problem with competing conceptions (only the usual cavils about Bach on the piano). But woe unto Gould that his next recording should be of the last three Beethoven sonatas; these performances had to be measured against the "standard" set by weighty German tradition, and particularly by the recordings of Schnabel.

It is a wonderful thing for us all that Gould possessed such a stubborn independence of mind that he refused to be cowed by considerations of tradition and the "proper" way of performing the works of an established composer. The attitude I have described so misses the mark because Gould's art was based on the notion that completely different and equally sublime performances of the same work are possible. From him we had no pretense that his conception of a work of music was somehow the right conception. He would have recoiled from Landowska's jibe at another pianist, "You play Bach *your* way, and I'll play him *his* way." Even if we knew how Bach, or Beethoven, or Mozart performed their own works, these conceptions could not have for Gould a privileged or definitive place. In this respect, Glenn Gould's idealism is far from being Platonic in character: there is no one eternal form of the Beethoven Opus 111 Sonata. There are an indefinite number of ideals, each different from the others but capable of being revealed in a single ecstatic performance. The sense, moreover, in which each of these ideals is unique lies in the fact that they are not to be assessed according to some external super-standard: each sets its own standard of inner coherence.

Gould's unending effort to achieve ecstasy by his own lights in whatever way he thought it might be revealed in a score, coupled with his refusal to bow to any tradition of performance, is the source of so much of the critical nonsense that has been written about him over the years. So often the dismissals of Gould's art involved the application to one of the supreme geniuses of twentieth-century performance a canon of criticism for a music student. In fact, the whole world of music is in my view oppressed by the heavy hand of authority (much more so than, for example, the worlds of painting and literature). Every person who learns to play an instrument is sooner or later instructed about the "right way" and the "wrong way" to interpret some musical work. Beyond all those humble, but implicitly authoritarian, music teachers are the scholars who specialize in genres and composers, people who write learned books to tell us in general about the "right way" with this or that composer. How could we expect anything but misunderstanding—and intermittent outrage—in response to Glenn Gould, a performer who made it his point always to find a new way, and who refused to pay the necessary obeisance to scholarship and tradition.

At the outset of this discussion, I expressed the belief that Glenn Gould has achieved a more lasting place in the history of music than any other performer since the invention of the phonograph. If true, this is because he was so much more a creative artist than other performers. In actuality, the distinction between creation and performance tends to disappear when properly considering his art. For Gould, performance was an act of creation. Further, his activity as a creative performer places responsibilities on us as listeners. Because of the power of his intellect and the scope of his imagination, Gould makes not only keyboard interpretation, but listening itself into an active experience. I know of no pianist who required more of his listeners. They are never allowed to bathe passively in a pleasing wash of sound. They are to be surprised and provoked, and at those sublime moments thrown into the ecstatic state, moved by a stunning vision of the expressive unity of a work of musical art.

"The purpose of art," Gould once wrote, is "the gradual, lifelong construction of a state of wonder and serenity." If his recordings are our evidence, Glenn Gould not only achieved this for himself: he made it possible for us to share his ecstasy.

A public rehearsal at Massey Hall, Toronto, 1960. (Glenn Gould Estate, David Wulkan)

ART OF
THE FUGUE
Glenn Gould

Bach was forever writing fugues. No pursuit was better fitted to his temperament and there is none by which the development of his art can be so precisely evaluated.

He has always been judged by his fugues. In his last years, still writing them at a time when the avant-garde of his day was occupied with more melody-oriented endeavours, he was dismissed as a relic of an earlier, less enlightened age. And when that great grass-roots Bach movement began in the early nineteenth century, his partisans were well-intentioned romantics who saw in those massive, glaciated choruses from the *St. Matthew Passion* or the *B Minor Mass* insoluble, if not indeed unperformable, enigmas, worthy of devotion primarily because of the faith they so triumphantly exuded. Like archaeologists, excavating the substratum of a forgotten culture, they were impressed with what they found, but pleased primarily by their own initiative in finding it. To the nineteenth-century ear those modulatorily ambivalent choruses can scarcely have fulfilled any classical-romantic concept of tonal strategy.

And even today we who feel we understand the implications of Bach's work and the diversity of his creative impulse, recognize in the fugue the prime forum for all of his musical activity. There is a constant proximity of fugue in Bach's technique. Every texture that he exploited seems ultimately destined for a fugue. The most unpretentious dance tune or the most solemn choral theme seems to beg an

answer, appears eager for that flight of counterpoint which finds in fugal technique its most complete realization. Every sonority that he sampled, every vocal-instrumental combination seems carved out in such a way as to admit a multitude of answers and to lack completeness unless those answers are forthcoming. One feels that just beneath the surface, even in those most *gemütlich* moments when we find him vending coffee in an cantata or jotting airs for *Anna Magdalena,* lies a potential fugal situation. And we can sense his almost visible (or audible) discomfort when he must repress the fugal habit and endeavour, from time to time, to join that simplistic search for thematic control and modulatory conformity with which his generation was primarily concerned.

The fugue,however, did not go into eclipse with Bach's death. It continued to be a challenge for most of the younger generation who were growing up, though they didn't know it yet, in his shadow. But it was being phased out—employed, when at all, as a blockbusting finish to large-scale choral works, or as pedagogic therapy for budding melodists whose alberti basses required enlivening. It was no longer the focal point of musical thinking and an overdose of fugue could cost a young composer of the day dearly in terms of public favour. In an age of reason the fugue seemed essentially unreasonable.

The technique of fugue may have come more easily to Bach than to others but it is none the less a discipline which no one picks up overnight. And we have, as witness to that fact, Bach's early efforts at fugue, among them those ungainly toccata fugues written around his twentieth year. Interminably repetitious, rudimentarily sequential, desperately in need of an editor's red pencil, they frequently succumb to that harmonic turgidity against which the young Bach had to struggle. The mere presence of subject and answer seemed sufficient to satisfy his then unselfcritical demands. The first of the two fugues contained within the *Toccata in D Minor* for harpsichord reiterates its basic thematic proposition on no less than *fifteen* occasions in the home key alone.

In such works, the inventive aspects of fugue were necessarily subservient to an examination of the modulatory function of tonality and despite the prevailing contrapuntal inclination of that generation, it was a rare fugue indeed that established a form relevant to its material demands.

This, in fact, is the fugue's historic problem—that it is not a form as such, in the sense that the sonata, or at any rate, the first movement of the classical sonata is a form, but rather an invitation to invent a form relevant to the idiosyncratic demands of the composition. Success in fugue-writing depends upon the degree to which a composer can relinquish formulae in the interests of creating form and for that reason fugue can be the most routine or the most challenging of tonal enterprises.

A full half-century separates those awkward teenage attempts at fugue from the most determinedly anachronistic of the later ones—*The Art of the Fugue*. Bach died before the completion of this latter work but not before having indulged a degree of fugal gigantism which, by the clock at least, stood unchallenged until the neo-baroque exhibitionism of Ferruccio Busoni. Despite its monumental proportions, an aura of withdrawal pervades the entire work. Bach was, in fact, withdrawing from the pragmatic concerns of music-making into an idealized world of uncompromised invention. One facet of this withdrawal is the return to an almost modal concept of modulation; there are but few occasions in this work which Bach invests with that infallible tonal homing instinct that informed his less vigorously didactic compositions. The harmonic style employed in *The Art of the Fugue*, though rampantly chromatic, is actually less contemporary than that of his early fugal essays and often, in its nomadic meandering about the tonal map, it proclaims a spiritual descent from the ambivalent chromaticism of Cipriano di Rore or Don Carlo Gesualdo.

Most of the basic key relationships are exploited for structural relief and continuity—there is even the occasional full close on the dominant as Bach terminates a major segment within one of the multi-theme fugues—but only rarely is this fluid and modulatorily shifty opus endowed with that purposeful harmonic determinism for which Bach's middle-period fugue-writing was notable.

Between the immature efforts of his Weimar days and the intense, self-entrenched concentration of *The Art of the Fugue* Bach wrote literally hundreds of fugues whether designated as such or not, of all instrumental combinations, and which reveal in its most fluent form his well-nigh impeccable contrapuntal technique. For all of these, and for all subsequent efforts in the form, the yardstick is the two volumes of his *Forty-Eight Preludes and Fugues — The Well-Tempered Clavier.* These astonishingly variegated works attain that rapport between linear continuity and harmonic security which totally eluded the composer in his earlier years and which, because of its anachronistic bias, plays but a minor role in *The Art of the Fugue.* The tonal flair which Bach exhibits in these works seems inexorably wedded to his material and possessed of a modulatory scope that enables him to underline the motivic quirks of his themes and counter-themes. In realizing this conceptual homogeneity Bach is not only stylistically uninhibited but indeed manages to determine his harmonic vocabulary on an almost piece-by-piece basis.

The very first fugue of *Volume 1,* for example, tolerates only the most modest of modulations and in its stretto-ridden way resourcefully characterizes the fugue subject itself—a bland, diatonic model of academic primness.

Other fugues, like that in E Major from *Volume 2,* exhibit much the same sort of modulatory disinclination and here so tenacious is Bach's loyalty to his six-note theme, and so diffident the modulatory program through which he reveals it to us, one has the impression that the intense and fervently anti-chromatic ghost of Heinrich Schütz rides again.

There are other fugues with longer, more elaborate themes in which the unravelling of the motivic mystery is inseparable from a modulatory master-plan, and the B Flat Minor fugue from *Volume 2* is a good example. Here an energetically spiralling subject of four bars' duration

is put through the customary expository paces and as the three remaining voices enter in turn, Bach minimizes his accompanimental dilemma by retaining as a counter-theme a sequence of alternately ascending and descending semi-tones.

Later on, the unassuming compliance of this subsidiary strand pays handsome dividends, for what Bach has in mind is a very different order of fugue than that represented by the C Major or E Major fugues discussed above. He sets forth his material in many different harmonic guises and spotlights some structural phenomena latent within it at each of the major modulatory turning-points. Thus, when he dissolves into the mediant and establishes his theme for the first time in a major key (D flat) a canonic duet ensues between the theme itself, now ensconced in the soprano part and, one beat delayed and two octaves plus one note lowered, an imitation in the bass. For this episode the chromatic counter-theme temporarily vacates the scene and in its stead, subsidiary voices append their own quasi-canonic comments.

No sonata or concerto of a later generation ever prepared its secondary thematic area through a more judiciously rationed series of events. But, for Bach, this is not, in any Rococo sense, a secondary area—merely one more way-station on his continuing quest for the relationship between motive and modulation.

His return to the home tonality is signalled by the first of several inverted presentations of the theme

and eventually elaborated to include original and inverted statements simultaneously.

These in turn sponsor a suave, chromatic, inner-voice dialogue with which Bach embarks upon an almost promiscuous modulatory sequence. But, in due course, tonal rectitude prevails and in the closing moments the composer emphatically renounces all foreign entanglements, remains solidly encamped within the original B Flat Minor tonality and lest there be any doubt that the harmonic adventures of this piece were inseparable from his superbly paced revelations of its primary motive, takes his exit cue with both an original and inverted statement of the themes set forth in an unabashedly virtuosic exhibition of double thirds.

In many cases within the *48*, there is, as between the fugues and their anticipatory preludes, a true communion of interest and of spirit. Sometimes the preludes are just prosaically prefatory—the C Major and C Minor from *Volume 1* perhaps falling within that etudish category. But one could not ask a more complete identification with the melancholic rumination of the five-voice C Sharp Minor Fugue (*Volume 1*) than is provided by its languorous and wistful prelude. Upon occasion, the preludes are themselves fugally oriented—that in E Flat Major from *Volume 1* for instance, offering for all its unacademic neglect of expository proprieties entanglements of fugal texture which quite overshadow the rather glib and conventional proper fugue which it precedes. Bach also, upon occasion, uses the preludes as probes with which to examine those neatly-formulated niceties of binary balance and thematic altercation which were becoming the primary preoccupation of most of his colleagues. (The *F Minor Prelude*

from *Volume 2* calls to mind one of Signor Scarlatti's less indulgently tactile creations.)

Like *The Art of the Fugue*, *The Well-Tempered Clavier*, or excerpts therefrom, has been performed on the harpsichord and piano, by wind and string ensembles, by jazz combos, and by at least one scat-scanning vocal group as well as upon the instrument whose name it bears. And this magnificent indifference to specific sonority is not least among those attractions which emphasize the universality of Bach.

There is, none the less, a real tactile awareness about most of the *48* preludes and fugues, and in the absence of any accurate poll, one can safely say that the great majority of its performances are given on the modern piano. One cannot, therefore, entirely sidestep considerations pertaining to the manner in which that instrument should be employed on its behalf.

Throughout the twentieth century there has been a continuing debate about the extent to which the piano should accommodate the interests of this score. There are those who contend that "If Bach had had it, he would have used it"; the other side of this argument is buttressed by the notion that since Bach did not make allowances for future technology he wrote, by and large, within the limits of those sounds with which he was familiar.

Bach's compositional method, of course, was distinguished by his disinclination to compose at any specific keyboard instrument. And it is, indeed, extremely doubtful that his sense of contemporaneity would have appreciably altered had his catalogue of household instruments been supplemented by the very latest of Mr. Steinway's "accelerated action" claviers. It is, at the same time, very much to the credit of the modern keyboard instrument that the potential of its sonority—that smug, silken, legato-spinning resource—can be curtailed as well as exploited, used as well as abused. And there is really nothing, apart from archival consistency, to prevent the contemporary piano from faithfully representing the architectural implications of the baroque style in general, and Bach's in particular.

Such an approach, of course, necessitates a discriminating attitude toward those questions of articulation and registration which are inextricably bound up with Bach's composing method. It demands, at the very least, the realization that an over-indulgence of pedal will almost inevitably bring the good ship "Contrapuntal Ambition" to grief upon the rhetorical rocks of romantic legato. It also necessitates, I think, some attempt to simulate the registrational conventions of the harpsichord, if only because the technique which informs all of Bach's attitudes toward theme and phrase design is based upon an appreciation of dynamic dialogue. If one could express it in cinematic terms, Bach was a director who thought in terms of cuts rather than dissolves.

There are, to be sure, occasions when the linear continuity of his works is of such tenacity that clearly articulated cadence-points are simply not to be found, and which consequently allow no convincing opportunity for that alternation of tactile effect which is the piano's answer to the harpsichord's lute-stop or coupler-shift manoeuvers. Such situations exist very frequently in *The Art of the Fugue*, scarcely ever in the toccata fugues, and in the *48*, to degrees dependent upon the harmonic premises employed from one work to the next. (In a fugue like that in C Major from *Volume 1* the continual stretti overlap makes such pivot-points rather more difficult to ascertain than is the case, for instance, with *Volume 2*'s B Flat Minor Fugue.)

Issues of this kind pose undeniable problems of adaptation when one performs the masterworks of the baroque on a contemporary instrument. They are foremost on any list of practical considerations which, however idiosyncratically, a conscientious executant must seek to resolve. Ideally, however, such problems should serve as a catalyst for that exuberant and expansive effort of re-creation which is the ultimate joy that all analytical considerations and argumentative conclusions must serve.

Seeking solitude on a Toronto park bench, winter 1976. (CBS Don Hunstein)

THE QUEST FOR SOLITUDE
William Littler

It was in early April that I met Glenn Gould in Hamburg. This April. Six months after his death. He was sitting at the water's edge, on a lonely bench, bundled up in his customary coat, scarf and gloves. He did not speak, of course, nor, out of consideration for the traditions of sane behavior, did I address him. We were simply two Canadians abroad on a rainy day in a city we loved. I was on my way to the Staatsoper and he, less mobile, was sitting in the window of a record store, ornamenting the jacket of an album of Bach toccatas.

Seeing him there reminded me of the time several years ago when a kidney ailment forced the then peregrinating pianist to spend an entire month in Hamburg as a guest of the Vier Jahreszeiten Hotel. The convalescence, it transpired, was not only luxurious in its appointments but, as the patient later confessed to Jonathan Cott in a *Rolling Stone* interview, "...the best month of my life—in many ways the most important—precisely because it was the most solitary...."

Now to most travelling keyboard virtuosi this confession would constitute grounds for confinement not in a hotel but in a more abundantly padded institution. A whole month, in a city of strangers? Yet this is how Glenn Gould remembered it: "There is a sense of exaltation—I'm careful about using that word, but it's the only word that really applies to that particular kind of aloneness. It's an experience that most people don't permit themselves to know.... And sooner or later I'm going to spend a winter in the dark; I'm convinced of that, too."

GLENN GOULD VARIATIONS

The speaker didn't get to spend his winter in the dark but he did live much of his life in it. Not for him that dawn's cheery greeting. He came to hate the daylight, to sleep through what he could of it and to shut out the rest with the blinds of his Toronto apartment.

Toronto is the city Glenn Gould lived in primarily as a matter of convenience. The convenience happened to be greatest at night, when anonymity was easy to find and the fruits of solitude could more readily be picked. But the country offered both in fuller measure and he repaired to it, to his family cottage on Lake Simcoe, or even to a northern Ontario motel, whenever circumstances permitted.

His fellow Ontarians, indeed his fellow Canadians, did not always understand Glenn Gould's quest for solitude. To many of them he was the hermit of St. Clair Avenue, the public figure who refused to behave publicly, the eccentric whose social contacts required the mediation of a Bell telephone line.

He even catered to this reclusive image in his occasional interviews, going so far as to tell Elyse Mach (in her book, *Great Pianists Speak for Themselves*, New York: Dodd Mead, 1980) that "the recording studio and the kind of womblike security that it gives is very much integrated with my life style. I guess it's all part of my fantasy to develop to the fullest extent a kind of Howard Hughesian secrecy...."

Secrecy? Well, he did at one point take the nameplate off the letterbox of his Park Lane penthouse. And one of his favorite pastimes involved interrupting long nocturnal drives with the pleasures of surreptitious eavesdropping on conversations in roadside diners. The carefully edited overlapping conversations in his radio documentaries owe their origin to real-life experience.

But the object clearly had less to do with the achievement of secrecy for its own sake, in the Howard Hughes sense, than with the quest for a kind of isolation that permitted intellectual concentration and control. Whether in a hotel room in Hamburg, a cottage on Lake Simcoe, a penthouse in Toronto or its extension, a studio with 24-hour room service in the suburbs, Glenn Gould sought out private environments whose very banality fostered the life of the mind he so actively lived.

This is why he did not need Paris, London, or New York. In later years he even resisted visiting Manhattan to make recordings, preferring to produce his own for CBS from tapes recorded during off-hours in a mid-town Toronto hall. What he did need was an environment where familiarity freed him from anxiety and made mental work possible. He fervently believed that, as he wrote in reviewing Geoffrey Payzant's *Glenn Gould, Music and Mind* (Toronto: Van Nostrand Reinhold, 1978) for the *Globe and Mail*, "solitude nourishes creativity and...colleagual fraternity tends to dissipate it."

And creativity was what Glenn Gould was about. Not to put too fine a point on it, he liked playing God. It delighted him to make something out of nothing, the way he did in his radio documentaries by assembling, through hundreds of hours of meticulous tape editing, conversations between people who had never met. He called the process "creative cheating" and he used it just as openly in assembling his CBS albums.

To appreciate his devotion to this process is to understand in part why he had to leave the concert stage in favor of the studio. You can't stop the Appassionata Sonata in mid-movement, take a second run at the development section, and expect your Carnegie Hall listeners to thank you for the interruption. This non-take-twoness, as he called it, inclines the concert artist toward a recreative rather than a creative approach to musical performance.

It is fascinating to speculate, at this point, on the forces that instinctively made Gould a creator rather than a re-creator. Geoffrey Payzant may be on the right track when he quotes Anthony Storr's *The Dynamics of Creation* (London: Secker & Warburg, 1972) to the effect that: "Since most creative activity is solitary, choosing such an occupation means that the schizoid person can avoid the problems of direct relationships with others. If he writes, paints or composes, he is, of course, communicating. But it is a communication entirely on his own terms....He can choose (or so he often believes) how much of himself to reveal and how much to keep secret."

We do not have to accept the conclusion that Gould's creative impulses originated in schizophrenia to find in this analysis both an interesting possible explanation for his behavior patterns and a vote of confidence for his assertion of a correlation between solitude and creativity. Indeed, the latter correlation operates as a subliminal and not so subliminal theme throughout all six of Gould's major radio documentaries, beginning with the significantly titled Solitude Trilogy (*The Idea of North*, *The Latecomers* and *The Quiet in the Land*) and including as well his documentary portraits of Leopold Stokowski, Pablo Casals and Arnold Schoenberg.

This, I submit, is no accident. Being a loner, being self-absorbed, being a citizen of a country whose very history and geography have adopted isolation as a liturgical theme, he naturally gravitated toward subjects whose exploration would help him understand his own condition. For there is a sense in which all these documentaries are aspects of a portrait of Glenn Gould.

Among them, *The Idea of North* appeared first, as a centennial project of CBC radio's *Ideas* series in December of 1967. It is also the one he appears to have been most driven to complete. "The north has fascinated me since childhood," he explained in the liner notes to the subsequently released record album. "The idea of the country intrigued me, but my notion of what it looked like was pretty much restricted to the romanticized, art-nouveau-tinged Group of Seven paintings which, in my day, adorned virtually every second school-room and which probably served as a pictorial introduction to the north for a great many people of my generation."

Though the grown-up child subsequently took the 1,015-mile ride of two nights and one day north by train from Winnipeg to Fort Churchill, his fear of flying denied him a comprehensive first-hand view of Canada's great frontier. No matter. It was not what the north looked like that mattered to the radio documentarian, it was its power as a metaphor: "I found myself writing musical critiques, for instance, in which the north—the idea of the north—began to serve as a foil for other ideas and values that seemed to me depressingly urban-oriented and spiritually limited thereby."

Listening to his subsequent sound documentary, with its painstakingly fabricated, spliced-together conversations aboard a clickety-clacking train, one hears character after character feed this thesis. Here is a place where nonconformists can live and flourish, says one of them. The north is not so much finding as seeking, argues another. It is a place where you try to become truthful with yourself.

And so, what emerges is not as much a geography lesson as a sequence of philosophic observations—musical in their technical construction, for as a musician Gould liked to exercise his craft—but concerned with deeper questions of self-realization and even ultimate salvation.

"*The Idea of North* is itself an excuse," he rather more modestly put it, "an opportunity to examine that condition of solitude which is neither exclusive to the north nor the prerogative of those who go north but which does, perhaps, appear, with all its ramifications, a bit more clearly to those who have made, if only in their imagination, the journey north."

A different kind of solitude attracted Gould's attention in *The Latecomers*, his 1969 CBC radio portrait of life in Newfoundland, Canada's newest province. He wrote of this enterprise: "it was obviously to be about the province-as-island, about the sea which keeps the mainland and the mainlanders at ferry crossing's length, about the problems of maintaining a minimally technologized style of life in a maximally technologized age."

But it was just as obviously about people who talked into Gould's microphones about wanting to be themselves, striving to be self-sufficient in isolation, fearing the disappearance of time in which to meditate. And although he was holding those microphones, the interviewer might as easily have been the one facing them.

The people in *The Quiet in the Land*, the Mennonites of Red River, Manitoba, occupy yet another solitude as a religious community long separate from the mainstream of Canadian life. In them, Gould found spokesmen for a deliberately simplified kind of existence that, as one speaker put it, enables you to do a few things in life and do them really well.

That same speaker talked of reading in Sören Kierkegaard that "purity of heart is to will one thing." It dovetails nicely with the Anabaptist tradition of trying to work out your own destiny in the midst of other people and of being in the world though not of the world.

A lapsed churchgoer, Gould was nevertheless raised as a Presbyterian and many of these ideas obviously carried resonances from his youth. It took him several years to polish and refine *The Quiet in the Land* before submitting it for CBC radio broadcast in 1977 and it would hardly have been like him to spend that much time in uncongenial company.

I referred earlier to the notion of isolation as a liturgical Canadian theme, which in a sense makes Gould's preoccupation with it a validation of his citizenship. He was, in fact, quite at home in the country that Canadian hoboes familiarly refer to as Big Lonely, although as he explained to Ulla Colgrass of *Music* magazine, he found the exclusionist tendencies of current Canadian nationalism rather silly: "I really haven't much sympathy with barriers, maybe because I haven't found any objections to my own participation in the musical life of other countries."

Gould said of Toronto in John McGreevy's television series *Cities*, that it belongs on a very short list of cities "which, for want of a better definition, do not impose their 'cityness' upon you." By extension, Canada itself offered him a non-pressuring environment in which to live and work. "I think there are tremendous virtues within the country," he observed in the *Music* magazine interview, "and I personally am more at home with the somewhat reserved, quieter Canadian spirit than with the more energetic American spirit and being Canadian I therefore understand the wish to preserve it...."

But like the Mennonites, he remained more in than of the world of measurable geography. His real world housed the interior landscape of the mind. And by dwelling there in solitude he became, arguably, a more intense communicator with the outside world than his abandoned life of concert touring would ever have permitted.

As Gould's collaborators in media projects testify, he cared a great deal about his viewers and listeners. He took the act of communicating very seriously, spending countless hours on clarifying his arguments and polishing their delivery. Even the supposed ad libs in his recorded interviews had to be scripted in later years.

At its deepest level we may never know whether all this stemmed from a will to communicate or a will to control. Certainly the will to control appeared obsessive in his editing procedures. He took positive pride in the fact that he had to submit the first draft of a two minute, forty-three second speech in his radio documentary on Richard Strauss to no fewer than one hundred and thirty-one edits—about one per second.

On a more personal level, Gould applied the same kind of control to his contacts with other people. In this the telephone became his prime agent. As his private as opposed to what one might call his public years went on, he progressively decreased personal and increased telephonic contact with even long-time friends and acquaintances. Anthony Storr might have had some interesting things to say about this.

All the same, Gould did communicate and communicate powerfully through his recordings, through the electronic media and through his occasional forays into print. And for all his reservations about the twentieth century, this kind of communication in isolation would scarcely have been possible in an earlier age. As he admitted to Elyse Mach some years ago, twentieth-century technology enabled him "to exist as far as possible from the outside world and have contact with it electronically."

At least as far as the listening experience is concerned, Gould offered the rest of us the same option, having argued in *High Fidelity* that modern recording technology has created "a new kind of listener—a listener more participant in the musical experience," who enters into communion with the tone art in the privacy of his living room. The efficacy of this option has not gone unchallenged. In his chapter on Gould in *The Virtuoso* (London: Thames and Hudson, 1982), Harvey Sachs accuses his subject of going "off the deep end," of exalting "advanced forms of dial twiddling to the status of creativity."

But surely it is not so much the dial twiddling aspect as the direct, one-on-one encounter between music and listener that is most significant in this relationship. Traditional musicians would argue that the presence of other people, i.e. an audience, by no means undermines the relationship, but for Gould music was something to be approached in a contemplative state. A religious attitude? In a way of speaking, yes, almost a monastic attitude. But then, for him, music was not a social, it was an individual experience. And if the dichotomy appears to be a false one to some of his critics, it does seem to have gone a long way toward justifying Gould's ways to Gould.

And to the extent that a man must work his own way to salvation, Glenn Gould took great strength from his subscription to the solitary attitude. It gave direction to a life that might otherwise have been caught up in the outer-directed swirl of success. It enabled him to take the infinite pains that are traditionally ascribed to genius. It let him be himself.

Posing for publicity still to promote the film version of his documentary "The Idea of North."
(CBC Harold Whyte)

REMINISCENCES
John Lee Roberts

When I moved into an apartment in Toronto's Rosedale in 1957, Glenn and a very small group of friends used to get together regularly to read plays by Shakespeare and other playwrights. In the summer a few of us also played badminton in Rosedale Park (Glenn usually sat on a bench and read scores while this was going on). It was the year he made his European debut with the Moscow Philharmonic Orchestra, performed in Leningrad, Vienna and Berlin, and undertook many other engagements as well. Even though he was either away or consumed by his work, Glenn always squeezed in reading sessions if there was a gap in his schedule and enough members of the group could be assembled. With us he could relax and escape from a life of concert-giving which he found distasteful and was beginning to regard as a complete circus. When on tour, he often phoned me in a depressed frame of mind about problems he was having with pianos, performances which he was dissatisfied with for one reason or another, his dread of flying, or the state of his health. (Glenn always seemed to have more will than strength.)

For Christmas that year he gave me very elegantly engraved writing-paper inscribed, *Lower Rosedale Shakespeare Reading and Badminton Society, President John Roberts.* We all laughed about it, but the group lived on, with one or two people leaving and one or two joining. Occasionally visitors were allowed.

Patiently waiting for his cue in a recording studio, 1955. (CBS)

I first got to know Glenn in 1955 in Winnipeg. He invited me to have breakfast with him in his hotel room the morning after he had performed the Piano Concerto, No. 1 in C Major by Beethoven with the Winnipeg Symphony Orchestra, using his own highly individual cadenzas. He had received tumultuous acclaim and afterwards backstage he was surrounded by so many admirers there was hardly room to breathe. I had arrived in Winnipeg a few months earlier from Australia via England and was a neophyte radio producer with the CBC. Glenn asked me about Australian animals, so I gave him a demonstration of a hopping kangaroo and topped it with the call of a much-loved Australian bird, the kookaburra. After he stopped laughing, it became clear that Glenn had a great affinity with animals: "They don't have words to waste and are more trustworthy than some humans I know."

Soon I became the producer of the CBC Winnipeg Orchestra, of which Eric Wild was the conductor. Apart from jointly choosing the programs with him, I was, of course, responsible for the microphone pick-ups and writing the scripts. Glenn often phoned or wrote to me concerning these broadcasts as well as other radio programs and some telecasts on which I was working. His comments were always very encouraging and also perspicacious. He had an enormous interest in and knowledge of Canadian musical life and gave me all kinds of useful advice and helpful information.

In the Lower Rosedale Shakespeare Reading and Badminton Society, Glenn's favourite role was Richard II. However, we progressed from play reading to extemporizations. In this way he got us to assimilate electronic music sounds which he conducted and often structured, although in essence the improvisations were aleatoric creations. We also did character extemporizations, and it was in the course of these that he invented various personalities, some of whom he went on to develop and use in the lighter moments of his career. Sir Nigel Twitt-Thornwaite (an Edwardian startled to be living in modern times), Duncan Haig-Guinness (an agreeable honest-to-God Scot), Karlheinz Klopweisser (a turgid musicologist), and Theodore Slutz (a Bronx type who appeared stupid and spoke slothfully, but often hit the nail on the head), all came to life in the course of various sessions and caused general hilarity. Glenn eventually moved to a penthouse—he used my name instead of his when scouting around for an apartment, so I was relieved when he finally signed the lease—and we sometimes taped our sessions there in order to get more out of them. He was a clever mimic and found it amusing to phone me pretending to be someone else. Sometimes he would call saying it was Pierre Boulez, Leonard Bernstein, the prime minister of Canada or the president of the CBC, and he even made one attempt at pretending to be my landlady.

Glenn had a razor-sharp mind and could quickly see through people and situations. He was an extremely moral person, was often outraged by the injustices of society and not infrequently helped various humanitarian causes or people in difficulties, although he did so as anonymously as possible. Glenn set extremely high standards for himself and his work. He was irritated or exasperated and frequently saddened when those around him did not strive for something similar.

Every now and again Glenn would invite me to go for a car ride. He loved driving and found it relaxing. On one occasion we drove to the Caledon Hills. It was 1962 and a moment when a long sombre winter was yielding to the insistence of spring. Glenn's singing of the Quintet in F Minor by Brahms trailed off into silence and we drifted into talking about the cyclical nature of life. His comment was that the human life-cycle is absurdly short, given the potential of individuals. It was obvious that such a thought played on his mind. We stopped the car by the Credit River and, well muffled in winter coats, we walked toward the rushing water bearing away debris from the last fall. Back in the car he said that when all is said and done, it is always the "great statements" which are immortal and live on as food for future generations. It had started to drizzle and the windshield wipers were going apace. Looking straight ahead he said something which he had said on other occasions—he intended to stop performing in public, adding that in any case live concerts would be overtaken by the presentation of music in the electronic media. The audiences of the future would be able to experience music in the privacy of their own homes, operating their own equipment. For Glenn the beauty of this development was that he could address each person individually and in this way the collective aspect of mass audiences, which he found so repugnant, would be done away with. Both recordings and equipment on which to play them would constantly improve. A listener would not have to be passive. If someone wanted to combine the first movement of a Beethoven Sonata recorded by Glenn with recordings of other pianists playing the other movements, then why not? He felt his life had become too cluttered and intended to remove what he considered to be debris. Public concerts had to be swept aside. For Glenn live performances were ephemeral: here today and gone tomorrow. However, a recording was a document or ideally a statement of lasting value and importance.

As far as money was concerned, he said he would always make enough to satisfy his needs which were after all "very simple." He dreamed of removing himself out of sight from the musical world and of living in the country. Manitoulin Island in Lake Huron was a potential isle of retreat which he thought about for years. Wawa on Lake Superior was another place of escape where he felt at one with nature. On one occasion there, through his motel window, he saw an alienated but noble creature walking towards him out of the darkness—a wolf—which came close enough to look him in the eye. The memory of this event seemed to be imprinted on Glenn's mind forever afterwards. Perhaps for a moment it was a mirror image.

On another occasion, also a car trip, Glenn was introducing me to a new concept he had of the Piano Concerto No. 1 in D Minor by Brahms. He was to perform it with the New York Philharmonic in the near future (April 1962) and had decided to broaden the overall outline dramatically by placing the first and last movements at extraordinarily slow tempi. Through singing, conducting with any hand which could be freed from the steering wheel, plus incisive clicking noises when all else failed, he made it clear that the work was to take on the proportions of a vastly extended and towering musical monument. All this was very different to the performance which I heard a few years earlier in the privacy of the Gould family's cottage on Lake Simcoe. On that occasion—he had just finished learning the work away from the piano, relying on his photographic memory—the outer movements were fast, extremely intense and dramatic.

When explaining his new approach to the concerto Glenn employed three different tempi—all slow—using the introduction to the first movement as a point of departure and repeating it more slowly in each case. With great conviction he made it clear that he preferred the slowest. In response to my concern about how conductor and soloist could hold the work together without it losing tension and cohesiveness as well as sounding idiosyncratic, Glenn laughed and with a sweep of the hand said, "Ah, that is the challenge."

Later in the year, in a Chinese restaurant in Orillia where they always turned off the pop music when Glenn walked in and put on the Gould recording of Bach's Goldberg Variations, he confirmed that his performing career was definitely in the process of winding down. He said his last public concert would be in 1964. All the pundits, including Columbia Records in New York, were telling him that his recording career would be finished if he abandoned public concerts. "Well we'll see," said Glenn. "It will be a terrific challenge."

Meeting an enormous challenge, preferably a superhuman one, was a pronounced characteristic of all the dimensions of Glenn's career. He seemed to have a fundamental need to test whatever abilities he was engaging to the ultimate. It is ironic that someone who felt that his well-being was being threatened by the circus of concert giving—by the notion of the artist as a travelling road show—and even felt that the possibility of a long life was endangered through air travel, should have continually pushed himself, in exploring the by-ways of his career, to the point of endangering his health. By this I mean that after he gave up playing in public in 1964 he began working longer and longer hours and sustaining a degree of intensity and commitment to the various avenues of his career in the mass media which few of his associates could keep up with. His radio documentaries were put together with consummate art and contained thousands of tape splices. In fact they took hundreds of hours to put together. Glenn had a vision of what he wanted to achieve in terms of content and continuity of structure (the latter overlaid with musical forms) and with a sustained concentration hardly equalled by anyone either before or since, he kept editing sessions going beyond the small hours of the morning—sometimes they finished at 4 A.M. Through simultaneous juxtapositioning of characters' voices, and through structural approaches such as using sounds of the sea as a *cantus firmus* in "The Latecomers," he was in fact pushing back the frontiers of the radio medium itself. For him this manner of working within radio was a new way of composing, which he explained carefully in an article for the *Canada Music Book* called "Radio As Music."

When I made a presentation on the emergence of the radio documentary as a major art form at a conference of the International Music Centre (IMZ) in Salzburg in 1972, relying heavily on Glenn's documentaries, the older generation of radio directors were totally scandalized. In contrast, younger producers were fascinated and no doubt very influenced by Glenn's opening up of the medium. Marshall McLuhan was a speaker in another part of the conference and the fact that he was at an event which combined music and media interested Glenn very much. While having enormous respect for McLuhan, Glenn confessed that his own discussions with him were not so much dialogues as McLuhan monologues. Like McLuhan, Glenn formed many perceptions about the future by watching a great deal of television, and to help him he had two videorecording machines in his studio at the Inn on the Park in Toronto. "Marshall does not communicate by answering questions, but performs more like a medium. I'm perhaps somehow closer to the 'message,'" he said with a laugh.

There were also videotape editing sessions at the CBC in the small hours of the morning and putting together television programs—each one making a major statement in its own right—a challenge which occupied him night and day at different points throughout his life. In devising an engaging program mix, Glenn often agonized over what to include and what to exclude. For the television program "The Flight from Order" in the CBC *Music of Our Time* series, he solved a missing link problem by making his own remarkable transcription of "La Valse" by Ravel. He lavished enormous amounts of time on television scripts, scripts for radio programs in which he introduced his own performances, as well as scripts for other radio programs. His literary articles occupied him no less. In fact it was not unusual for his scripts to metamorphose through fifteen or more drafts which he read to a small select group of "sounding post" people, often late at night.

The superhuman effort which it took to meet the challenges of "found" talents such as writing and documentary making was in contrast to his one entirely natural gift for playing the piano. Reading notes had never been difficult for him, and he did not know how he produced his prodigious technique. It was just *there*, ready to respond to the commands of his mind in performances which were not just interpretations, but re-creations.

At the beginning of his career he came to the conclusion that because of his rather long arms he would have to sit low at the keyboard to get the results he wanted, and it was his father who came up with the chair that went on to become his trademark. Bert Gould also made wooden blocks which, when used under the legs of the piano, put Glenn in an even lower position. Glenn's mother taught him piano at a very early age and he was not unmindful of the debt he owed her. Although later he studied with Alberto Guerrero, Glenn considered himself largely self-taught because of his natural gifts and very individual way of playing, which he felt went against the grain of most piano instruction. Nevertheless, I believe as Glenn grew older he had a certain nagging tension in the back of his mind because he did not know how he achieved what were perceived to be staggering results as a performer. He loathed "pianistic talk," told me on more than one occasion that he was incapable of teaching anyone and disliked talking to musicians who suggested that anything in a particular work was technically difficult. His comment to me after flawlessly sight-reading the Piano Concerto in A Minor by Grieg was, "I just try not to look at the battlefield." In other words, the challenge of performing lay not in realizing the notes of a score, but in arriving at a re-creation which would satisfy him. He was accused by some of not respecting the wishes of composers or of incorrectly interpreting ornaments in the music of Bach stylistically. Glenn paid no attention to such criticism. He felt that any score had to be probed and that if he had no fresh view of a work there was no point in performing it. In fact, he very often had a number of visions of a work and the challenge was deciding which one of them he would finally accept. It was no wonder then that making recordings appealed to him so much. Through a system of "takes" he was in a position, if need be, to put a variety of possibilities on tape through splicing and choose a composite realization which satisfied him. This is not to say that all his recordings were intricately spliced together in this way. Sometimes there were very few splices at all, and the idle talk of those who suggested that he became incapable of playing a work right through in a spontaneous fashion should be written off as complete nonsense.

It was his staggering ability to breathe new life into music, to recreate it and if necessary defy all tradition in doing so, which contributed to his uniqueness. A particular kind of détaché playing often used in contrapuntal music to achieve linear clarity, an individual kind of lucidity used in Romantic and other music, an extraordinary rhythmic precision, a sense of pulse and drive, unusual choices of tempi (sometimes freakishly fast), an ability to sustain tension in a whole variety of ways (for example, from note to note over long lines and throughout major structures), all contributed to his magic. One could go on and on. When called for, his playing could reflect a rare sense of pathos, a quality of robustness or an extraordinary sense of inner quiet and peace. But no doubt it was his total grasp of structure, almost with an x-ray perception, which contributed to his ability to recreate music rather than interpret it. Aaron Copland once said to me that the thing which made Glenn unique among performers was that when he played Bach, it was as though Bach himself was performing. When Glenn played the five Beethoven piano concerti in London in 1959 with the London Symphony Orchestra conducted by Josef Krips, a who's who of pianists came from near and far to hear him. Among them was the great pianist Gina Bachauer. Later she described his performances as being extraordinary musical revelations. "I learned a great deal from him" she said to me later in Toronto with great modesty, and went on to describe him as "a once-in-a-century phenomenon."

Ecstasy was Glenn's word for the state of mind he reached for when performing. He certainly was not concerned with outward appearances at all, hence the incongruities of his own dress (odd socks, clothes sometimes coming apart at the seams and, at least on one occasion, odd shoes). Furthermore, Glenn was unable to perform without singing and, if he had a free arm, conducting as well. He once told me during his concert-giving days that he had more than occasionally tried to stop singing along with his own performances, but the concentration this took detracted from his playing and made him nervous and tense. Many times Glenn also expressed his frustration with the piano as an instrument. He often felt it was much too limited and was incapable of realizing everything he felt and perceived about the works he was performing. Before Glenn began to talk so much of the ecstasy he experienced in playing the piano, he often used another word— spontaneity. He prided himself in doing a minimum amount of practice and said that too much practice spoiled his spontaneity. During one of our conversations he calculated that in the previous five weeks he had barely done any practice at all. His seemingly eccentric habit of not shaking hands, not carrying anything excessively heavy, and of soaking his hands in warm water was necessary to him for a particular reason. By not using his muscles unpianistically and taking great care of his hands, he was always in a state of preparedness for playing the piano. He had to feel that if someone snapped his fingers at him and said "play this" or "play that," he could do so instantly. "Try me," he said to me on one occasion. I asked him to play specific parts of the Burleske for Piano and Orchestra by Strauss, the Sonata No. 7 by Prokofiev, the Beethoven Sonata Opus 33 No. 3 as well as other works, all of which he could do instantly without warming up.

Glenn was essentially concerned with things of the mind and the spirit. In fact his increasing remoteness over the years enabled him to create a very special internal world of his own. "My life has become cluttered again," he would sometimes say. As the years passed his private world contained fewer and fewer personal contacts and made him even more dependant on his own internal resources. However, all this was an evolutionary process. In the twilight of his concert career he asked his few friends not to go to his concerts. Audiences had to be totally anonymous. In 1961 he became a co-director of the Stratford Music Festival with Leonard Rose and Oscar Shumsky and I often accompanied him on car trips to and from Stratford attending what were for me spell-binding concerts. However, it was in either 1962 or 1963 that he begged me and my wife, Christina (by that time I was engaged), to accompany him but not attend the performances, a request we respected. After 1964 he seldom consciously performed for

Filming in a Toronto studio, late 1950s. (CBC)

At a recording session, mid-1960s. (CBS Don Hunstein)

friends and increasingly gave the impression that he was uncomfortable being watched at the piano. The exception always was fellow performers and the people responsible for cameras and microphones. However, this is not to suggest that he did not play at all when he came to see us. He liked our rather ancient Mason and Risch because it reminded him of his own old Chickering, which had been the workhorse piano of his youth. Whether at our place or his, whenever there was a discussion about music, he often rushed spontaneously to the piano to illustrate a point. On one occasion at our house he started looking at the Preludes and Fugues of Mendelssohn which he found on the music-stand. Although he knew the Preludes and Fugues for organ by the same composer, he had never before encountered those for piano, and took time to play them through. He had a certain quiet admiration for Mendelssohn. At the end of the evening he left, carrying the score with him. He sometimes walked off with books and scores which he never intended to return. But he always said, "I grant you equal rights." After he "borrowed" a rare edition of early music given to me by my father, I "borrowed" books and records. (He got tense if anyone touched his scores.) Later he took a fancy to a dramatic award-winning photo taken in Australia by my father, and called "Gathering Storm." It hung in his penthouse for years. Glenn asked for my parents' address in Sydney, wrote them a letter of thanks, and enclosed it in a package containing all the records he had made up to that time.

Glenn had always been a night-person, but as he grew older he deliberately chose to work through the night and sleep during the day. Although his long telephone conversations, which became something of a legend in themselves, allowed him an electronic or media communication with others, he was obliged to emerge during the day to make his activities coincide with the availability and working hours of colleagues. (Sometimes he would provide details of the small amount of sleep he had had in a previous week.) His schedule was always impossibly demanding, and even after it was discovered that he had high blood pressure, he continued to maintain an extraordinary pace. However, he always thought he could cope because he was on constant medication and took his own blood pressure at regular intervals.

In order to sustain his work schedule, Glenn had always gone to great pains to avoid being sick. The few people close to him knew to stay well away if they had a cold. He also developed certain ideas after reading various articles. For example, he thought second-hand articles should be avoided because one never knew if they had been handled by people with diseases. It was also important to live as close as possible to the summit of a hill because one was less likely to develop cancer. Glenn's spirits sank very rapidly when he was ill. He liked to feel he was in total control of himself every instant of his life. This meant that he did not drink: "even after one glass, one's thinking is not so crystalline." Glenn told me that in every way he was determined to stay in the driver's seat with his own life. Although he sometimes felt the burden of his own genius he was grateful that he had been spared the cog-in-a-machine life of the less fortunate. He was sometimes very possessive of his closest friends, but it was an attitude he took in their interest rather than simply his own. He insisted that I go to a chiropractor and finally took me to his. On one occasion he absolutely ordered my wife and me not to take a certain flight. He had had a dream the night before about a plane crash. We were more than a little unnerved, but felt we had no choice but to take it as scheduled. Glenn then started to beg and entreat us not to fly that day at all. His persistence upset me and made me extremely tense, but we took the flight anyway. However, he was a marvellous friend. Although he had a fear of hospitals, when I was seriously ill, he was the first person to see me and came every day in spite of his horrendous work schedule. In fact, his loyalty and devotion to those he cared for helped them through turns in fortune and in coping with the dark moments in their lives.

Glenn was very fortunate that the CBC was able to provide him with vehicles to test his ideas and help him meet the whole variety of challenges he continued to set himself at regular intervals. In fact, Glenn grew up with the CBC. His broadcast recital debut on what was then the Trans-Canada Network took place in 1950, and he continued to give radio recitals throughout the fifties, sixties and well into the seventies. Most of the music he presented this way developed an after-life through being used in recordings for Columbia, later CBS Records.

When I arrived in Toronto in 1957, I was one of two radio producers who had been promoted to the rank of program organizer as part of an attempt to set up a properly organized CBC music department for the first time. For several years afterwards I was a constant visitor to the Gould home on Southwood Drive in the Beaches area of Toronto. Glenn and his parents were extremely hospitable people and I often went with them to their cottage on Lake Simcoe, where the living room had been enormously extended to make a studio for Glenn. The cottage was a very special place for him. It was associated with happy childhood memories and was a place where he could escape to between concerts, be with his family, walk with his dog Banny and work in total seclusion. At Southwood Drive our "sessions" often lasted until 3 A.M. Not only did Glenn have a prodigious talent for reading orchestral scores at the piano, but he had a large number of them stored in his memory. In most instances they emerged more as self-contained piano transcriptions than anything else. (Bearing this in mind, it should be noted that the few piano transcriptions which he later recorded were simply the tip of an iceberg.) I can remember him performing "Pelléas and Mélisande" by Schoenberg with his eyes mostly closed. Another example was the "Four Last Songs" of Richard Strauss. He also had whole opera scores in the back of his head. Once he started Wagner's "Tristan and Isolde," Glenn would be lost in another world, often oblivious to the presence of anyone else. He returned from England with a score of Sir William Walton's "Troilus and Cressida," which he gave me as a present. After handing it to me, he performed from memory several segments which had stuck in his mind and which he admired.

Because Glenn had constantly listened to CBC Radio throughout his life, we spent many hours talking about programs and programming. These discussions included concepts of series which might be undertaken, an exchange of views on young artists we thought were promising, and a widening of the repertoire which the CBC was presenting. He had always been a champion of Schoenberg, Berg and Webern, and went through a lot of their music with me. Glenn was very interested in contemporary music, but had pronounced likes and dislikes as well as some blind spots. He kept himself well informed about what was going on in the arena of international contemporary music, but he largely distanced himself from it.

In the fifties and early sixties, Glenn was very interested in composing, although these energies were later channelled more and more into the making of radio documentaries and other media projects. His String Quartet was performed at Stratford in 1956 and he was delighted when the Symphonia Quartet made a commercial recording of it. Following this he started several works which he expected would go through long gestation periods. He had plenty of ideas, in fact he once said to me he had too many. Although Glenn agonized over a number of works for weeks on end, he never got around to finishing them. This was probably because he was so self-critical that he could not get them to evolve in a way that satisfied his exacting standards and powers of invention. I also think it concerned him that the musical language he was still using belonged more to the last century than the present.

Glenn was above all an innovator and a futurist. I remember him saying that he really wanted to write music destined not for the concert hall but for the electronic media. He wanted to try his hand at writing and arranging music for films. Through lack of opportunities, it took him until 1972 to go through the learning process with *Slaughterhouse-Five*. In the last year of his life he wrote the music—using Brahms as a point of departure—for the film *The Wars*, for Primedia in Toronto. It also allowed him to make a personal contribution to a project which he felt was a powerful and important anti-war statement. Before his death he said to me that he was anxious to continue working with Primedia on other films, and that in one of his future careers he wanted to conceptualize films, do the writing himself, compose the music and direct them as well.

Glenn sometimes acted as a catalyst. When I first arrived in Canada he was one of two people who led me in the direction of Canadian music, an area which was to become a life-long interest and lead to the commissioning of a large number of Canadian works by the CBC later in my career. He also played a catalytic role in the "Stravinsky and the CBC" saga.

In 1961, while having supper with Glenn, I explained to him that I had been trying without success to make contact with Stravinsky. My purpose was to invite Stravinsky to come to Canada the following year to undertake special radio and television projects in honour of his eightieth birthday. Shortly afterwards, Stravinsky's close colleague and friend Robert Craft was due to arrive in Toronto to conduct a recording of the Piano Concerto by Schoenberg with Glenn as the soloist, for Columbia Records. Glenn had chosen both Craft and the CBC Symphony Orchestra. After the recording sessions finished, Glenn invited both Craft and me to the Benvenuto, an out-of-the-way restaurant where he ate every evening. In the course of a very long discussion—we were the last to leave the restaurant—Craft agreed to try to persuade Stravinsky to fit three major CBC projects, consisting of radio and television programs as well as a radio documentary, into his already overcrowded schedule for the following year. Of course, all the rest is history. In fact, Stravinsky had a love affair with Canada. Apart from CBC broadcasts, Columbia Records became part of the overall projects, with the result that some of Stravinsky's most significant recordings were made in Toronto, even though in those days all the equipment had to be flown in from New York. In addition, the CBC introduced works of Schoenberg to Canadian audiences. These were conducted by Robert Craft and were also recorded by Columbia, in separate sessions.

Stravinsky and Craft made numerous visits to Toronto during the next five years. (Stravinsky gave the final public concert of his career with the Toronto Symphony in 1967.) All this focused world attention on Canada and the CBC. As Glenn had been the catalyst in this whole development, it is ironic that he never performed any of Stravinsky's music. I used to tell him that he had a blind spot about it. Except for some of the early works, Glenn simply was not interested in Stravinsky's music. However, Stravinsky was enormously impressed with Glenn. Some years earlier, after hearing him perform the three last piano sonatas of Beethoven at a public concert in the United States, Stravinsky had written Glenn saying that up until that moment these works had eluded him. Glenn's performances had been a total revelation.

On one of his visits to Toronto, Stravinsky asked me to invite Glenn to lunch. Columbia was going to make a recording of the Capriccio for Piano and Orchestra by Stravinsky and the old man's dearest wish was that Glenn should be the soloist. The lunch took place in the Park Plaza Hotel where Stravinsky and Craft always stayed. Stravinsky hinted, but Glenn avoided any proposal coming into focus and confessed afterwards the event had been an ordeal. He had no interest in the Capriccio. I felt it was a work he simply did not know and begged him to look at a score I had of it, but to no avail. Once Glenn had made up his mind about something there was no changing it.

In 1961 Glenn became very interested in a documentary I was devising on music by royal composers. However, it was not so much the music as the process which fascinated him—the creation of a broadcast made up of segments of interviews, a text based on a great deal of research, all interspersed with very carefully chosen and interrelated music. In no time he said that he wanted to try his hand at making documentaries and asked if the CBC would accept one from him on Schoenberg. This led to "Arnold Schoenberg: The Man Who Changed Music," which was broadcast in August of 1962 and later by the BBC under the title "Schoenberg in America." This in turn led to a succession of other remarkable documentaries, including another on Schoenberg called "Schoenberg The First Hundred Years: A Documentary Fantasy." The solitude trilogy, "The Idea of North," "The Latecomers" and "The Quiet in the Land" were very important milestones in Glenn's life, because they allowed him to make his own statement about the human condition. Although he considered them a whole new kind of music because their structures were drawn from musical forms, they were developed outside the Music Department and his subjects were people in everyday life. While Glenn was associated with some of the most stimulating intellectuals of his day, he was in fact most at home with everyday people and was endlessly fascinated by remarkably interesting but unsung characters he encountered at different times.

In 1965 I became supervisor of music for the English Service of the

CBC. By that time Glenn had established himself internationally as one of the greatest pianists of the century, an innovator of extraordinary importance in the presentation of music in the electronic media and a thinker who was attracting world attention.

In spite of all the dire predictions, Glenn's recording career with Columbia Records was flourishing. I asked him what he wanted to do for the CBC. Finally it was decided that he would do four major recitals a year, introduced by himself, and two documentaries. However, because of the increasing amount of thought and time that he put into all projects, I found it difficult to keep him on schedule with this commitment. I tried to help by providing him—rather illegally—with a corner of the Music Department at CBC Toronto. By arranging some dividers it was turned into a office. I also hoped that Glenn, who had at least one idea a minute—I called him a twittering machine— would prove a stimulating person to have around CBC staff producers.

Glenn's CBC Radio career was branching in several different directions simultaneously. Apart from his radio recitals, which were all highly individual, Glenn became involved with a variety of other programs. The *Ideas* Unit of CBC, which thrives on innovation, was a marvellous vehicle not only for documentaries but for other programs such as the revealing one he did on the extraordinary British pop singer Petula Clark. He acted as commentator for a series called "The Art of Glenn Gould." It allowed him to include the "Conference at Port Chilkoot" which gave scope to his satirical inventiveness in a spoof on a music critics' conference. On *Music of To-Day* he presented a long series of programs on Schoenberg in which he exploited in different ways material from the interviews he had on hand from his two very major documentaries on the same composer. On *Sunday Supplement* he discussed the phenomenon of the synthesizer recording "Switched-on Bach," and *The Scene* gave him a chance to give controversial views on competitive sports, games and the effect of technology on the arts. *Arts National* gave him a five-week run at introducing the music of his choice, to talk about himself and play his own programming games. Other radio series which gave free rein to his many and rare talents were *CBC Wednesday Night*, *CBC Thursday*

Music, *Mostly Music* and *Listen to the Music*. Among the audio documents which he considered important were various Gould projects released by CBC Learning Systems, Radio Canada International Transcriptions of the Quintet in F Minor by Brahms, and an interview conducted by Vincent Tovell called "At Home with Glenn Gould."

Glenn always attached great importance to his documentaries, in which he explored and developed contrapuntal radio. This exploration of a new field of his own invention became so demanding in terms of studio and technicians' time that I realized the CBC was not equipped to provide the kind of backup he needed for the future. Over supper one night I suggested he should buy his own equipment, use technicians on a part-time basis, and set up his own company or a new enterprise to undertake the making of radio documentaries and recitals which the CBC would buy back from him. The result was that the CBC entered into a long-term agreement with Glenn.

The arrangement also suited him for another reason. Glenn disliked having to go to New York to record and had come to the conclusion that if CBS Records could send up a producer from the Big Apple he would be able to make his commercial recordings in the Eaton Auditorium in Toronto, which he felt was a perfect recording studio. This meant that his CBC recitals were recorded there too. Glenn became more and more concerned with experimenting with microphone pickups. Out of every hour in the recording studio, an increasing amount of time was spent in the control booth listening analytically and critically to the music taped. He was in fact developing yet another career—this time as a producer. In fact, it was his extraordinary gifts as a producer which allowed Glenn to piece together a recording of the Ophelia Lieder by Richard Strauss, performed by soprano Elisabeth Schwarzkopf with Glenn in New York some years earlier. Glenn was always a great admirer of Elisabeth Schwarzkopf and he regarded the possibility of recording with her as a very great privilege. My lips are sealed as to what happened at the session. All that needs to be said is that at the conclusion there were barely enough "takes" to cover an entire performance. The fact that the recording did appear, and that it represents a pinnacle of the artistry of Schwarzkopf and Gould, is a tribute to Glenn as a producer, and to CBS Records for letting him have his way in saving what appeared to be an uncompleted project.

Another example worth mentioning is a taped recital Glenn recorded as the CBC's contribution to the main radio concert series of the European Broadcasting Union. It was eventually broadcast all over Europe and in the United States as well. I arrived at a meeting of the music committee of the EBU (of which I was a member) in Helsinki and quickly discovered that preliminary reports of the recital's being "unsatisfactory" were true. At first there were complaints about the technical quality of the broadcast, but these seemed to disappear quickly when I said that an identical tape would eventually be used by CBS Records when the broadcast was turned into a commercial recording. What appeared to worry some of my colleagues was that for early music the microphone had been moved closer to the piano in order to give a more percussive or harpsichord-like sound, but that for other works such as the "Variations Chromatiques" by Bizet there was a totally different pickup. For the Bizet the microphone was placed so as to give the piano a more mellifluent sound. These changes of perspective were considered undesirable in a broadcast, because in the view of some members of the committee the perspective created by the distance between the instrument and the listener should not change. Neither should the sound of the piano. After all, such things did not happen in a public recital. However, when I explained that Glenn was using the occasion to be innovative in radio broadcasting, a colleague from Geneva quickly said, "Gentlemen, I am sure you will agree that Mr. Gould's recital is the finest the EBU has ever been privileged to broadcast. Is there anyone who disagrees?" By that time no one did, and the project went ahead to enormous acclaim. It was in fact a great and very individual Glenn Gould statement.

Glenn always looked upon his career in the media as a "higher calling." His programs for television were particularly important to him. He made his television debut in 1952, on the opening night of the CBC's television station in Toronto, CBLT. A turning point in his career was a 1961 project called, "The Subject is Beethoven," in which he performed the Eroica Variations and the Sonata for Cello and Piano

Opus 69 with Leonard Rose. Apart from the insightful performances themselves, Glenn's commentary was so articulate and communicative that the program was repeated shortly afterwards. It was not so much that the viewers understood all the details of what he said, as that they were captivated by his warmth, enthusiasm and conviction, in other words, by his personal magnetism. Glenn was very touched when some viewers wrote to say that they had never before encountered serious music and that his program had sent them hurrying to local record shops where a whole new world began to open up for them.

Another landmark was a CBC program called "The Anatomy of a Fugue" which ended with his own witty composition, "So You Want to Write a Fugue?" I remember him saying sometime afterwards that the frustrating thing about television was that it was a much more unwieldy medium than radio and that although television producers were interested in innovation, what was lacking was the opportunity to experiment with the presentation of music away from the actual making of programs themselves.

In 1966, *Duo*—a major CBC telecast—offered him the chance to work with Yehudi Menuhin, something he had wanted to do for years. The combination of two such rare talents in works by Bach, Beethoven and Schoenberg gave the CBC a musical result seldom achieved on television anywhere. The BBC, with the co-operation of the CBC, made a four-part series with Glenn in 1967. Then, in 1968, he introduced a CBC television series called "The World of Music," which included not only Canadian programs—in none of which he played—but also others from France, Great Britain and the U.S.A.

Glenn was just as excited about presenting his own television programs as he was about performing in them. In 1970, in a telecast called "The Well-Tempered Listener"—an all-Bach program—he conceived a program in two sections. The first was fugal in approach, consisting of the interweaving of the voices of Glenn and his interviewer, Curtis Davis from NET, with musical illustrations, as well as with an animated film by Norman McLaren and René Jodoin of the National Film Board of Canada. In the second part Glenn performed Preludes and Fugues from Book II of the Forty-Eight Preludes and Fugues. The program was of particular interest, because in addition to the piano, harpsichord and organ were used. The producer was Mario Prizek.

Also in 1970, CBC TV and NET presented a visual realization of Glenn's radio documentary, "The Idea of North." The script was of course provided by Glenn and is based, as is the radio documentary, on the commentary of people he met on a train journey to Fort Churchill, Manitoba. Although this is not the Far North, it is certainly polar bear country. Glenn never went to the Arctic islands because he refused to fly. However, this did not matter to him at all. "The Idea of North" is not so much concerned with geography as it is a state of mind, of finding oneself and of mining internal personal resources. In the television program, Glenn's contrapuntal use of the voices of characters (several speaking simultaneously) was realized to his satisfaction although he said to me, "In my next life I want to be a film director."

Glenn was both delighted and amused when he was asked by CBC television, with only a day's notice, to replace the distinguished Italian pianist Arturo Benedetto Michelangeli in a performance of Beethoven's Emperor Concerto with the Toronto Symphony and conductor Karel Ancerl. It amused him because during his concert career he had developed a certain reputation as a canceller of concerts and he now found himself substituting for someone else.

His television career took a new twist when he made a four-part series for French TV produced by the French film director Bruno Monsaingeon in 1974. These programs, in which Glenn not only performed but was interviewed by Monsaingeon, caused a sensation in France, and resulted in a wide-ranging discussion of his views and performances in the national press. They were also the beginning of a series of programs directed by Monsaingeon which continued until the end of Glenn's life. The association with Monsaingeon ended with the filming of the *Goldberg Variations*. A few days after his death, CBC Television presented the film as a tribute to Glenn, and shortly after that CBS Records released an audio recording of the Goldberg Variations: thus Glenn's international career had gone full cycle. It began with a recording of the Goldbergs and ended with another even more remarkable than the first. It was recorded on a Yamaha piano Glenn had found in New York and which he described as the piano of his dreams. And it was recorded in the same New York studio he had used for the original recording. He hurried to do this because the studio was to be demolished shortly.

When Glenn died, many acquaintances suddenly realized they had not seen him for a long time. After Glenn set up his own recording operations, he moved his office from the CBC and took a studio at Film House. Later he moved into a small suite at the Inn on the Park which he arranged as a studio. The demands of his work and his unusual working hours had turned him into more of a recluse than ever. His long telephone calls with people amounted to visits, but he still saw a few friends—mostly in his studio where he could offer them supper by taking advantage of room service. When I visited him this way we would talk a great deal about present and future projects and listen to acetates of new recordings. We also looked at videotapes and his own projects-in-the-making. In this way, and in unedited form, I first saw film projects such as *The Wars* and the *Goldberg Variations*. He also enjoyed showing *Glenn Gould's Toronto*, a film produced by John McGreevy, in which Glenn Gould the recluse emerged to discover his own home town. Glenn thought of it as a divertimento and liked the "movement" in which he sang to the animals at the Toronto Zoo. (As a child he was inclined to sing to animals, particularly cows, because they proved the most attentive of all!)

In the course of our last sessions together, Glenn played me tapes of two conducting projects. A group of musicians had been put together for him at his expense and the result was a recording of the Piano Concerto No. 2 by Beethoven, in which he used a student as the soloist, and a superb recording of the Siegfried Idyll by Wagner. Glenn had toyed with conducting at various times in his career and years ago, in order to encourage him, I had invited him to conduct the CBC Vancouver Chamber Orchestra. Although he was pleased with the result he said he found the physical demands of conducting were not in accord with the physical demands of playing the piano. "If I conduct," he said, "I am forced to practice and I tend to think too much about things I can normally do spontaneously." He added that he had to make a choice, and that playing the piano was important because he subsidized other areas of his career with income from it. He felt he was going through a new learning process with his two private conducting projects and planned to continue with others.

For years Glenn insisted he would retire from playing the piano at fifty. "That will be enough of Gould," he used to say. However, as digital and videorecording technology advanced and videocassettes improved, he began to think he should re-record some of his repertoire and also add to it. At any rate, he had to make up his mind, because his contract with CBS Records was coming up for renewal. After procrastinating a little more, he finally went ahead and signed a new contract. This represented a continuation of an association with CBS Records which had already lasted for more than two decades and produced a legacy of recordings, the importance of which was not to be fully understood until after his death. Glenn was hoping to make some recordings as a conductor. He seemed to have become much more sanguine about reconciling the physical demands of conducting and playing the piano. In fact, it is clear that he was about to add a new dimension to his career when death overtook him.

I think Glenn sometimes had the impression fate was looking over his shoulder. In his concert-giving days he sometimes called me long distance to say he had changed his flight, the reason being that he felt the one he was on was "unlucky." In 1958, after he set off for Europe, I got a call from him. "Greetings from Reykjavik, Iceland," he said. In truth, he was still in New York. He had decided to change his trans-Atlantic trip and was waiting for an Israeli Airlines flight. He explained that because Israeli Airlines had so few planes they undoubtedly maintained them better than other companies. At other times, he explained that he had postponed doing certain things because his vibrations told him it was the wrong moment.

Glenn had a penchant for playing guessing games. If he was going to be interviewed, or something interesting had just happened to him, his friends always had to guess what it was. I often failed to guess correctly. Two interviews I failed to guess were those for *Rolling Stone* and *Der Spiegel* and something else which defeated me was the *Globe and Mail* review of Geoffrey Payzant's book, *Glenn Gould, Music and Mind.* (The review, which was at once witty and scintillating, was written by Glenn himself in the third person.)

In everything Glenn did, I was conscious of his feeling for structure. It made little difference whether he was extemporizing bedtime stories for our children, inventing a new guessing game, writing an article, or speaking his mind about something, his thoughts were instantly well organized and structured. In fact, his whole life was structured so that he could lead a contrapuntal existence. He had the ability to undertake a number of projects simultaneously, give each one a life of its own, and bring them all to brilliant fruition.

Sometimes he had two or three levels of thought unfolding simultaneously, dealing with different subjects, and would have a stream of music progressing at the same time in his mind. He would suddenly stop in mid-sentence and say, "Do you know what work is running through the back of my mind?" I of course had to guess. One such work was "Metamorphosen" by Richard Strauss. However, the last time I talked to him it was the "Four Last Songs" by the same composer, written at the end of his life. As I talked to Glenn, I thought how exhausted he looked. "Shall I guess where you are?" I asked, and he replied, "Yes." "Are you into the fourth song yet?" "Yes, that's just where I am," he said. Months afterwards I remembered the last words of that song, based on a poem by Joseph von Eichendorf.

> We sense the night's soft breath
> Now we are tired, how tired!
> Can this perhaps be death?

Conducting a radio session in a CBC studio, mid-1970s. (CBC Robert C. Ragsdale)

TOWARDS A
CONTRAPUNTAL RADIO
Robert Hurwitz

He opened the door and stuck out his hand. It was to be shaken. Moments earlier, as I took the short walk from the house phone to his room at the Four Seasons Hotel in Toronto, I wondered what I was going to do when I met Glenn Gould for the first time. Shake his hand? One of the parts of the "legend" of Glenn Gould had to do with handshaking: he didn't do it. He soaked his hands in warm water for at least a half hour before concerts (which he stopped playing in 1964) and recordings (which he continued to make until his death this past October), and once, so goes the legend, he sued a man who shook his hand too hard. But when he opened the door, unshaven, slightly hunched and smiling, there was his right hand in front of me, as if to dispel a myth. And as I reached out to complete the greeting, he pulled it back, just a bit, as if to say shake, but not too hard.

For many of those who were fortunate enough to have seen Glenn Gould perform, or who, like myself, were too young to have attended his concerts but who grew up with his recordings, there was a legendary quality about him unlike that of any musician of our time. He was foremost, of course, a brilliant performer, and the more than 90 recordings that are his legacy are an accurate and comprehensive statement of what he had to say as a pianist and as a musician. Everything about the way he played seemed so *different*. He had a unique sound and a particularly unusual manner of playing the instrument, and while some might question his performance of a familiar (Bach, Beethoven, Mozart) and unfamiliar (Gibbons, Bizet, Sibelius)

253

repertoire, it was hard to deny that the interpretations were those of a remarkable and original musical mind.

The legend was fueled by the fact that Gould did what no other musician of his stature had done: he retired from performing in public when he was only 32 years old. But he did not retire from being a musician or a creative force. While continuing to make as many as five albums a year for CBS, he also composed music and transcribed for piano the orchestral music of others (from Wagner's *Meistersinger Prelude* to Ravel's *La Valse*), he wrote magazine articles (a few titles: "In Search of Petula Clark," "Glenn Gould Interviews Himself About Beethoven," "Křenek, the Prolific, is Probably Best Known to the Public at Large as—Ernst Who?"), performed for television (more than a dozen programs for Canadian, French and German TV), scored for motion pictures (*Slaughterhouse-Five* and the as-yet unreleased *The Wars*), and invented a new form of radio documentary called "contrapuntal radio." His involvement with radio and television was so significant, in fact, that a few years ago Gould told me that he had been asked to head the Canadian Broadcasting Corporation (he turned it down). These non-performing activities took up most of Gould's time in recent years, and he brought to each the same originality and passion that characterized his piano playing.

The way Glenn Gould lived created an atmosphere of legend around him. Here was a man who wore gloves during recording sessions (in fact, the gloves were cut off at the fingertips; it was his joke for some CBS recording engineers). A man who, when he played in public, would drink a glass of water or read a magazine during a pause in a concerto. (It's reported in his reviews; the *New York Times* wrote, about a 1961 performance of the Beethoven Fourth Concerto, "What's next? Can we look forward to Mr. Gould's playing Beethoven next year with a seidel of beer and a ham sandwich to occupy himself during the orchestral tuttis?") A man who wore layers of clothing under heavy overcoats, gloves and scarves in mid-summer (he was dressed that way when I first met him—in August). A man who sang when he played (you can hear him on the recordings). A man who wouldn't shake hands for fear he might get hurt. A man who communicated only by the telephone; a man who shied away from personal contact. The most frequently quoted statement about Glenn Gould was, appropriately, "That nut's a genius" (George Szell).

And so, armed with stories and myths, I confronted the Glenn Gould "legend" about ten years ago, when I was 24. At the time I was a publicist for CBS Records and I was in Toronto, where Gould lived, on other business. I had spoken to him on the telephone a few times before—usually on minor matters—and our talks were always polite and to the point. I knew he was a recluse, but nonetheless I suggested—a bit brashly, it seems now—that we might be able to meet. He told me, very politely, that he was extremely busy and would most likely have no time, but to call anyway.

Although he had an apartment in Toronto, he was staying at the Four Seasons Hotel, and recommended it to me. After I checked in, I called him on the house phone, and again he told me that he really couldn't see me. Then he launched into a 15-minute tale—I was still standing in the lobby, listening—about a BBC crew that was in town to make documentaries about three Canadian "institutions"—Prime Minister Trudeau, the Mounties and himself. He was about to reach the punchline when he said, "This is going to take too long; why don't you come up to my room for a moment so I can finish the story."

Nine hours later, we shook hands as we said goodbye. All that I'd heard about Gould's "eccentricities" seemed true when I met him, and yet it didn't really matter. That is, behavior that might have appeared eccentric in other people was not necessarily eccentric with Gould; his habits were absolutely consistent and finely tuned to the man. He was an extremely friendly and interested person, never condescending, a man of genuine warmth, kindness and humility. I was a virtual stranger; my connection to him was merely that I had updated his CBS publicity biography. Yet he accepted me, if not as an old friend, perhaps as a son of a good friend who was passing through the city. In all, he bore little resemblance to the legend.

After talking for a few hours that August evening, Gould bundled himself up in a dark overcoat and we drove in his large, late-model American car to a studio he had in town, to play some tapes for me.

He played a few of his latest recordings. Gould was never a passive listener: eyes closed, he sang and conducted as the music was played back, often as intensely as if he were at a keyboard.

Next we turned to the radio programs. Gould began writing radio scripts during the mid-1950s, but he was unsatisfied with his first efforts. They were too "linear"; he told an interviewer, "Radio programs came out sounding, in a word, predictable. It was always, 'Over to you, now back to the host and here for the wrap-up....'"

The first little radio drama Gould played was just like that: it was called "Glenn Gould on Sports," and in it he "interviewed" himself about sports and competition. He wrote all of the parts, and besides playing himself, he acted the roles of the "guests," including a kayak champion from a small Arctic village, as well as a Canadian welter-weight named Dominico Pastrano, who sounded like Brando in *On the Waterfront*—but with a Canadian accent. Gould said a few things about Team Canada (the national hockey team), the Fisher-Spassky chess matches, and pugilism, as well as taking a few digs at music criticism, which he felt often veers too closely to sports reporting. But the program was really about one of his favorite subjects: the "moral" advantages of technology. The program also provided another oppor-tunity for him to defend his decision to leave the "competitive" concert stage.

Where the sports program was a divertissement, the next radio show he played, "The Idea of North," was a symphony: in fact, Gould claimed that his primary "compositional" activity during the last two decades was the creation of these radio programs. For "The Idea of North" Gould interviewed five people who appeared to be traveling on a train towards the Arctic Circle in Canada. Like Gould, they sought solitude and were not intimidated by the isolation of the Canadian north. He interviewed them individually and then spliced together all of the conversations so that the five strangers seemed to be engaged in a dialogue. Sometimes, you heard three voices at the same time, as if Gould was creating a verbal equivalent to musical counter-point. He used other musical devices as well. Throughout the program, for example, the train is heard in the background, rolling northward; Gould called this the "basso continuo." Listening to this and other "contrapuntal" programs was like sitting on a crowded subway car during rush hour, hearing two or three conversations as you read the paper, a portable radio blaring across the aisle and the car rattling down the tracks.

Nonetheless, it would be wrong to simply equate the programs like "The Idea of North" with the music that Gould so closely identified with. Musical elements were borrowed to create a structure, to serve Gould's conception of man's relationship to his environment. This theme of isolation—one with which Gould clearly identified—was present in each of these programs whether they were about a community cut off from the world (the village in Newfoundland in "The Latecomers" or the Mennonites in "The Quiet in the Land"), or those individuals like Arnold Schoenberg or Richard Strauss, who were estranged from the mainstream of the musical world during their lifetimes.

About a year after the first visit, I saw Gould once again at the Four Seasons, this time to observe the final mix of his radio documentary on Schoenberg. By the time I reached Toronto he had already spent several months on the program. He had begun work on the documentary by driving down to New York (he wouldn't fly) to conduct studio interviews with composer John Cage, conductors Erich Leinsdorf and Denis Stevens, and *Mahler* author Henri-Louis de la Grange. A fifth interview, with composer Ernst Křenek, was conducted over the phone. The process for creating the verbal half of the program was similar to that of "The Idea of North": after interviewing each man separately, he edited himself out of the conversations and spliced together their comments so that it sounded as if they were talking to one another. He also created sections where two conversations would go on simultaneously. Finally, there was a single reel, seamlessly stitched together, that contained the verbal text of the program.

He then transcribed the material, creating a written script and, away from the studio, began looking for musical equivalents to choreograph the words of his actors. When I arrived, he was ready to mix the music, and for this crucial part of the program, Gould was not leaving much to the moment. An example: following the transition from comments by Leinsdorf to those of Křenek, the script reads,

"Overlap of Pierrot excerpt and E minor canon occurs during 2nd line on words, 'to be right numerologically'; overlap should begin on the flute notes G and E and continue throughout tonic and momentarily into dominant harmony if possible."

Assembling these programs was long and difficult, and like most studio work, tedious. He worked evenings (he usually slept during the day) and the night I was in the studio, he was beginning to put on the music tracks with a CBC engineer. Gould acted as producer, assistant engineer (when the engineer's two hands weren't enough) and maestro. Overdressed as always, a yellow Bic pen constantly in his right hand, he spent the evening conducting music (and comments) during rehearsals, false starts, "almost perfects," and very few "takes." After ten hours, he and his engineer had completed a few minutes of the program. It was not quite "…and now back to the host."

There is a great deal of counterpoint in the Schoenberg documentary: at one point, for example, Křenek and Cage speak simultaneously while a Gregorian chant and the music of Guillaume Dufay, Guillaume de Machaut and Karlheinz Stockhausen are all mixed together (and clearly heard) in the background. Yet instead of sounding busy or confused, there is a clarity, even a calmness, to this moment; and one can derive a similar satisfaction to what is often found from listening to music. What Gould wrote about "The Idea of North" seems relevant here as well: "The point about these contrapuntal scenes is that they test the degree to which one can listen simultaneously to more than one conversation or vocal impression. It's perfectly true that, in the dining room scene, not every word is going to be audible, but by no means is every syllable in the final fugue from Verdi's *Falstaff*, either."

As is true in hearing contrapuntal music, the focus of the listener to these programs tends to shift from one idea to another. Indeed, in the Schoenberg documentary, it's sometimes difficult to figure out whether the principal focus is the dialogue or the music. And the music—by Schoenberg, Brahms, Mahler, Webern and many others—is so closely allied with the verbal track that the pieces Gould chose often sound as if they were written especially for the program, like a soundtrack on a film.

Gould's documentaries are not always easy to listen to, and, as with some music, one can only begin to get a full sense of his intentions either by repeated listenings (hard to do without tapes of the programs, which at best are infrequently broadcast), or by having a copy of the script (limited in distribution, one would suppose, to personal acquaintances). But although these programs are serious works of art, they are not inaccessible. They often project a great sense of fun, and can be as highly spirited as, say, a Gould performance of a Bach fugue. In fact, during the best moments of these programs, one clearly sees the hand of Gould the pianist: he is a conductor, a guide; he seems to be saying, here, *listen to this*, the lines of the music or the documentary text appearing like those in a book underlined by a yellow magic marker.

While Gould's radio documentaries were arguably a great achievement, there are a number of reasons why they have gone largely unnoticed. Perhaps foremost is the fact that the radio drama no longer holds a pre-eminent place in our television culture. Of course, it's hard to compare these programs with those of an earlier time, for Gould used an original conception that was unlike anything that had ever been done. Additionally, the idea of "contrapuntal radio" would have been impossible without the resources of multi-track tape machines, which have been used only in the last 25 years. Another reason why these programs aren't known is that they were rarely broadcast outside of Canada. Then, too, we tend to undervalue accomplishments outside of one's primary field. Although the radio documentaries took up more of Gould's time than any other activity—including music—he was generally perceived by the musical community as, say, the politician who also paints, or the conductor who also races cars.

And so, when people talk about Glenn Gould today, the subject always goes back to two things: the way he played the piano, and his early withdrawal from public performing. Of the latter, a great deal has been written since he left the concert stage in 1964. Much of the comments implied that Gould's retirement resulted from a flaw in his character, and writers used examples of his eccentric behavior to confirm this theory. Even since his death, much of the comment regarding Gould and his departure from the stage has focused on the weakness in his personality. Donald Henahan wrote in the *New York Times*, concerning Gould's recordings, "It is not a musical performance so much as Gould's idealized image of himself, engraved in vinyl, a dream of how he would like to have played. An interesting document, to be sure, and perhaps one that should interest psychologists as much as musicians. At any rate, rest in peace, Glenn Gould. You need nevermore have any fear of facing a live audience." And William H. Youngren in the *Atlantic* wrote that Gould "never grew up emotionally. Instead, he remained a rebellious adolescent, his view of the world shaped by the melodramatic absolutism so obvious…in the elaborate theories he constructed to explain his withdrawal from the concert stage."

Gould, of course, was not oblivious to criticism. He took it seriously enough to answer his critics, if not in kind, then by taking his favorite targets and making them characters in satirical magazine articles (for example, transforming *New York Times* music critic Harold Schonberg into Homer Sibelius) and in his radio documentaries (which included not only music critics but a resident psychoanalyst as well).

There was always a hopeful public that "knew" someday Gould would return to performing, but it never happened. He believed that the concert hall was not the best place to perform or to hear music, and that by using technology (that is, recordings), one could come close to realizing a musical ideal. In this respect, he would surely have agreed with Henahan's criticism, except, of course, that Gould saw as a virtue what Henahan judged to be a weakness.

Gould also defended his decision on "moral" grounds. After I left CBS, he told me (in an interview that appeared in the *New York Times*): "I happen to find all of the live arts immoral because one should not voyeuristically watch one's fellow human beings in testing situations that do not pragmatically need to be tested. Those who stand in opposition to technology do so because they think that there is something inherently wrong with making life simpler than it ought to be, that if you can take a series of problems and reduce these problems by a splice, in some way you are performing an anti-human act."

Finally, Gould was simply not comfortable with the life of a public figure. He was a throwback to an artist of another time, a man who felt comfortable only when he worked in solitude and even obscurity. He did this not necessarily for neurotic reasons, but because he believed that only in isolation, undistracted, could he fully command his intellect and imagination.

Gould wrote extensively about the concert hall/recording question. Some of his opinions, like his prediction that the concert scene was dying and would be extinct by the end of the century, were little more than polemical wishful thinking. But other ideas were far ahead of his time. He was one of the first musicians to see recordings as a creative end in themselves, something beyond a "faithful reproduction" of the concert hall experience. The recording artist, he felt, should have similar advantages to painters, novelists or filmmakers—to create in solitude and to have final control of all aspects of their creations, something concerts could never provide. He was one of the first to perceive how profoundly recordings would change the way the music was performed and heard.

Gould died just as digital recording was becoming more accepted. This latest technological breakthrough is perhaps the final bridge between live and studio performances, for it eliminates technical problems, like tape hiss and distortion (and in the compact disc format, warpage and surface noise) that mar analog recordings. Recorded music can now sound as if it were live, even if it comes from dozens of takes and contains hundreds of splices.

Just prior to his death, CBS released Gould's first efforts using digital technology, a two-record set of late Haydn sonatas and a recording of the *Goldberg Variations*; one hopes that there will be compact disc versions of these recordings so that the full impact of the digital process can be heard. As brilliant as these records are from a sound perspective, they do not diminish the value of Gould's earlier recordings on technologically inferior equipment. His recording career developed during a period when a large number of technical advances were being made (his first records were made before stereo). Nonetheless, there is still a consistent level of intensity in almost all of his albums, making them not only important documents, but living statements, full of passion, intelligence, wit and, perhaps with the exception of his notorious Mozart recordings, his great commitment to music. The American composer Elliott Carter, writing in *Flawed Words*, spoke of a characteristic of performance that seems apt in regard to Gould:

"From a purely musical point of view," Carter wrote, "I've always had the impression of improvisation of the most rewarding kind when good performers take the trouble to play music that is carefully written out as if they were thinking it up themselves while they played it—that is, when with much thought and practice they come to feel the carefully written-out piece as part of themselves and of their own experience, which they are communicating to others directly from themselves in the moment of performance, in an alive way."

I saw Gould for the last time this past April when I was once again in Toronto. Gould was staying in a different hotel, the Inn on the Park, where he also had his studio. When I asked what he was up to, he put me through a game of "20 Questions." (The answer: he had recently hired an orchestra to test his aptitude as conductor; not, of course, with the intention of performing in public, but because he wanted to make a concerto recording, first as a pianist and then—on a different take—as the conductor.)

As usual, there was a wide range of programs to be listened to and to be watched. First, there was a travel show—"Glenn Gould's Toronto," part of a series that included "Studs Turkel's Chicago," "Jonathan Miller's London," and so on. Gould wrote the program, narrated it, and starred in many scenes. He also played a rough cut of a film he had recently scored about the First World War called *The Wars*, since completed but not yet seen in the United States. As he did in *Slaughterhouse-Five*, Gould mostly used versions of his own recordings, adapting them to the action; in this instance, much of the soundtrack consists of his performances of Brahms *Intermezzi*.

And finally, there was a truly extraordinary performance on video of Gould playing the *Goldberg Variations*, shot at CBS's 30th St. Studio in New York when he made the audio recording. I looked at the image of the TV Gould during this performance; at times I could not help looking at the real Gould. As always, he sang and conducted as he watched, as if every ounce of energy was as involved in listening to the music as he was in actually performing it. He was extremely satisfied with both the recording and the film, as well he should be; he had, after all, made his life's work of projects such as these, the fruits of our age of technology.

We had met in the late afternoon, and now it was four in the morning. Time had gone by quickly. I was exhausted but, as always, exhilarated by our meeting, and once more was surprised at the extraordinary warmth and friendship Gould projected. He insisted upon helping me find my way back through the maze of underground corridors at the hotel, and as we shook hands goodbye, I was already looking forward to when I would see him again.

Late 1960s, a pause during a recording session at CBC. (CBC)

WELL-TEMPERED GOULD
Curtis Davis

"Ah, good evening, sir!" The calls would always come during the late evening, usually after 11:00. "I have something for you to hear, and I want you to tell me, within the first eight bars if you can, where, when and by whom this music was composed." There would follow the sounds of a recording wafting over the phone, and the caller's unmistakable chortle when a guess fell short of the mark. "No, it's not Janáček, and it's not Sibelius either, though at least you're in the right country there." Armed with that clue, on I would guess through my litany of Kilpinen, Kokkonen, Merikanto, and any other obscure Finns I could think of, until my caller could stand no more. "No," he would interrupt, "none of those, but you'd never guess him anyway. I've only just discovered the fellow myself, and having fallen in love with this work, I thought you should hear it. It's the Third Symphony by Aulis Sallinen."

Of course I knew from the first words that it was Glenn at the other end of the line. Such opening gambits usually brought on not less than half an hour's talk ranging from the glories of the Nordic life to the home computer which would eventually permit any listener to influence directly the interpretation offered by any recording. Not infrequently Glenn would insist that my wife, Julie, get on the other phone so he could read aloud to us his latest bit of outrageous critical prose, or one of his dialogues in German, Scotch and Bronx dialects, a skill in which he was not many notches below Peter Ustinov.

I had first met Glenn in the late 1960s when we began discussing a film version of his CBC radio documentary "The Idea of North." I was then handling cultural programs for NET. Glenn's 1956 recording of the Bach *Goldberg Variations* had been a prized recording for years, to which many others had been added, but curiously I had never seen him in public. His American appearances were not all that frequent, but I had even managed to miss his celebrated encounter with Leonard Bernstein in 1962 when the New York Philharmonic maestro impishly disassociated himself from the very performance he was about to conduct of the Brahms D Minor Concerto, on the ostensible grounds that he could not subscribe to the interpretation of his chosen soloist, Glenn Gould. This has always reminded me of the statement by Florence Foster Jenkin, the famed New York socialite coloratura of the 1940s, "Some people said I couldn't sing, but nobody can say I didn't sing." In this case, nobody can say Lenny didn't conduct. The clear winner, hands down, was Glenn Gould—and I missed it!

By 1970 we had completed "The Idea of North" and the next year we shared on-camera roles in a TV special for NET and the CBC on the music of Bach called "The Well-Tempered Listener," a show full of visual surprises and metaphors in which the taped dialogue was, on one of the rare occasions Glenn allowed it, unwritten and unrehearsed. From that time on, after I left NET in 1972, Glenn and I remained friends—"close" is unlikely to be appropriate. I took every opportunity I could on my Toronto visits through the 1970s to reserve a spare evening for him. Glenn would pick me up at the Chelsea Inn, driving either his king-size Cadillac or his Mercedes, over whose infirmities he would sympathetically cluck, as over an ailing aunt.

Glenn was by this time largely a recluse, seeing few people, and centering his life on his recordings, radio and TV shows, and numerous articles. An exceptionally devoted hypochondriac, he rarely travelled without cap, overcoat and galoshes, even in summer, and a big shaggy muffler flung around his neck. Direct human contact was not his strong suit. On rare occasions, upon opening the door for me, he might extend his hand, gloved now only in winter, with another "Ah, good evening, sir," and I would grasp it lightly. More often he would simply wait for me to settle into my seat, and we would roar off north to his tiny suite at the Inn on the Park, as I anticipated a long night of talk and music with one of the rarest spirits and most honest men it has ever been my privilege to know.

I had to calculate the choice of those nights with care, for I knew that Glenn would rarely release me before 3:00 or even 4:00 A.M. He liked nothing more than a captive audience of one. The last time I saw him, in May of 1982, toward the end of the night he did say, "You know, we really should be taping these things. It's a pity to waste all that brilliance on just the two of us." That was typical of Glenn's extravagance, but I wish we had. Now, far, far too soon, one is forced to reply, "Ah, good evening, sir."

I've speculated often as to why Glenn chose to leave the public arena. To attribute it to hypochondria or misanthropy is as superficial as to accept his own stated reasons for it, namely that public performance has become irrelevant and recordings are now the only valid medium of musical communication. I think it was something else altogether. Glenn was a born explorer, speculator and creator. These are essentially solitary activities, requiring enormous energy and concentration. Had he remained chained to the life of a touring artist, towards which he was always unsympathetic, he would not have had the independence he required. It was a difficult choice, but frankly I'm glad he made it. We may only have had a bit more than a decade to enjoy his extraordinary public performances, but at least we did have those, about as much as we got from Maria Callas. If he had not closed himself off from the world, we could not have had his bountiful flow of recordings, radio, TV and published essays.

Glenn's fascination with the art of recording, and his unmatched command of it, was most clearly revealed to me the first time we sat down together to listen to his radio documentary "The Idea of North." Glenn had been pestering the CBC for years to let him do a documentary, and they thought they finally had him benched when they said "OK, but only if it's not about music." What he produced was one of the most provocative groundbreaking works of radio ever heard, and one of the few now available on disc. This paean to the siren song of cold bleakness had been conceived for stereo with that meticulous calculation of weights and balances one should expect from Glenn, with his lifelong love affair with the Arctic.

What I heard was an opening in which voices entered sotto-voce at far left, far right, left center and right center, only to be supplanted at the hubbub or climax by Glenn Gould himself at dead center, like the boys' choir breaking into the opening fugue of the St. Matthew Passion. Glenn's introduction, to the accompaniment of the sounds of old-fashioned steam engine noises, signalled the program's departure toward the North. At one point during the playing of the tape, as I remained glued to the only ideal dead-center spot in the room for proper binaural listening, Glenn couldn't refrain from interrupting the playback, explaining, "I want you to pay special attention to this next part. It's in A-B-A-C-A-D-A-C-A-B-A form." I can't recall any other producer ever uttering such a line.

The instant appeal of "The Idea of North" for me, besides its lyrical visionary humanistic content, was the formality of its construction, worthy of any Baroque master, or perhaps Bartok's *Music for Strings, Percussion and Celesta* (though Glenn wouldn't have cared much for that comparison, harboring a lifelong distaste for the music of Bartok). Alban Berg in *Wozzeck* or *Lulu*, with his subliminal rondos, fugues, sonata forms and canons, did not go further. I believed immediately that it could serve as the basis for a marvelous film.

All the characters in the documentary were real people, recorded by Glenn in separate interviews. The garrulous old trainman was something between Tiresias and Prospero, a sometimes cynical but wise and kindly commentator who had seen them all come and go, whose observations had much the same function as those of a Greek chorus, telling us what we didn't yet know, or giving us a view of the meaning of events. The other four characters—for that is how Glenn treated them, manipulating their recorded musings to suit himself, inventing dialogues that never existed in reality—all had different reasons for travelling north. For one it was employment, for another adventure, for yet another a government reassignment, for the last an escape. Each greeted the prospect of the frozen North with mixed anticipation and dread. They remained individual in their commonality, and when combined by Glenn they added up to a powerful mystical statement of that attraction we all feel at some time toward the unknown, and the ultimately unknowable.

To get "The Idea of North" going as a film took some finessing. I was tied up at NET, and Glenn was busy with his jammed agenda of recordings and a new radio music series for the CBC. We needed a producer-director, and as this was to be an NET-CBC coproduction, I preferred it to be an American, otherwise it could so easily fall into the "you pay, we do" trap (like so many coproductions with England). I also felt it should be somebody without a past producing history with Glenn.

The ideal candidate turned out to be Judith Pearlman, who also knew the radio documentary and thought it should be a film. I had never worked with her before, but her solid reputation combined with her energy and imagination recommended her highly. Besides, I thought it might be marginally easier for a woman to work with Glenn on this show. Judith was also quite a competent pianist. For some Canadian members of her crew, however, being an American, a New Yorker and a woman amounted to quite enough strikes against her.

Glenn's support of Judith throughout the project was impeccable. When the first "day for night" footage shot on the train from Winnipeg to Fort Churchill turned out to be less than ideal, Glenn helped her find fresh ways to use it. If the CBC bureaucracy got a bit "shirty," Glenn found paths through its labyrinths. When the demands of an urgent news documentary forced a hiatus in the middle of editing, Glenn secured a quiet unoccupied CBC radio studio for Judith with a splendid Steinway on which she could practice alone to her heart's content, armed with music supplied by Glenn.

It was in this way that Judith eventually heard Glenn perform "live," a privilege I had never enjoyed or requested. She did ask him once for permission to attend a recording session, which he gallantly but firmly refused. Now, after so many months of hard work, a woman alone away from home and among sometimes grumpy professional men, Judith was surprised one day when Glenn arrived at her studio. Their chat turned toward the music of Richard Strauss, and she asked if he had ever heard *Die Frau Ohne Schatten.* He went straight to the keyboard and began the first act from memory, singing out all the parts in basso, falsetto, and tenor squeak, before her incredulous eyes and ears. This was followed by some Bach, and his latest craze for the English Virginalists, and even a little Brahms, played just for her alone.

Later in the editing hiatus, Judith found herself at Glenn's studio as he played for her the tape he had just edited for broadcast of Chopin's Sonata No. 3 in B Minor. Glenn was never noted as a Chopinist, having given up this music soon after his earliest teen-age recitals. Offering his first mature Chopin interpretation to a nationwide radio audience was a characteristic act of bravado and self-confidence. Judith critiqued the performance in some detail, particularly as the tape had been spliced from several "takes." The unspoken implication was that Glenn might not be able to reproduce the performance "live."

Some days later Glenn again visited Judith in her CBC studio. He led the talk into the Romantics, and, warming up on some Schumann and Beethoven, launched without a further word into the Chopin sonata, playing it right through to the end without a pause. Judith has described it to me as one of those transcendent musical experiences one hopes to have at least once in a lifetime. It convinced her that Glenn had robbed the world, and himself, of one of the rarest gifts any interpreter can offer, that of direct public communication at the highest level, an achievement granted to only a handful of artists in any generation.

Glenn loved being outrageous. I've rarely met anyone who enjoyed laughter so much, though my image is not that of a belly laugh, but of a figure slouched on a secretarial chair, his stockinged feet up over the audio console board, cackling lightly at something I'd just said, or more often at his own wit. Fortunately he shared this with his readers and his mental image of their startled faces was one of his greatest sources of relish, whether he happened to be suggesting that Ludwig van Beethoven didn't write much of value after he went deaf at the age of 32, or when choosing to open his long tribute to Leopold Stokowski with the words "I am not by nature a stage door John." Curiously, he rarely liked to hear ordinary jokes, as they are so often made at the expense of others. His generosity extended to not wanting to hear people made fun of, just as he would never gossip about fellow artists, even though he was willing to critique their performances explicitly.

Glenn had spoken to me, more than once in recent years and again on our last visit together, of his desire to give up the piano. As we sat viewing his phenomenal video remake of the Bach *Goldberg Variations*, part of a TV series on the Leipzig master and Glenn's testament on the subject, he thought he might choose his imminent fiftieth birthday as the occasion to leave the keyboard, and perhaps devote himself to conducting, an art at which he had already begun to try his hand. I am not so romantic as to be able to think of it as a premonition. It was simply one of those self-willed decisions of which Glenn was entirely capable.

That Glenn Gould managed to maintain himself in the forefront of pianists and recreative musicians of our time, despite his absence from public performance for nearly two decades, is a measure of his capacity to continue expanding his horizons, and ours. We can ask little more of art, or of human relations. His recordings were awaited eagerly, year after year, for these were not simply the mechanical transcription of a public interpretation, appropriately cleaned up for posterity, but a mutual voyage of discovery in companionship with the listener. Glenn played not as others played, but like an excited Champollion having just discovered the Rosetta Stone, and being finally able to begin deciphering signs whose meanings had remained closed to us all for an uncounted age. His listeners world-wide understood this compact, and looked forward to the long-distance exchange, separated by time and space. Like the imaginary dialogues of "The Idea of North," the combination of Glenn-plus-listener added up to a larger whole.

For a generation Glenn Gould has proved to be the only musical artist who succeeded in preserving an existence and audience strictly through the modern reproductive media of our day. To my mind it makes him comparable to a Chaplin or a Spielberg, or perhaps to Frank Lloyd Wright for when we walk through the architect's spaces we learn more about ourselves each time. Glenn's records, broadcasts and articles happily constitute a heritage on which we will continue to feed for a long time to come. Future listeners will almost hear him say, "Now I want you to tell me within eight bars where, when and by whom this piece was composed," and then as the Bach or Beethoven or Byrd unfolds, hear him go on, "Never mind, it isn't fair. I've only just discovered this fellow myself."

Testing a piano in the basement of a concert hall, mid-1950s. (University of Michigan News Service)

Glenn Gould Variations, New York City, 1982. (CBS Don Hunstein)

THE WELL-TEMPERED LISTENER
Glenn Gould & Curtis Davis

Davis: I've been wanting to ask you, Glenn, what are the earliest recollections you have of hearing the music of Bach?

Gould: My own performances, I'm not sure. No, I wasn't all that precocious, it's simply that I wasn't much attracted to multi-voiced things until I was a teenager. I was definitely homophonically inclined until the age of about 10, and then I suddenly got the message. Bach began to emerge into my world then and has never altogether left it. It was one of the great moments of my life, and although it was not with the Bach fugue, it was with a fugue, and its relevance is entirely fugal. I was exposed to my own performance of the Mozart fugue, Kochel 394, the C major one (singing). I was learning it when I was an early teenager (I don't remember exactly how old) and suddenly a vacuum cleaner was struck up beside the piano, and I couldn't quite hear myself play (I was having a feud with the housekeeper at this particular time and it was done on purpose). I began to feel what I was doing, the whole tactile presence of that fugue as represented by finger positions. And it's represented also by the kind of sound that you might get if you sit in the bathtub or in the shower and shake your head, with water coming out both ears. It was the most luminously exciting thing you can imagine, the most glorious sound. It took off all of the things Mozart didn't quite manage to do—I was doing it for him—and I suddenly realized that there was a particular screen through which I was viewing this, and which I had erected between myself and Mozart. It was exactly what I needed to do, and exactly why, as I later understood, this certain mechanical process could indeed come between myself and the work of art that I was involved with. It was a great moment, and although this was not a Bach experience, it was the first great recognition of what the contrapuntal experience properly is. How really involving it is, of what a great number of layers it in fact consists, and precisely in what way one might go about enhancing those layers. It was a very private experience, of course, because it had sealed off all areas of that room, even the acoustics, if there were any to talk about now that the vacuum cleaner was on. The vacuum cleaner became the void in which I was working. And that fugue and my relation to it was the only thing that existed. That was the first great contrapuntal awakening.

Davis: You know, as a sometime composer, I think it's fair to say of all composers that they want the audience to hear absolutely every note they write, and one of the frustrations for the listener is not always being able to discriminate every note that the composer has written. I wonder how you find yourself approaching the music of Bach in order to try to make every single one of the notes heard?

Gould: I think one approaches it in many different ways, perhaps, depending on the time of life in which that approach finds you, your moods at the time, the audio perspectives that are available to you, the audio perspectives that are available to other people and that influence you. It's very difficult to make all of those things, all of those incredibly complicated statements of Bach available; I think it's impossible to do it by any means other than through the phonograph and through recording. I don't think that one can ever do it, ever hope to do it, in a concert hall at all. Because the acoustics are unrealistic, one just doesn't have enough after-the-fact, or with-the-fact control of the performance, of what you're doing at that time.

Davis: I assume for that reason the introduction of stereo has meant alot, and the introduction of even more channels could mean even more to this separation.

Gould: I had a fascinating experience a couple of weeks ago. I sat in a studio in New York and took a couple of Bach fugues—the E Major Fugue from the 2nd volume of the *48*, and the F Sharp Minor Fugue from the same book, and also B Flat Minor from that book; fugues that I've played all my life—and I had almost the performing experience of a lifetime. I played the entire piece with its four parts, or three parts or whatever it represented, and then having done that (it lasted 2½ or 3 minutes), I put on a set of earphones and had fed to me my own clicktrack, which in this case consisted of somebody saying, 4, 3, 2, 1, m and the mm constitutes a beat. Then I went back to the bass voice and started playing it along with my control-performance, hearing only what I had just done, and hearing a muffled version, as one must necessarily do with earphones, of what I was doing. And having put down the bass voice in this fashion, we did the tenor and alto and soprano and so on. The extraordinary thing was that having known these pieces at least twenty years, I saw them and heard them afresh in the most extraordinary way. I had never realized things about the inner voice aspects of those fugues which are manifestly clear; they are simply there to be apprehended by anyone who takes a close look at that score, and yet I had never discerned them in that fashion. I'm sure that if you took a student, or indeed anyone who was at all interested in music and suspicious of the contrapuntal experience (because a lot of people are), if you took him into a studio, and had him do precisely that, let him listen to one voice at a time (which I really think is the ideal way to understand music), I'm sure it would change his whole notion of what Bach was, what the Baroque represented, what that whole incredibly involved experience of Baroque counterpoint really meant.

Davis: Do you foresee at some point presenting that experience to the public in the form of a recording?

Gould: I would like to try. It isn't quite feasible yet: it isn't feasible in my own case, until I learn to play duets and trios and quartets with myself successfully, which (laughs) I certainly did not do on this occasion. It was a disastrous and unsound performance. I would love to see performances of that kind presented in four-corner stereo, a speaker in each corner of the room; it would be a totally unreal performance and one would not in any sense be confronted with the spectacle or the sense of the awareness of somebody up there on that podium playing at you. You would be in the centre of the problem, so to speak, and I think that's really what the listener should try to do and the way in which performance experiment with Bach must continue. It must try to bring the listener into the centre of the problem.

Davis: When you've successfully solved that problem for yourself, I can see a hotel cocktail lounge advertising "featuring the Glenn Gould Quartet."

Gould: (laughing) On Muzak. But speaking of Muzak in the hotel lobby or dining room—there's a connection between Bach and any music manufactured that way. There is a real Muzak-like significance to the nature of the fugue itself, or in the nature of any music that involves the kind of live-a-life-of-its-own on behalf of each voice, because the prime function of a fugue is to suggest an experience that is essentially open-ended. I would like to think that one could dip in and dip out of an experience of music just as easily as you get into an elevator (with a bit of Mantovani for 35 seconds) to get to the 19th floor. At which point you move into the Peter Nero zone, and you get somebody else's wall-to-wall musical decoration. I think that, in a sense, this is what Bach was about, because obviously he was quite ready to accept all forms of interchangeability, as between different performing forces, as between keys....

Davis: This is certainly true of the C Sharp Major, which was originally a C Major fugue running some 19 bars; only...

Gould: Was it?

Davis: ...in this version in C Sharp Major it now runs 35. So obviously Bach himself could be of two minds about how long the fugue could be and how many episodes to throw into it, and whether it should have a terminal point after 19 bars, or after 35 bars.

Gould: Yes, Did it change at all as between its incarnations in C and C sharp because I didn't have...?

Davis: Yes, the theme, the thematic materials and a good many of the details are the same, but in book two of *The Well-Tempered Clavier* it's very much expanded.

Gould: Because it's a strange fugue, it's very dense, and it doesn't have any of the conventional expository notions within it. The third entry, I think, is upside down, right away, and that's a bit Webernesque, even for Bach, at that period.

Davis: This points up, however, that since he appears to have redone it, and expanded it, and put it into C sharp—primarily in order to have it occupy an appropriate point in *The Well-Tempered Clavier* key scheme, and there had to be a piece in C sharp, just as there had to be a piece in C—well, he didn't happen to have a piece in C sharp around. He did have one in C and moved it up to C sharp, but in the process he expanded it considerably.

Gould: This must have been much less important to him (even though he set out quite conspicuously to write preludes and fugues in every key) than to Scriabin or even to Chopin, who had theories about keys and what they meant, and which were languorous, brisk, bright, lascivious, and which forced pure thoughts upon the imagination. Obviously Bach didn't have this if he could transfer from C, which is a pure, upstanding, academic and solid-citizen key, to C sharp, which is a slightly "dirty old man" key. You know, if he can really do that, obviously he wasn't much concerned with the Scriabinesque theories of key. I've often wondered whether the key affiliation that people profess (or that composers in particular profess) hasn't more to do with sheer tactile consideration than it does with anything that's truly oral.

Davis: It's easier to play C than it is C sharp.

Gould: It's easier to play C, and it's more satisfying to play C sharp because there is a velvet stroking feeling that comes from playing C sharp, and there is nothing but endless memories of Hannon exercises when you play C.

Davis: Do you suppose that to some degree the fugues he may have written in C were more academic because they would have been regarded as training pieces for his children?

Gould: Oh, that's a very good point. I never thought of that. Yes. I'm sure that's true.

Davis: If C is the key in which we all start out if we ever touch a keyboard at all.

Gould: True, true, it didn't occur to me.

Davis: What also troubles me, as a composer, about what has been happening to music and musical perception is that in Bach's time and in practically all of the music up until the beginning of this century, you were not usually expected to be able to hear or discriminate at one time, more than three tones sounding simultaneously—four at the very most—and in a fairly regularized series of relationships. Now, in the 20th century, we have to be able to discriminate five, or six or seven simultaneously sounding tones and an entirely new relationship. And I suspect this is one of the reasons that composers at this point are so far ahead of the public.

Gould: Very true. Of course the whole idea of what music is, of what music can consist, has changed so much in the last five years. I feel something quite remarkable happening and I'm pleased to see it happening, in a way, because I think that we come by a very hide-bound notion of what music, in fact, was. I think that much of the new music has a lot to do with (and I don't mean to sound like that chap, Marshall something-or-other) the spoken word. With the rhythms and the patterns and the rise and the fall and the inclination of the spoken word. And the human voice. I've worked a lot with the spoken word because I've been doing radio documentaries. It has occurred to me in the last five years that it's entirely unrealistic to see that particular kind of work—that particular ordering of phrase and regulation of cadence which one is able to do taking, let us say, the subject of an interview like this one, to a studio 'after the fact' and chopping it up and splicing here and there and pulling on this phrase and accentuating that one and throwing some reverb in there and adding a compressor here and a filter there—that it's unrealistic to think of that as anything but composition. It really is, in fact, composition. I think our whole notion of what music is has forever merged with all the sounds that are around us—everything that the environment makes available—and in that sense I think that the contrapuntalists, especially the Renaissance contrapuntalists, and Bach as he represented them historically in a sense, were the first practical men. As composers, they were the first people who recognized that it was possible and feasible and realistic to expect the human mind and the human ear to be aware of many simultaneous relationships, to follow their diverse courses and to be involved in all of them. Not to expect a particular precedence accorded to any one of them, not to expect any bowing or scraping on the part of the two or three remaining voices to one that was uppermost or lowermost, or *canto firmus*-most, or whatever. I think these were the first realistic people in the sense that they understood some aspects at least of this environmental compote which was to become music and which is now, perhaps for the first time, truly becoming music. I don't know whether you believe in that, but....

Davis: I do believe in it, even though it took some time to take hold. That is, Italian opera is still of the 19th century, one in which the other three or four, however many, voices do bow and scrape—scrape particularly—to the leading one. But are you suggesting that musical notation as we now know it is on the way out?

Gould: Oh I think so, definitely. There's no reason that it shouldn't remain, as long as it suits a purpose, but the great problem with musical notation is the barline because the one unrealistic fact about Baroque counterpoint, or Renaissance counterpoint, amidst all its other realistic acceptances, was the fact of that barline and the fact that the composers, not even the greatest of them, and not even Bach who managed some incredible leaps, were able to find a way of getting rid of a certain element of simultaneity. There was always the feeling that if your fugue subject was (humming) and then you answered (hummungp), that this presupposed the accompaniment to (pumpumpum) would be in some way more than harmonically relative. It would be also rhythmically relative, even though, if you had (bmmbmmbmm) as he does against (bumpbump), there is no particular statistical mathematical way or reason other than one of convenience and barline conformity for that (bmbmbm) to be exactly on the dot of the beats (making musical sound) in the right hand. That's one of the great things about performance practice that we've begun to discover. That very often it wasn't on the dot of that beat, that they in fact had a glorious improvisatory sense and they knew precisely in what way (given a certain discipline and training and a sense of taste and so on), those beats and barlines could be expanded so as to accommodate something a little less than simultaneous. But it didn't lead to solving the notational problem: it created a tremendous notational quandary, and we still don't know how to read Baroque scores as they were read by those who were really in.

Davis: So that in that sense the Baroque score is as much a bare blueprint without all the performance indications as some of the aleatory or improvisatory scores are today, which are really only the barest suggestions as to where you ought to start thinking about the noises you're going to make.

Gould: Exactly. I think if you could read a Baroque continuo part, with as much imagination as I'm sure old JSRB really did, sitting there at the...surrounded by his ten faithful....

Davis: Most of them children.

Gould: Most of them children (laughs). It was the forerunner of all aleatoric scores. And you know, one of the funny things to me is that many historians speculate that the piano sonata, the violin sonata, the string quartet, the symphony, were great miracles of art, that somehow in the later years of the 18th century, something congealed and all of the proper architectural impulses that had been abroad in the day in house design and furniture design, and all such things, got into music and a certain kind of welcome symphony resulted, and that this was indeed one of the great miracles of art. And when that occurred, as we know, the reputations of composers like Bach had to be eclipsed temporarily. But to me the great wonder of the classical sonata is not that it was invented, in the sense that it took a long time to be arrived at, but that anyone ever really wanted to bother doing it. I don't see why it was ever regarded as a great advance of art that an incredibly autocratic principle sprang into being. Whereby if you wrote an ideal sonata (and you could; the conservatories were full of them in those days; Bizet wrote an ideal symphony in the French fashion and at the age of 17, or whatever it was) you did things according to a certain kind of prescription that was failsafe, because once you had assumed that so many things went into the prescription of what a symphony was, what a concerto was, once you had assumed that the first theme ought to be upright and powerful, and brisk, and delineated clearly, and the second theme should be less forceful and more lyrical, more relaxed more tranquillo and more midnight-coloured and so on; once you'd assumed those things and you'd done all those things, you could then take your symphony or your prospective string quartet or sonata or whatever it was (they're all the same really) to your teacher, and say, "There is my symphony, sir, and I have done all these things, and as you will see, my first theme is impeccably a Mannheim M skyrocket (bumbumbum) and my second theme is (humming) and he's marvelously lyrical." And he'll say, "Aha, my boy! But you see, it is not quite tasteful, because the second theme, it comes too late, no, it comes too—some would say it comes too early, but no, I think it comes too late—it's, how shall I say, you see, it is something which only a great master, which you are not yet, my boy, could arrive at it." This attitude towards what taste was, and the role that taste played, just simply got in the way in the later 18th century and certainly in the 19th century, whereas one of the great refreshing things about the Baroque is that taste really didn't play a very strong part. The very fact that you can dip in and out of the Bach experience, that you can satisfactorily merge with another and play half a dozen, or play twenty-four at once, or play one only, or play half of one only, and be equally satisfied and not feel that you've missed out on something, is the greatest argument against that kind of imposed taste which always had to do with dimension of experience, always had to do with what the middle point was in relation to the end. Because in Bach you just don't get that notion of taste as revealed through dimension. For instance, if I were to make an experiment and take X number of fugues, only a portion of each of those selected, and make a compote out of it, put them together, adjoin them with good taste, proper splicing points and so on, and make one massive contrapuntal structure out of that lively collection of fugues, would you, in effect, as a listener be disturbed by the lack of taste not only of my doing this, but of the kind of decision that I would have to be authorized to make in order to make them adjacent one to the other, instead of leaving them as separate and bound pieces of music for your perception, one at a time? If I were to make one vast glut out of the fugue, would you personally be offended?

Davis: Well, I don't know whether it's fair to say offended. I think rather I'd be flabbergasted, because it seems to me that while you can

take these many bits of audiotape and cut them all up and splice them back together in a form that will suit you, you will encounter some evidences of musical illogic.

Gould: Oh, well, in that case grant me a modulatory prerogative, allow me to modulate, and to transfer the keys from one key to another. Would you then be offended?

Davis: I would not be offended, any more than I'm offended by what Bach does to Vivaldi. You have perfect freedom to do what you want with Bach's music as Bach felt he had perfect freedom to do what he wanted with Vivaldi's. If however you have exercised ghastly good taste, if you've done your homework properly, the result will be persuasive.

Gould: But doesn't it strike you as humanly good that the element of taste should be ruled out of a listening experience. I mean if we are going to absorb an environment (sorry to sound like Marshall what's-his-name again), then surely the question of taste is, in a certain sense, irrelevant; because your notion of the environment in which you must live, and work, and think and do your very best cogitating is not going to be mine; because your cogitating is necessarily going to be about different things, and have a different past, and we're moving toward a different sort of future. Is it realistic to think that one autocratically imposed terminal-bound statement can satisfy both of us equally? Is it not more realistic to think that a condition in which the ideal work of art which could satisfy not only the two of us, but all future generations, could exist and could be brought out in some laboratorily controlled way? Is it not possible to think that that could only be done through a notion in which the form itself is applicable to that work which didn't have a terminus, didn't have to come to an end, didn't recognize that kind of boundary, because of course the thing about Bach (if you think in religious terms, in theological terms) is that, unlike all of the sonata writers and unlike all of the symphony makers and the string quartet writers, he didn't have the urge (I wouldn't say he didn't possess the tools, because I think he as a composer would know very well that he did possess the tools), he didn't have the urge to demythologize his material, within any given work. I mean, the notion of the sonata and the symphony is precisely that, really, if you put it in theological terms, that the composer had such ultimate power over the material and over all the decisions that went into the material (and his characters as represented by the material if you see voices as characters in that sense), as a transformation of vocal impulse into characterization; that he could (if he chose) by textural alterations, by changes of pace, by all of the things of which a sonata or a symphony could be disrupted, and the events, the whole course of events changed, he could, in a sense, demythologize his characters; he could actually make one feel a sense of metamorphosis, a sense of implicit plot context in relation to what he was doing. So there was a very aggressive attitude abroad in the world of the symphony and sonata basically and, if you think about it, the sonata and symphony writers who are heroes are not unlike generals. They're not unlike the Napoleon figures. Beethoven was very like Napoleon, really; he is that great hero-general who commanded all the Mannheim leitmotifs and held it all together. I love Beethoven's music, as you know, so that has nothing to do with it. Nevertheless, there was a very aggressive impulse whereas in Bach's case it was a kind of mystic acquiescence before something that was absolutely inevitable, and which once started, could not be stopped.

Davis: In talking about the nature of a fugue and the experience of the fugue, it has seemed to me that there are times in which you can think of the fugue simply as a dialogue, and the changing character of the fugue is very much like the differences in the kinds of things we elect to talk about, depending upon the circumstances in which we find ourselves—whether it's a dialogue at the edge of a lake, or a dialogue at a cocktail party, or a dialogue on the corner of 42nd Street or some other crowded city, or a dialogue in bed—almost inevitably the nature of the environment in which you find yourself is going to affect the kind of dialogue in which you engage.

Gould: Well, do you have pictorial associations of any particular kind with a fugue or with fugues in general, with contrapuntal music as opposed to homophonic music?

Davis: I have almost no pictorial associations with music at all. That may seem strange, particularly in a society in which so much musical education insists that there must be pictorial associations to the point where you refer to the sonata form and wonder why musicians ever found it necessary to invent it. I often wonder what made it necessary for composers to invent tone painting, or the tone poem as it's come to be called, where these pictorial associations are forced upon you.

Gould: But are there conventional images that are associated with counterpoint? Because one thinks of certain kinds of music as leading onto imagery, one thinks of, my goodness, what? Strauss tone poems as having to do primarily with colours, perhaps—with violent colours much of the time. But, are there images that many people associate with counterpoint? Presumably there could be a generation growing up that has learned to correlate a contrapuntal experience with a certain kind of visual image. What would it be? Something very inner and post-expressionist, sort of Rorschach blot.

Davis: I think there are probably as many possible pictorial associations with, let's say, a Bach fugue, which does not contain anything that could possibly be remotely associated with the visual, other than by a kind of literal "Mickey Mouse" effect. When the notes go up you think of clouds, and when the notes go down you think of grottoes. But leaving aside that kind of literalness, it would probably take someone who had a very strong visual sense already, someone who reached through the eyes first, let's say a film-maker like Norman McLaren, who might make direct visual associations with a Bach fugue that wouldn't occur to either of us.

Gould: That's true...

Davis: There is, I suppose, an animation-like aspect to Bach as regards his performance anyway, because one can certainly think of it as existing as an infinite number of tempi—as being taken frame by frame, separate, fragmented, valued for that individual frame.

Gould: It feels that way looking at it from the point of view of its composition. It feels rather like having to put the piece together note by note by note, one at a time, to get each one exactly right and exactly in its right place—just the way you would put together animation cells to be able to ultimately simulate in motion that which, by the time it arrives in the form of a motion projected as a film, has to seem completely natural and flowing and appropriate to the character that you're trying to portray. And yet in its technical execution, it has only been put together very, very slowly, piece by piece, painstakingly, and none of that must ever be apparent.

Davis: Do you think that film observation—I mean the whole cult of film, the cult of cinema which is the new great super-art, the art that Wagner thought he was inventing and seems to be becoming more and more that for many of us, certainly is for me—do you think that film-making is going to influence the way in which we listen to music (and I don't mean by that the kind of music that accompanies film), the way in which we think now in terms of dissolves rather than the hard cuts one automatically gets when you're flashing through the family photo album? Do you think that in addition to the sort of Muzak-like contact and jump-cutting here and there, the whole notion of the dissolve, for instance, will have a feed-track effect on our perception of music?

Gould: Yeah, it may very well be that what film will ultimately do is change both our ears and our eyes and the ability of the eye to lead the ear and the ear to lead the eye. This is something that film is exploring more and more by off-setting the track, by leading the ear into the next scene before you have visually left the preceding scene or doing the reverse, introducing visually something that is about to happen while the track continues to hold on something that you have just been leaving. And in that sense it's a construction which is not all that unrelated to the principles of counterpoint, where something new is introduced while something that was going on is still going on but isn't...

Davis: And isn't ready to be let go of just yet.

Gould: I've a feeling that it's changed our sense of distance, and I know that since film became more and more important to me in the last decade or so, I've begun to think of music dimensionally in a way that just hadn't occurred before. You see, I have a feeling that what we're going to do eventually is forget about this funny notion that we've carried over into the recording of music strictly as a legacy, and a very poor one, of the concert hall. Which is to say that we should sit the listener down in front of his stereo speakers and confront him box-like with an experience. I don't think that we're supposed to confront him with anything at all, and I think that one way in which that can be broken through (and I'm trying this now because I think that it's the salvation of audio recording at a time when video recording may very well play a large part in our future), is to think in terms of multiple perspective—multiple perspectives which represent and which choreograph and which set forth the work as purely and as analytically as we can. I mean, why should we think in terms of one Bach fugue as being represented by one particular set of microphones, stationed in front of the piano and remaining there throughout, and I don't mean in terms of upping and downing the track or lowering it a bit in order to add emphasis to something like that. I mean precisely in the way in which a film track would have multiple perspectives applied to it to represent the kind of situation it was in—the horse leaning over and kissing the girl from the farm next door; that kind of scene as against the intimate shot by the Bonanza fireplace. But no one's ever thought of doing this except in relation to one symphony as against the next symphony.

Davis: Would it be fair to say or to suggest that, for example, in the opening of the Beethoven Hammerclavier Sonata, you might take those opening big chords in a very close microphone perspective, practically inside the piano lid and, the minute the sound got soft again, the minute the next musical idea came in, all of a sudden your microphoning was taken way off in the distance until it gradually approached the piano like...

Gould: Precisely, that way you could convey precisely what the motion of that piece is, just as an animator could convey to you what it's all about. You wouldn't violate the music; there would be no sense in violating the music. What you would violate is the ubiquitous, too-long-held perspective of the concert hall, which has kept us going and in business for a long time but...

Davis: Well certainly the two experiences can be complementary to one another and even though the concert hall experience has admitted severe limitations I think it would be nonetheless worthwhile recalling that music is a performed art...

Gould: Yes, but must it always pass through the mediation of a performer who is just that? I mean is it not possible that some sort of masterful technician could guide it much more successfully?

Davis: Well I think you have this in the Walter Kraals recording which is a very masterful guidance.

Gould: One of the great recordings.

Davis: By a superb—but more than just the technician—a technician-musician, and he has done a job which only his technical expertise could allow him to do. And yet the whole recording is informed with a great sense of musicality and exercise of individual initiative on his part as a performer...

Gould: No, he had an interesting thing to say about that recording. I produced a programme for the CBC in which he was interviewed and he said that one of the most remarkable things that he felt in sitting down to his Moog Synthesizer was he didn't have to set down the bass track or the treble track, unless he felt like it. He could set down a middle track first, bearing in mind what would be required from the bass and the treble ultimately, without necessarily getting caught in that vertical-horizontal crossbar that infects all of us with a certain notion of decorum of what is appropriate about where the climax really is, and in what way it should be stated—just as the Italians are always churning out the top line. In this sense it's a most enfranchising thing to think about, and even to hear him say, the fact that one could, as he said, set a brick someplace in the middle of the wall and not be bound by gravity because of the knowledge that the other bricks would be put in later.

Davis: But those bricks have already been provided—there by the composer—and he has that building blueprint to go by.

Gould: Yes, but if you think in terms of what that comment represents in terms of post-facto judgment as opposed to the kind of frantic decision-making that went on in your platforms of hallowed memory, it's a great idea. I can't think of anything quite as liberating as the notion that one can sit there at the piano, at one's keyboard or with one's Swingle Singers or whatever, and think in terms of Bach as a series of bricks many of which are yet missing and any one of which or any group of which can have predominance as one chooses. The sense of anonymity that Bach relinquished in writing fugues comes to you and without becoming Napoleonic, without becoming a sort of take-charge-generalissimo of the troops in the old romantic sense, you become the composer—you the performer become the composer. That sense of identity-confusion is the most delightful thing about playing Bach.

Davis: What on the concert platform do you recall as among the most frantic instant processes of Bach decision-making?

Gould: The ones that I couldn't remember.

Davis: I think at that point all of us are ready for a concert experience via this medium, and you begin it.

Gould: I feel challenged.

(Gould plays *The Well-Tempered Clavier*)

Chatting between taping sessions with director Bruno Monsaingeon, 1980. (CBC)

THE LAST PURITAN
Bruno Monsaingeon

Los Angeles — Late July 1972

I happen to be spending a few days in the company of Yehudi Menuhin who came to give two concerts in California. Tomorrow, he will travel back to Europe while I will be flying to Toronto where I am to meet Glenn Gould for the first time. I mention this to Yehudi, curious as I am to know his feelings vis-à-vis an artist whom I admire but have never met despite having exchanged a voluminous written correspondence in the past few months. Much to my surprise, I learn that Yehudi and Glenn know each other personally; that they have in fact played together. Yehudi undertakes to relate the occasion:

"It dates back to 1965; Glenn Gould had invited me to participate in one of his television appearances and had asked me to play with him sonatas by Bach and Beethoven and... the Schoenberg *Fantasy*. As you well know, Schoenberg is not amongst those 20th century composers for whose music I have an immediate and irresistible appeal. When I arrived at Glenn's place in Toronto for our first scheduled rehearsal, I met a man of genius to whom the Schoenbergian structures and idiom were natural elements. We worked on the *Fantasy* together and he magnificently managed to convey to me the profound understanding and true love he had for that music. *It was a revelation.*"

Toronto—One day later

I let into my hotel room a very odd individual muffled up in a sizeless overcoat and wearing cap, scarves, gloves and overshoes despite the hot weather outside. In the course of the subsequent first 15 hours of uninterrupted conversation, I feel submerged by his intensity, his warmth and his humour. Our mutual admiration for Menuhin provides us with a most opportune conversation opener:

"Two days prior to taping sessions, Yehudi came to Toronto, hardly knowing the Schoenberg *Fantasy*. While we were working on it, I witnessed his progressive immersion into the work of which he finally gave an intensely poetic and heart-rending reading—*It was a revelation.*"

Such was the appropriate beginning to what was to prove an incredibly productive ten years of collaboration between Glenn Gould and myself. This collaboration resulted in two series of films, the last one designed to represent his musical testament—containing the *Goldberg Variations* as the ultimate installment we were given to complete—and for which we had further plans for a few years to come.

I was still more or less a kid then and he was approaching his 40th year. My professional activity as musician and film-maker had hardly begun, whereas he had already been the subject of a legend. Moreover I was living in France where he had never set foot ("The French nation has known worse crises than my absence," he said to me) and towards whose music and art, a few exceptions aside, he felt no inclination; and I often wondered what might have been the common ground on which our friendship was founded and without which no long-term association would have been possible.

I suppose that more than age analogy, more than geographic rooting, and more even than community of experience and interests, it is a community of preoccupations that is most likely to fecundate friendship. Here I was attempting to give musical form and expression to films, confronted with a great man who was convinced that his best musical thought went into recordings and that the best analogy to be found vis-à-vis the making of a record involving musical interpretation was in the filming process—a man who was convinced that concentrated communication required isolation from the world with which one eventually wanted to communicate and that the whole apparatus of preconception, production and post-production was editorial afterthought. And yet of all pianists, he was in a sense the one who needed least the assistance of the editorial blade because of the unparalleled infallibility of his technical resources and the superb lucidity of his conceptions.

Let us imagine for a moment that we are in the audience at one of the concerts that established Glenn Gould's international reputation in 1955—we immediately know that we are dealing with the foremost pianist of the century. Such an assertion, however, does not mean very much, because what he is bringing lies in an altogether different and elevated sphere. By deserting the blood-thirsty arena of public concerts to confine his activity to the hermetically sealed privacy of the recording studio, Glenn Gould was assigning a new role to the interpreter and defining a new concept of interpretation. Engaged in the structure of the music, detached from the instrument which he had mastered to perfection, Glenn seemed to be possessed with a kind of clinical ecstasy when he played. Thinking as a composer, he identified creatively with the work performed and could therefore allow himself a critical and non-servile attitude towards the score. Harnessing the undissipated intellectual power that only solitude can give, he could engage himself in a manifold enterprise as pianist, composer, writer and broadcaster: a kind of meditation in action on the concept of communication in the era of technology and the "charitable" machine. Technology, he hoped, would be a redeemer. A sin had been committed at the end of the 18th century and if technology helped to put less emphasis on the notion of individual and separate identity, as well as on the hierarchical subdivisions that art seems to imply, composer, interpreter and listener should be in a state to reclaim the unity shattered by the artistic concepts of the Romantic age.

Blessed as he was with the conjunction of an incomparably compelling intellect and seemingly limitless pianistic gifts, yet also distrustful of fingers he saw as dangerous agents full of thought-dictating potential, Glenn could dispense with practicing, that chore of a musician's daily routine. Indeed, the only time I ever heard Glenn practice the piano happened a few days before he was scheduled to record the Webern *Concerto for Nine Instruments* for his CBC television series "Music in Our Time." As usual, he had studied the score away from the piano. Its intricate parts had become so integrated in his mind that he suddenly discovered he had to go to the piano to force his fingers to "unlearn" the parts of the other instruments involved in the piece! In fact, the whole concept of repetitiveness on which the practice of music has so far been based, appeared to him entirely nonsensical and deprived of the creative spark that makes music an ecstatic experience. A new vision of the same work was of course always possible, but it would not be conditioned by the deteriorating influence of overexposure. If Glenn decided to record a work again—that happened only two or three times in 26 years of recording endeavours—his decision was based on technological reasons as well as on the conviction that he could establish an entirely new relationship to the work in question and envisage it from a completely different and coherent angle. Of this attitude, I was the privileged participant when, amongst many other ventures, I directed the film of Bach's *Goldberg Variations* which he re-recorded one year before his death. The filming sessions, which coincided with those of the sound recording, took place over a period of several months during which I would travel back and forth from Europe, and he between Toronto and New York. We kept in daily contact, spending countless nights on transatlantic calls singing to each other over the telephone the variations that remained to be filmed so as to make sure that we would finally achieve a perfectly integrated structure of picture and sound.

Glenn no doubt represented a threat to the musical profession as we know it, and the implications of his thinking reach far beyond the limits of esthetics. The musical world, particularly in North America, if hopefully less so in Europe, is poisoned. Competition and the search for power have spread their venom. Paradoxically, it is by making use of electronic media, or more accurately, by taking shelter behind the protective shield they offer, that Glenn Gould resisted the falsely satisfying temptations of the world: public opinion did not reach him; he did not seek approval; nor did he sacrifice his genius on the altar of the public relations system. Indeed he thought that the artist should be granted anonymity. In this quest, he was reaching back to the status of the Medieval illuminators and cathedral builders who served a purpose larger than themselves. The frantic ambition for a glamorous yet transient position whereby too many artists degrade their role to that of entertainers had for a long time been discarded from his mind, if the temptation ever existed. Instead, he had become the controller and the doer of an art whose impact is all the stronger in that it is immune to acceptance. No applause from the few friends who had access to him and to whom he gave the warmest and most affectionate of welcomes was needed to achieve a state of intense private communion with him. This solitude, which was a recurrent theme in his works, resembled that of a fictitious character, his brother in literature, Adrian Leverkühn in Thomas Mann's *Doctor Faustus*. However, Glenn's pact was not with the devil, but with a God of absolute purity and integrity. In his own writings, he had become the theoretician of a purified humanity, the austere and penetrated moralist who, away from the sterile pursuit of worldly honours and pleasures, brought into accord his life and his faith: "The last puritan."

GLENN GOULD: THE CREATOR
Yehudi Menuhin

No supreme pianist has ever given of his heart and mind so overwhelmingly while showing himself so very sparingly. This great phenomenon that was Glenn, a jewel produced by geological eons, presented a great rift in the continuity of the expected and the ordinary. Yet these similes are purely figurative, for his was an ephemeral presence and only the recorded echoes of his thoughts and passions remain forever to enlighten and inspire us. The key to successfully probing this phenomenon is Gould's essentially creative nature.

Glenn Gould the creator, almost unwillingly trapped onto a keyboard, was reduced to a recreative role normally filled by performing intermediaries attempting to entertain, astonish or bewitch an audience. So great were his dominating creative powers that they determined the structures and patterns of his life—one of the principal effects of which was his very private use of time, of hours, seasons, and years.

His extremely selective and parsimonious choice of friends and projects, together with the concomitant and more obvious rejection of people—intruders, either to his world of thought or presence, be they interviewers or concert audiences, or for that matter any bipeds not sympathetic and somehow not organically integratable to his world and work—sharpened that isolation which was the very condition for the release of his creative powers.

Studying a Schoenberg score with violinist Yehudi Menuhin, October 1965, for a CBC telecast. (CBC)

303

So great was the compulsion of his creative universe that he himself (the Glenn that one might but did not touch) was a very touching, tender and extremely sensitive, almost heart-rending, offering—a sacrifice on the altar of his own genius—for his fulfillment reposed entirely in the written and taped records of thoughts and feelings in music and words.

"In the beginning was the word...." To contemplate Glenn is to ask why God had to make the world, and why in just six days. And was He too but the victim of, the sacrifice to, a yet greater power, for if nothing can be totally self-generating, if God and Glenn are/were celibate, is it not reasonable to believe in the constant, greater creative element which permeates our universe and of which we, in our ordinary lives, recognize only the expected and accepted, in the usual acts of living and dying, but which in rare individuals takes over completely and in which the creative is revealed in all its awesome purity and power?

Glenn was a very modern, very North American, and more specifically, Canadian man in all the characteristically fundamental aspects of these concepts. Modern because the microphone, electronic tape, radio, television and film were indispensable means whereby the anachronism of a "great pianist" (which one automatically hears joined with "concert pianist") dispensing with his audience, could be resolved. This was only possible in our own days. But being Glenn this "solution" became a creative challenge; it became an art in which all possible recording techniques were integrated into the very fabric of his musical conception and re-cast in a *superior* way.

The same applies to his radio programs and his television epics, all constructed as would be a fugue, but using words and images as themes and counter subjects. Nothing was haphazard yet all was animated by a very human passion and a very human compassion.

His was an extraordinarily aristocratic figure in the early North American tradition, more at ease on the one hand with lumberjacks, gold prospectors and our wonderful train conductors, all born gentlemen and a breed unto themselves, and on the other hand with his closest friends and very few soulmates; he chose to shun everything and everyone in between. However, he drove the automobile with the same expert matter-of-factness as any North American and his mind was not above dealing nimbly on the stock exchange with the most promising and least-known gold mines, inspected personally on his summer jaunts to the north.

Elusive and yet as all-permeating as oxygen or thought, even though dwelling alone and changing the order of day and night, sleeping, working, thinking, reading, remembering and talking (over the phone mostly), acting and creating in his own time, his very presence was a living comfort to us who knew him. Perhaps one day when sufficient time has worked on sufficient love we may arrive at a truer appreciation of Glenn's genius.

NOTES ON THE CONTRIBUTORS

John Beckwith, composer, is with the Faculty of Music, University of Toronto.

John Dann is a Canadian sculptor.

Denis Dutton is with the Department of Philosophy, University of Michigan.

Robert Fulford is the Editor of *Saturday Night* magazine

Robert Hurwitz is a recording producer with Warner Brothers.

Herbert von Karajan is Conductor of the Berlin Philharmonic Orchestra and Director of the Salzberg Music Festival.

Richard Kostelanetz is a writer and editor of books and essays on contemporary culture.

William Littler is Music Critic for the Toronto *Star*.

Yehudi Menuhin is a violinist, philosopher, and co-author of the *Music & Man* television series.

Bruno Monsaingeon is a musician and and collaborator with Glenn Gould on several film projects.

Geoffrey Payzant is Glenn Gould's biographer and a professor of philosophy at the University of Toronto.

John Lee Roberts is the former head of the Music Department of CBC Radio.

Joseph Roddy is a writer and the profiler of Glenn Gould in *New Yorker* magazine.

Edward Said is with the English Department at Columbia University.

Robert Silverman is Editor and Publisher of *Piano Quarterly*.

BIBLIOGRAPHY

This bibliography includes articles by Glenn Gould that have appeared in various periodicals. It does not include scripts for radio, television film, or disc, or his program notes or liner notes.

"The Dodecaphonists' Dilemma." *Canadian Music Journal* 1 (Autumn 1956), pp. 20-29.

"Bodky on Bach." *Saturday Review* 43 (November 26, 1960). pp. 48, 55.

"Let's Ban Applause!" *Musical America 82* (February 1962), pp. 10-11, 38-9.

"An Argument for Richard Strauss." *High Fidelity Magazine* 12 (March 1962), pp. 46-9, 110-11.

Arnold Schoenberg: A Perspective. Cincinnati: University of Cincinnati, 1964.

"Strauss and the Electronic Future." *Saturday Review* 47 (May 30, 1964), pp. 58-9, 72.

"Address to a Graduation." *Bulletin of the Royal Conservatory of Music of Toronto* (Christmas 1964), not paginated.

"An Argument for Music in the Electronic Age." University of Toronto *Varsity Graduate* 11 (December 1964), pp. 26-7, 114-27.

"Dialogue on the Prospects of Recordings." University of Toronto *Varsity Graduate* 11 (April 1965), pp. 50-62.

"The Ives Fourth." *High Fidelity/Musical America* 15 (July 1965), pp. 96-7.

"The Prospects of Recording." *High Fidelity Magazine* 16 (April 1966), pp. 46-63.

"Yehudi Menuhin: Musician of the Year." *High Fidelity/Musical America* 16 (December, 1966), pp. 7-9.

"We, Who Are About to be Disqualified, Salute You!" *High Fidelity/Musical America* 16 (December 1966), pp. MA-23-24, 30.

"The Search for Petula Clark." *High Fidelity/Musical America* 17 (November 1967), pp. 67-71.

"The record of the decade, according to a critic who should know, is Bach played on, of all things, a Moog Synthesizer?" *Saturday Night* 83 (December 1968), pp. 52, 54.

"'Oh, for Heaven's Sake, Cynthia, There Must Be Something Else On'!" *High Fidelity/Musical America* 19 (April 1969), pp. MA-13.

"Should We Dig Up the Rare Romantics? No. They're Only a Fad." *New York Times*, November 23, 1969.

"His Country's 'Most Experienced Hermit' Chooses a Desert-Island Discography." *High Fidelity Magazine* 20 (June 1970), pp. 29, 32.

"Admit It, Mr. Gould, You Do Have Doubts about Beethoven." Toronto *Globe and Mail Magazine* (June 6, 1970), pp. 6-9.

"Liszt's Lament? Beethoven's Bagatelle? Or Rosemary's Babies?" *High Fidelity Magazine* 20 (December 1970), pp. 87-90.

"Rubinstein." *Look* (March 9, 1971), pp. 53-8.

"Gould Quizzed." *American Guild of Organists and Royal Canadian College of Organists Magazine* (November 1971), pp. 31-2.

Introduction, *Bach's Well-Tempered Clavier 1*. New York: Amsco Music Publishing Company, 1972.

"Glenn Gould Interviews Himself about Beethoven." *Piano Quarterly* 21 (Fall 1972), pp. 2-5.

"Hindemith: Kommt seine Zeit (wieder)?" Trans. Peter Mueller. *Hindemith-Jahrbuch* 1973/III, pp. 131-36.

"Data Bank on the Upward Scuttling Mahler." Toronto *Globe and Mail*, November 10, 1973.

"Glenn Gould Interviews Glenn Gould about Glenn Gould." *High Fidelity Magazine* 24 (February 1974), pp. 72-8.

"Data Bank on the Upward Scuttling Mahler." *Piano Quarterly* 22 (Spring 1974), pp. 19-21.

"Today, Simply Politics and Prejudices in Musical America Circa 1970…but for Time Capsule Scholars It's Babbit vs. Flat Foot Floogie." Toronto *Globe and Mail*, July 20, 1974.

"Conference at Port Chilkoot." *Piano Quarterly* 22 (Summer 1974), pp. 25-8.

"The Future and Flat-Foot Floogie." *Piano Quarterly* 22 (Fall 1974), pp. 11, 12, 14.

"An Epistle to the Parisians: Music and Technology, Part 1." *Piano Quarterly* 23 (Winter 1974-5), pp. 17-19.

"Glenn Gould Talks Back." *Toronto Star*, February 15, 1975.

"Křenek, the Prolific, is Probably Best Known to the Public at Large as—Ernst Who?" Toronto *Globe and Mail*, July 19, 1975.

"The Grass is Always Greener in the Outtakes." *High Fidelity Magazine* 25 (August 1975), pp. 54-9.

"A Festschift for 'Ernst Who'???" *Piano Quarterly* 24 (Winter 1975-6), pp. 16-18.

"Streisand as Schwarzkopf." *High Fidelity Magazine* 26 (May 1976), pp. 73-5.

"Bach to Bach (and Belly to Belly)." Toronto *Globe and Mail*, May 29, 1976.

"Fact, Fancy or Pscho-history: Notes from the P.D.Q. Underground." *Piano Quarterly* 24 (Summer 1976), pp. 40-43.

"On Mozart and Related Matters: A Conversation with Bruno Monsaingeon." *Piano Quarterly* 24 (Fall 1976), pp. 12-19.

"Boulez by Joan Peyser." *The New Republic* 175, no. 26 (December 25, 1976), pp. 23-5.

"Portrait of a Cantankerous Composer," Toronto *Globe and Mail*, March 18, 1978.

"Stokowski in Six Scenes." *Piano Quarterly* 26 (Part 1: Winter 1977-8; Part 2: Spring 1978; Part 3: Summer 1978), Part 1: pp. 7-10; Part 2: pp. 47-54; Part 3: pp. 26-9.

"A Hawk, a Dove, and a Rabbit Called Franz Joseph." *Piano Quarterly* 26 (Fall 1978), pp. 44-7.

"Review of Payzant 'Music and Mind.'" *Piano Quarterly* 26 (Fall 1978), pp. 15-18.

"Memories of Maude Harbour -or- Variations on a Theme of Artur Rubinstein." *Piano Quarterly* 28 (Summer 1980), pp. 27-30.

"Glenn Gould Interviewed by Jim Aitken." *Contemporary Keyboard* 6, no. 8 (August 1980), pp. 24-36.

"Glenn Gould Interviewed by Tim Page." *Piano Quarterly* 29 (Fall 1981), pp. 14-24.

Articles under the Pseudonym Dr. Herbert von Hockmeister

"The CBC, Camera-Wise." *High Fidelity/Musical America* 15 (March 1965), pp. 86P-87P.

"Of Time and Time Beaters." *High Fidelity/Musical America* 15 (August 1965), pp. 136-7.

"L'Esprit de jeunesse, et de corps, et d'art." *High Fidelity/Musical America* 15 (December 1965), pp. 188-90.

PUBLISHED COMPOSITIONS

Cadenzas to the Concerto No. 1 in C Major for Piano and Orchestra by Beethoven, Op. 15. Great Neck, New York: Barger & Barclay, 1958.

"So You Want to Write a Fugue?" For four-part chorus of mixed voices with piano or string quartet accompanied. New York: G. Schirmer, 1964.

String Quartet, op. 1. Great Neck, New York: Barger & Barclay, 1956.

DISCOGRAPHY

All titles listed are on 33-1/3 rmp phonodiscs. All record releases are Columbia Records unless otherwise indicated. In Columbia releases of certain periods, the letter prefix "MS" indicates stereo, and "ML" indicates mono.

All items are listed by composers alphabetically; works by one composer are listed alphabetically by title in English. Sometimes there are variants in the title of the same work as printed on different recordings. Examples: Berg, Sonata Opus 1 and Berg, Sonata; Morawetz, Fantaisie and Morawetz, Fantasy in D Minor. The titles as given on the recordings in question have been used here.

The year of recording (in boldface type) is followed by the year of release (in roman text type). Year of release applies to the first release in North America only. Releases elsewhere, and re-releases in North America, are not included. In many Gould discs the material has been recorded at different times, months or even years apart. The year of recording as given in this Discography merely indicates that in the year mentioned Gould included among his activities the recording of part or the whole of the work listed.

Bach's *The Well-Tempered Clavier* Volumes I and II are listed as WTC-I and WTC-II respectively.

The short form "trans." indicates transcribed.

Musical performances by Gould are on piano except J. S. Bach, *The Art of the Fugue*, Fugues 1-9 (organ) and G. F. Handel, Suites 1-4 (harpsichord).

Musical Performances by Gould

ANHALT, I
Fantasia for Piano. Columbia Masterworks 32110046 (stereo), 32110045 (mono) (**1967**, 1967).

BACH, J. S.
Art of the Fugue, Fugues 1-9. MS 6338, ML 5738 (**1962**, 1962).
Concerto No. 1 in D Minor. Columbia Symphony, Bernstein. ML 5211 (**1957**, 1957).

Concerto No. 2 in E Major. Columbia Symphony, Golschmann. MS 7294 (**1969**, 1969).

Concerto No. 3 in D Major. Columbia Symphony, Golschmann. MS 7001, ML 6401 (**1967**, 1967).

Concerto No. 4 in A Major. Columbia Symphony, Golschmann. MS 7294 (**1969**, 1969).

Concerto No. 5 in F Minor. Columbia Symphony, Golschmann. MS 7001, ML 5298 (**1958**, 1958).

Concerto No. 7 in G Minor. Columbia Symphony, Golschmann. MS 7001, ML 6401 (**1967**, 1967).

English Suites 1-6. M2 34578 (**1971**, **1973-6**, 1977).

French Suites 1-4. M 32347 (**1972-3**, 1973).

French Suites 5, 6. M 32853 (**1971**, **1973**, 1974).

Fugue in E Major from WTC-II. ML 5186 (**1957**, 1957).

Goldberg Variations. MS 7096 (**1955**, 1956).

Goldberg Variations. M 31820 (**1980**, 1981).

Goldberg Variations. IM 37779 (**1981**, 1982) (digital).

Inventions and Sinfonias. MS 6622, ML 6022 (**1963-4**, 1964).

Italian Concerto. MS 6141, ML 5472 (**1959**, 1960).

Little Bach Book. M 36672 (**1955**, **1979**, 1980).

Overture in the French Style. M 32853 (**1973**, 1974).

Partitas Nos. 1, 2. MS 6141, ML 5472 (**1959**, 1960).

Partitas Nos. 3, 4. MS 6498, ML 5898 (**1962-3**, 1963).

Partita No. 5. CBC International Service Program 120 (**1954**, 1954).

Partitas Nos. 5, 6. ML 5186 (**1957**, 1957).

Partitas for Keyboard. M2S 693.

Partitas, Inventions. D3S 754.

Preludes, Fughettas & Fugues. M/MT 35891 (**1979**, 1980).

Sinfonias. (See Inventions and Sinfonias.)

Sonatas (three) for Viola da Gamba and Harpsichord. Leonard Rose, cello. M 32934 (**1973-4**, 1974).

Sonatas (six) for Violin and Harpsichord. Jaime Laredo, violin. M2 34226 (**1975-6**, 1976).

Toccata No. 7 in E Minor. MS 6498, ML 5898 (**1963**, 1963).

Toccatas, Vol. 1. M/MT 35144 (**1976**, 1979).

Toccatas, Vol. 2. M/MT 35831 (**1963**, **1979**, 1980).

WTC-I, Preludes and Fugues 1-8. MS 6408, ML 5808 (**1962**, 1963).

WTC-I, Preludes and Fugues 9-16. MS 6538, ML 5938 (**1963**, 1964).

WTC-I, Preludes and Fugues 17-24. MS 6776, ML 6176, (**1965**, 1965).

WTC-II, Preludes and Fugues 1-8. MS 7099 (**1966-7**, 1968).

WTC-II, Preludes and Fugues 9-16. MS 7409 (**1969**, 1970).

WTC-II, Preludes and Fugues 17-24. M 30537 (**1971**, 1971).

WTC, Bk. 1 (Complete). D3S 733.

WTC, Bk. 2 (Complete). D3M 31525.

BEETHOVEN, L. v.

Bagatelles, Op. 33, Op. 126. M 33265 (**1974**, 1975).

Concerto No. 1 in C Major. Columbia Symphony, Golschmann. Y 30491 (**1958**, 1958).

Concerto No. 2 in B-flat Major. Columbia Symphony, Bernstein. ML 5211 (**1957**, 1957).

Concerto No. 3 in C Minor. Columbia Symphony, Bernstein. MS 6096, ML 5418 (**1959**, 1960).

Concerto No. 4 in C Major. New York Philharmonic, Bernstein. MS 6262, ML 5662 (**1961**, 1961).

Concerto No. 5 in E-flat Major. American Symphony, Stokowski. MS 6888, ML 6288 (**1966**, 1966).

Sonata No. 1 in A-flat Major, Op. 2, No. 1. M2 35911 (**1974**, **1976**, 1980).

Sonata No. 2 in A Major, Op. 2, No. 2. M2 35911 (**1974**, **1976**, 1980).

Sonata in C Major, Op. 2, No. 3. M2 35911 (**1976**, **1979**, 1980).

Sonata No. 5 in C Minor, Op. 10, No. 1. MS 6686, ML 6086 (**1964**, 1965).

Sonata No. 6 in F Major, Op. 10, No. 2. MS 6686, ML 6086 (**1964**, 1965).

Sonata No. 7 in D Minor, Op. 10, No. 3. MS 6686, ML 6086 (**1964**, 1965).

Sonata No. 8 in C Minor, Op. 13. MS 7413, ML 6345 (**1966**, 1967).

Sonata No. 9 in E Major, Op. 14, No. 1. MS 6945, ML 6345 (**1966**, 1967).

Sonata No. 10 in G Major, Op. 14, No. 2. MS 6945, ML 6345 (**1966**, 1967).

Sonata No. 12, Op. 26, No. 13 and Op. 27, No. 1. IM 37831 (**1982**, 1983–to be released).

Sonata No. 14 in C-sharp Minor, Op. 27, No. 2. MS 7413 (**1967**, 1970).

Sonata No. 15 in D Major, Op. 28. M2 35911 (**1979**, 1980).

Sonata No. 16 in G Major, Op. 31, No. 1. M 32349 (**1971**, **1973**, 1973).

Sonata No. 17 in D Minor, Op. 31, No. 2. M 32349 (**1967**, **1971**, 1973).

Sonata No. 18 in E-flat Major, Op. 31, No. 3. M 32349 (**1967**, 1973).

Sonata No. 23 in F Minor, Op. 57. MS 7413 (**1967**, 1970).

Sonata No. 30 in E Major, Op. 109. ML 5130 (**1956**, 1956).

Sonata No. 31 in A-flat Major, Op. 110. ML 5130 (**1956**, 1956).

Sonata No. 32 in C Minor, Op. 111. ML 5130 (**1956**, 1956).

Symphony No. 5 in C Minor, trans. Liszt. MS 7095 (**1967-8**, 1968).

Thirty-two Variations in C Minor. M 30080 (**1966**, 1970).

Variations in E-flat Major, Op. 35. M 30080 (**1967**, **1970**, 1970).

Variations in F Major, Op. 34. M 30080 (**1967**, 1970).

BERG, A.
Sonata Opus 1. Hallmark RS 3 (**1953**, 1953).
Sonata. ML 5336 (**1958**, 1959).

BIZET, G.
Premier Nocturne. M 32040 (**1972**, 1973).
Variations Chromatiques. M 32040 (**1971**, 1973).

BRAHMS, J.
Ballades, Op. 10. IM 37800 (**1982**, 1983).
Intermezzos (ten). MS 6237, ML 5637 (**1960**, 1961).
Quintet in F Minor. Montreal String Quartet. CBC Transcription Service Program
    140 (**1957**, 1957).
Rhapsodies (two), Op. 79. IM 37800 (**1982**, 1983).

BYRD, W.
First Pavan and Galliard (**1967**), Sixth Pavan and Galliard (**1967**), A Voluntary (**1967**),
    Hughe Ashton's Ground (**1971**), Sellinger's Round (**1971**). M 30825 (1971).

GIBBONS, O.
Allemande, or Italian Ground (**1968**), Fantasy in C (**1968**), Salisbury Pavan and Galliard
    (**1969**). M 30825 (1971).

GOULD, G.
Glenn Gould Silver Jubilee Album. M2X 35914. Released 1980. Side 1: 3 Scarlatti
    Sonatas (**1968**), C. P. E. Bach's (Wurttemberg) Sonata No. 1 in A Minor (**1968**),
    Gould, "So You Want to Write a Fugue?" (**1963**). Side 2: Scriabin, Two Preludes,
    Op. 57 (**1972**), Strauss, Ophelia Lieder, Op. 67 with Elisabeth Schwarzkopf (**1966**),
    Beethoven-Liszt, Symphony No. 6 in F, Op. 68 (**1968**), A Glenn Gould Fantasy
    (**1980**, 1980).
"So You Want to Write a Fugue?" GG-101. Quartet of voices with string quartet
    accompaniment (**1963**, 1964).
String Quartet, Op. 1. Montreal String Quartet. CBC International Service Program
    142 (**1956**).
String Quartet, Op. 1. Symphonia Quartet. MS 6178, ML 5578 (**1960**, 1960).

GREIG, E.
Sonata No. 7 in E Minor, M 32040 (**1971**, 1973).

HANDEL, G. F.
Suites 1-4. M 31512 (**1972**, 1972).

HAYDN, J.

Sonata No. 3 in E-flat Major (1789-90). ML 5274 (**1958**, 1958).

Sonata No. 56 in D Major; Sonata No. 58 in C Major; Sonata No. 59 in E-flat Major; Sonata No. 60 in C Major; Sonata No. 61 in D Major; Sonata No. 62 in E-flat Major. I2M 36947 (**1980**, **1981**, 1982) (digital).

HETU, J.

Variations for Piano. Columbia Masterworks 32110046 (stereo), 32110045 (mono) (**1967**, 1967).

HINDEMITH, P.

Das Marienleben. M2 34597.

Piano Sonatas (three). M 32350 (**1966-7**, **1973**, 1973).

Sonatas (four) for Brass and Piano. Various soloists. M2 33971 (**1975-6**, 1976).

KRENEK, E.

Sonata No. 3. ML 5336 (**1958**, 1959).

MORAWETZ, O.

Fantaisie. CBC International Service Program 120 (**1954**, 1969).

Fantasy in D Minor. Columbia Masterworks 32110046 (stereo), 3211045 (mono) (**1966**, 1967).

MOZART, W. A.

Complete Piano Sonatas. D5S 35899.

Concerto No. 24 in C Minor, K.491. CBC Symphony, Susskind. Columbia MS 6339, ML 5739 (**1961**, 1962).

Fantasia in C Minor, K.475. (See Fantasia and Sonata in C Minor, K. 475/457.)

Fantasia in D Minor, K.397. M 32348 (**1972**, 1973).

Fantasia and Fugue in C Major, K.394. ML 5274 (**1958**, 1958).

Fantasia and Sonata (No. 14) in C Minor, K.475/457. M 33515 (K.475. **1966-7**; K.457, **1973-4**; 1975).

Sonata No. 1 in C Major, K.279. MS 7097 (**1967**, 1968).

Sonata No. 2 in F Major, K.280. MS 7097 (**1967**, 1968).

Sonata No. 3 in B-flat Major, K.281. MS 7097 (**1967**, 1968).

Sonata No. 4 in E-flat Major K.282. MS 7097 (**1967**, 1968).

Sonata No. 5 in G Major, K.283. MS 7097 (**1967**, 1968)

Sonata No. 6 in D Major, K.284. MS 7274 (**1968**, 1969).

Sonata No. 7 in C Major, K.309. MS 7274 (**1968**, 1969).

Sonata No. 8 in A Major, K.310. M 31073 (**1969**, 1972).

Sonata No. 9 in D Major, K.311. MS 7274 (**1968**, 1969).

Sonata No. 10 in C Major, K.330. ML 5274 (**1958**, 1958).

Sonata No. 10 in C Major, K.330. M 31073 (**1970**, 1972).

Sonata No. 11 in A Major, K.331. M 32348 (**1965**, **1970**, 1973).

Sonata No. 12 in F Major, K.332. M 31073 (**1965-6**, 1972).

Sonata No. 13 in B-flat Major, K.333. M 31073 (**1970**, 1972).

Sonata No. 14 in C Minor, K.457. (See Fantasia and Sonata in C Minor, K.475/457.)

Sonata No. 15 in C Major, K.545. M 32348 (**1967**, 1973).

Sonata No. 16 in B-flat Major, K.570. M 33515 (**1974**, 1975).

Sonata No. 17 in D Major, K.576. M 33515 (**1974**, 1975).

Sonata in F Major with Rondo, K.533/K.494. M 32348 (**1972-3**, 1973).

PROKOFIEV, S.
Sonata No. 7 in B-flat Major, Op. 83. MS 7173 (**1967**, 1969).

"The Winter Fairy" (from *Cinderella*), trans. M. Fichtengoltz. Albert Pratz, violin. Hallmark RS-3 (**1953**, 1953).

SCHOENBERG, A.
Fantasy for Violin and Piano, Op. 47. Israel Baker, violin. MS 7036, ML 6436 (**1964**, 1967).

Five Piano Pieces, Op. 23. MS 6817, ML 6217 (**1965**, 1966).

Ode to Napoleon Buonaparte, Op. 41. Juilliard Quartet; John Horton, speaker. M2S 767, ML 6437 (**1965**, 1967).

Piano Concerto, Op. 42. CBC Symphony, Craft. MS 6339, ML 5739 (**1961**, 1962).

Piano Pieces, Op. 33 a/b. MS 6817, ML 6217 (**1965**, 1966).

Six Little Piano Pieces, Op. 19. MS 6817, ML 6217 (**1964-5**, 1966).

Songs, Op. 1, 2, 15. Donald Gramm, bass-baritone; Ellen Faull, soprano; Helen Vanni, mezzo-soprano, MS 6816, ML 6216 (**1964-5**, 1966).

Songs, Op. 3, 6, 12, 14, 48, Op. Posth. Donald Gramm, bass-baritone; Cornelis Opthof, baritone; Helen Vanni, mezzo-soprano. M 31312 (**1964-5**, **1968**, **1970-1**, 1972).

Suite for Piano, Op. 25. MS 6817, ML 6217 (**1964**, 1966).

Three Piano Pieces, Op. 11. ML 5336 (1958, 1959).

SCHUMANN, R.
Quartet in E-flat Major for Piano and Strings. Juilliard Quartet. D3S 806 (**1968**, 1969).

SCRIABIN, A.
Sonata No. 3. MS 7173 (**1968**, 1969).

SHOSTAKOVITCH, D.
Three Fantastic Dances, trans. H. Glickman. Albert Pratz, violin. Hallmark RS-3 (**1953**, 1953).

SIBELIUS, J.
Three Sonatinas, Op. 67; *Kyllikki*, Three Lyric Pieces for Piano, Op. 41. M 34555 (**1977**, 1977; mixed 1977).

STRAUSS, R.
Enoch Arden. Claude Rains, speaker. MS 6341, ML 5741. (**1961**, 1962).

Sonata in B Minor; Five Pieces, Op. 3. M 38659 (**1982**, 1983-to be released).

TANEIEFF, S.
"The Birth of the Harp," trans. A. Hartmann. Albert Pratz, violin. Hallmark RS-3 (**1953**, 1953).

WAGNER, R.
Three transcriptions by Gould: *Die Meistersinger*, "Prelude"; "Dawn and Siefried's Rhine Journey" from *Die Götterdämmerung*; *Siegfried Idyll*. M 32351 (**1973**, 1973).

FILMOGRAPHY

Conversations with Glenn Gould, BBC (1966). In English. Four films, black and white, each 40 min.: 1. *Bach*, 2. *Beethoven*, 3. *Schoenberg*, 4. *Strauss*.

Glenn Gould, National Film Board of Canada (1960). In English. Two films, black and white, each 30 min.: 1. *Off the Record*, 2. *On the Record*. (Documentary profile of Gould.)

Glenn Gould, National Film Board of Canada (1960). In French. Black and white, 22 min. 45 sec. (Documentary profile of Gould.)

Slaughterhouse-Five, Universal Pictures (1972). Directed by George Roy Hill. In English. Colour, 104 min. (Music performed, arranged, and some of it composed by Gould.)

Spheres, National Film Board of Canada (1960). By Norman McLaren and René Jodoin. Colour, 7 min. 28 sec. (Animation, with music of Bach played by Gould on the piano.)

The Terminal Man, Warner Brothers (1974). Directed by Michael Hodges. In English. Colour, 104 min. (The music consists of Gould playing the *Goldberg Variations*.)

Les Chemins de la musique, Classart. Series of four: 1. *La Retraite*, 2. *L'Alchemiste* (pt. 1), 3. *L'Alchemiste* (pt. 2), 4. *Partito*.

The Wars, Nielsen Ferns and Torstar. (A feature-length film based on the book of the same name by Timothy Findley, for which Gould assembled music and composed one chorus part.)

Glenn Gould's Toronto, John McGreevy Productions-Nielsen Ferns Co-Production. One of a series of films about cities.

Radio as Music, Canadian Broadcasting Corporation. (A documentary film based on the radio script of the same name, about Glenn Gould's method of making documentaries and his concept of 'contrapuntal radio.')

Series of three films of Bach recordings by Glenn Gould, produced by Classart: 1. *Glenn Gould Plays Bach*, 2. *An Art of Fugue*, 3. *The Goldberg Variations*.

Music of Man: No. 8 Canadian Broadcasting Corporation-PBS Co-Production. Glenn Gould talking to Yehudi Menuhin. (One of a series of films on music throughout the world, past and present.)

RADIO
DOCUMENTARIES

Arnold Schoenberg: The Man Who Changed Music (1962).

The Prospects of Recording (1965). A study of the recording industry and the effect of recording on the life of modern man.

The Idea of North (1967). A view of the North and the people who live there. (Gould's first experiment with 'contrapuntal radio.')

Glenn Gould on the Moog Synthesizer (1968).

The Latecomers (1969). A study of outport life in Newfoundland.

Stokowski: A Portrait for Radio (1970).

Casals: A Portrait for Radio (1973).

The Quiet in the Land (1973).

Richard Strauss: The Bourgeois Hero (1979).